Red
1

Red
3

Red
2

Red
5

Red
6

Red
4

Red
9

Red
8

Red
7

Red
10

CLACT

LIFEGUARD CLUB

EURO
£5.

0 YEARS OF EXCELLENCE
The Red Arrows 2004
Hawk T1A XX227
The Royal Air Force Aerobatic Team
Rolls-Royce

AIRFIX
RED ARROWS HAWK
GIFT SET
1:48
MODEL KIT · MAGUETTE A MONTER · MODELLBAUSATZ · MAGUETTA PARA MONTAR
www.airfix.com
DOYUSHA
AH-64D
世界最強の戦闘ヘリコプター !!
Wing MUSEUM
F-22 RAPTOR
B-2
Enjoy Trouble-free Flying!
Sky Rider Glider
EXCLUSIVE!
Patented Wing Locks
Tail Wing Locks

SUPER
STOMP ROCKET
CAN TRAVEL 400 FEET
AIR-POWERED ROCKETS
DOYUSHA
F-15DJ
JASDF
Wing MUSEUM
AGGRESSOR
05
02
CLASSIC PROPS

RAF Aerobatic Team
The Red Arrows
reers.com

First published 2005 by
Dalton Watson Fine Books
1 Arundel Court, Elverlands Close,
Ferring, West Sussex BN12 5QE
England

1730 Christopher Drive,
Deerfield, IL 60015 USA

www.daltonwatson.com

ISBN casebound: 1-85443-217-6

To Lynda, Ella and Sam

For Bill, Queen, John and Jim Baker and Flight Lieutenant Matt Jarvis

RED

ARROWS

RICHARD BAKER

AUDITION

As a boy, I used to shove my flat hand into the slipstream of my Dad's open car window; it would lift abruptly and I would dream of flying aeroplanes. Forty years later, I am entering the alien world of aerobatics, a year-long story in pictures and interviews with the Red Arrows.

Here comes Wing Commander Bill Ramsey, the Red Arrows' Senior Supervisor. "Nervous?" he asks. My stomach tightens. "Not really, no," I lie. "Well you should be." An ex-Vulcan bomber man, known affectionately as 'the g-monster' because of his legendary resistance to high g-forces during aerobatics, he's about to unleash his aeronautical demons on me.

It's 15:00 hours on Friday 9 March 2004 and I'm on the apron at RAF Scampton, the Red Arrows' Lincolnshire base. I'm in the cockpit of Red 11, Wing Commander Bill Ramsey's BAE Hawk advanced trainer, my knees almost touching an array of instruments and dials. I'm sitting behind and high above the Wing Commander's front row seat, which is out of my view. But I see him adjust his top two mirrors so as to spy on me, the way Mum used to swing down the make-up mirror in the car to give me the evil eye.

This is my trial flight, my audition for a chance to fly in formation with the Red Arrows when they practise display aerobatics. To assess just how well (or how badly) their prospective guest photographer might cope with a ride in a Hawk, the Reds need to send me up in a replicated flight formation, and watch me. They need to see whether I, a middle-aged townie, can withstand forces that will accelerate my body to four or five times positive gravity, instantly increasing my weight to 400kg – about 880lb. If I pass out at the faintest hint of g, I won't be able to fly with them, because my flailing arms and rolling head might jog the flight controls and we could be doomed, or, at the least, very embarrassed.

And if ever there was an example of how not to react, how to disgrace oneself, there was the slip of a girl I saw earlier, who left a shade of pink and landed a deathly white, the contents of her breakfast decorating her life vest, mask and flying suit. This very unnerving spectacle was not what I wanted to witness pre-flight and yet, surprisingly, it has turned out to be the fillip I need to make myself grit my teeth – for this is the day when, for me, much is at stake for the coming months.

The canopy snaps shut, enclosing us in an acrylic bubble. The noises of the outside world become a remote whisper. My breath hisses through the mask and into my ears as if I'm listening to my breathing through an

Opposite While the engine idles before take-off, gloved fingers drum on the acrylic canopy.

Pages 2–3 Spectators are captivated by the display flying at the Clacton-on-Sea Air Show, Essex.
Pages 4–5 Smoke trails from some of Europe's leading aerobatic teams drift across alpine skies at Payerne, Switzerland, during Air 04. The smoke of the Red Arrows is on the far left.
Pages 6–7 Blues selling charity posters at the Clacton-on-Sea Air Show.
Pages 8–9 Merchandise shop at the RAF Waddington Air Show.
Pages 10–11 Local ladies shelter by the Red Arrows' promo trailer at the Southend-on-Sea Air Show, Essex.
Page 14 RAF Akrotiri, Cyprus, during spring training.

2
4
3
4
50
UHF
MAIN
OFF
BOTH
ADF
VOL
TONE
PRESET
MANUAL
GUARD
OFF ON
SQUELCH
SELECT
F
HDG
Up
Mid
Down
AC 1 Reset
AC 2 Reset
DC Reset
Altimeter
Isolate
Port
Stbd
Supply
Brakes
Hyd 1
Hyd 2 Reset
Hyd 2
RELIGHT-AUTO HOLD-IN
Aileron trim
Tailplane trim
Lift for Stand by
Close for Main
Rudder trim
Eng Start
Start

FT/MIN
X1000
HYD.1
FUEL
F.PR
AC 1
HYD.2
TRANS
SKID
AC 2
JP OHT
ECA
OIL
AC 3
Nav.
Anti-Collision
Panel
Emergy
Compass
White
Lower
Off
Upper
Red
Panel Lights
Port
Centre
Stbd
VHF
UHF
ILS
TACAN
I/C
RCVR TEST
MEGACYCLES
125.350
VHF AM
COMM
T/R GUARD
T/R
D/F
RETRAN
OFF
SQUELCH
AUDIO
Normal
Demist
Off
Flood
CABIN AIR TEMP
AUTO
Norm
Ground Crew I/C
ADR Status
FAIL
CODE
OFF
SBY
XMT
MODE
TEST
IFF/SSR
Oxygen On
ILS
MHz
ILS
OFF
VOR
OFF
RX
TX/RX
TACAN
X
Y
118
TEST
Lower
Seat
Raise
100
MANUAL SEPARATION HANDLE
Air

amplifier. I smell the rubber of the mask, cleaned with ethyl alcohol. I pull and push at the oxygen flow and see the 'doll's eye' on the instrument panel indicate how much I'm drawing from the jet's air supply.

I imagine many of the team peering through the windows of the squadron building, watching us depart. They've seen it before. *Homo sapiens* taking off full of bravado and alpha-male fitness and reduced, on landing, to a nauseous, gibbering sub-species. But surely, I reason, the human being in front is a guarantee of my safety? He looks like an ordinary, rather lanky, bloke, yet the brain behind those steely eyes can guide this supersonic flying machine with the technical skill and grace of any one of the Mercury Seven astronauts.

I hear the whine of the Rolls-Royce/Turboméca Adour turbofan spinning into life, the way wartime sirens gathered revolutions before wailing their warnings of catastrophe across town. I'm aware that the decibel level it's generating is dangerously high for anyone standing outside, close by, not wearing ear defenders, but it's considerably muted in the cockpit. When politely ordered, I fumble to remove my ejector seat pin and place it at shoulder height in its special receptacle – only to realize that my seat is now 'live'. If I were to pull the 'yellow and black' (the name RAF pilots call the thick, wide handle between my legs) at this precise moment I would be sent into oblivion by my rocket-powered ejection seat.

We rumble along yellow taxiway centrelines and the Wing Commander mutters his take-off checks. Then, as calmly as if he's telling me what he's thinking of having for dinner tonight, and amid lots of 'dum-de-dums' and 'hmm, hmm…hmmms,' he says: "The next time I say 'Eject, eject, eject!' it will be for real, not a drill."

We line up on runway 05 and, without more ado, we accelerate forward. And what a beautiful action it is; physics and nature turning our three-wheeler into a flying machine and pitching it high into the air. The interaction between airflow and speed, identified over three centuries ago by Daniel Bernoulli and Isaac Newton as the forces that generate lift, are carrying us high into the air by the time we cross the A15 – the highway beyond Scampton's perimeter fence.

The Wing Commander is flying a routine practice sortie, but it appears to my inexperienced eye as if he's scanning the air space between the horizons and picking areas to visit as if drifting around an expansive park pond in a pedalo, or just heading for the clearer patches between gray stratocumulus.

Pages 20-21 All the Reds love flying the Hawk. It's a pilot's aircraft, simple to start, all hand-to-eye, almost a step into a bygone era of aviation.

But then, perhaps satisfied that his punter isn't going to do anything silly, although the 'yellow and black' seems menacingly accessible between my legs, he utters a warning and piles on 4g by pulling into a hard turn.

•

Before flying with the Red Arrows I had to attend a series of briefings and kit-fittings. Health and safety lectures before a ride in a fast jet just aren't the same as those you get before standing next to a cement mixer wearing a hard hat. Hearing what might go wrong if I don't pay attention is as scary as the prospect of crossing the A15 in front of a heavy truck bearing down with all the menace of the Red Baron.

A dummy ejection seat on wheels sits outside the squips' (Survival Equipment Technicians) room, where pilots pick up their flying gear. Before you're allowed near a real seat, you undergo the Seat Brief, a lecture on this alarming safety device. How to connect, clip, turn, tuck, switch on and switch off while definitely not pulling the Personal Survival Pack (PSP) lanyard, thereby activating the emergency beacon that immediately scrambles a yellow helicopter search-and-rescue operation to your coordinates. My part of the contract, I'm told, is to pull the 'yellow and black' between my legs when ordered. I will apparently have eons of time to perform this unnatural feat, for rather than eject into the icy, very low pressure air at high altitude, we would dive to the warmer, more breathable heights of the lower atmosphere, and that would give us time to ready ourselves for departure through the canopy. Should the ejection fail, we should roll the jet over, detonate the Miniature Detonation Cord (MDC) to shatter the canopy, pull on a manual release handle and tumble out attached to parachute and locator beacon. The prognosis for this action would not be good, I'm assured, but all would be over quickly and painlessly.

Getting kitted out is not easy. I dress in woolly fell-walkers' socks, a combat green vest, full-length flying overalls and sturdy, shin-high black boots. A white helmet with a broad red arrow on the back is mandatory. I insert my forehead into it and rotate it back as I lower it, so as not to tear my ears. The mask is clipped over my nose and mouth and I'm shown how it toggles to alter the mike settings: 12 o'clock for off; 9 o'clock for on. In the event of noxious gases in the cockpit I can switch to 100% oxygen with a

FEET
1029
Rotation
101-4
UHF
Normal
FT/MIN
X1000
Batt
TEST
ON

ALT
mbar
62000 FT
GTS
ALT
°C
x100
TGT
FUEL
Kg
x100
FIRE
T6NL
E. OHT
START
HYD
C. PR
OXY
GEN
HYD. 1
FUEL
F. PR
AC. 1
HYD. 2
TRANS
SKID
AC. 2
JP. OHT
ECA
OIL
AC. 3

clip flicked quickly down, pressing the rubber seal hard against my face.

Now sealed into a device like a tenpin bowling ball, which muffles the noises of the outside world, I sit, nodding at Corporal Peter Stern, the cheeky, grinning squipper. He clicks down both visors, the first one clear, the second tinted green, and I imagine that the wide blue yonder is going to appear a sickly green colour. The screens will protect my face from the unwelcome puncturing of the cockpit canopy by, perhaps, one of those pheasants I hear gobbling at dawn most mornings in nearby Brattleby hamlet. I hear muted voices saying things like: "Don't wind him up Pete, he's worried enough, so keep it down." They think I can't hear behind my green shield and I feel like some hard-of-hearing nursing-home resident being given a blanket bath.

As I sit through the helmet-fitting, my mind projects various in-flight catastrophes that could befall me. What if I'm sick at high altitude and can't unclip the mask clamped over my face? On balance, motion sickness seems the least of my problems. What if the leg restraints running from the ejection seat over my shins don't snap taut on ejection, and so fail to jerk my legs and feet back, beneath the seat? Leaving my lower legs behind as I eject would be an unpleasant way to exit the jet.

I fret about these and other anxious anxieties, clarifying as many as I can while I'm still on the ground and able to ask. The squippers traditionally write an officer's name (or, in my civilian case, a nickname) on masking tape, which they stick over the red arrow on the back of each helmet they fit. They write 'Jibba Jabba' on mine, because of the many questions I nervously ask them.

Just for this first flight with the Wing Commander, I will wear a pair of extraordinary overtrousers and will belt myself into a complex of buckles and harnesses that snake around my legs and grip my groin. When we pull real g and my brain is drained of oxygenated blood, pressurized air from the engine will be forced into the trousers, pumping blood from my legs back up through my veins to my brain to restore full vision and consciousness. I give a practice blow down the connecting pipe that normally snaps into the jet's air system, and feel a dozen fleshy hands squeezing my thighs and loins. It is mildly gratifying. I'm glad of the g-pants on this trial flight, but after my test, I will have to fight the effects of high g-forces without their assistance. I won't be issued them because of the risk that, during an aerobatic manoeuvre, one of the straps might catch on the stick and jeopardize flight control.

According to Tom Wolfe in *The Right Stuff,* pilots and doctors must be

Pages 24-25 Each seat in the BAE Hawk has a full set of flight controls, but most non-flying controls are in the front cockpit only. The controls and instruments are ergonomically laid out and easy to reach. All the instruments are analogue type and most switches are lever type.

natural enemies. But the RAF periodically belts its doctors into the back seats of its jets so they experience the rigours of fast flight. In a way, we're all the Lab Rats Wolfe describes. Before I set foot inside a Hawk trainer and am introduced to the stresses it can impose when airborne, I have to visit a specialist in aviation medicine. I report to the Medical block, where my statistics are logged and a medic scratches his chin before he pumps my arm and measures me with rudimentary rulers and wall-mounted guides.

The grim reality of what I'm intent on experiencing is carefully explained to me by a charming but serious lady RAF doctor, who explains how to fight the onset of g-forces. She states that this will be somewhat different from the experience of flight on a 737 heading for Spain. I nod while she details what I must do when I start losing colour vision. From now on, a sunny March afternoon seems to darken under a cloud of alarming medical terminology: 'grunt'; 'bowel movements'; 'hypoxia'; 'disorientation'; 'inner-ear disturbance'; and 'monochromatic peripheral (tunnel) vision'. On her desk is a slip of paper inscribed with words waiting to be deleted to fit an appropriate verdict: 'fit/unfit to fly'; or perhaps 'borderline/hopeless risk' – words loaded with fate. The doctor is strangely uninformative about what ejecting might do to my 44-year-old flesh and bones. I gather I would lose consciousness as the rocket motor in my seat kicked me – exerting high stresses on my spine – up and away from a troubled aircraft, and that I would come round again while drifting down by parachute, hopefully on a warm afternoon like this one, rather than the iciest day in the year. I fleetingly recall the Seat Brief, when the correct techniques for hitting the ground were explained to me in two sentences: "Tuck your arms in, bend your knees and roll over. Been skiing, have you?" I don't know how many skiers bend their knees correctly *en piste,* but some 7,000 survivors of Martin-Baker ejection events apparently did. Yet, much as I like the idea of fraternizing with others who have experienced an extraordinary incident, I would rather not qualify for the ejection club tie and pin on my audition flight.

•

Back in the wide blue with the Wing Commander, the g-pants immediately inflate as we pull g, channelling blood up into my thorax. My arms sink and I try to raise my hands, first independently, then clasped as if holding

2
bar
Normal

a camera. My hands pull up so far but no farther, scarcely lifting from my thighs. The mask is pushed down my nose and my head and ears pulsate with the change of altitude and air pressure. An intense but brief pain spreads across my sinuses and I struggle to move the mask up. Then the g eases off and we're again in level flight.

I mumble a nasal agreement to my chaperone's questions ("Yes. OK. Thanks.") and we quickly pull another, then a third turn, accomplishing even more g. The indicator climbs to 4g, then to 4.5g and each time, my facial tissues and the blood inside them sag. I feel powerless, as if I've sunk into a vegetative state. Seen from the cockpit, from inside the acrylic bubble, the ground beyond the red wing with its RAF roundel changes at every blink, an accelerating landscape of farms and ploughed fields and hamlets whizzing by. To us up here there's little noise except the sssss-shhh of our breathing and the odd transmitted advice from Air Traffic Control. But I know the decibel count is rising in the kitchens, gardens, orchards and fields below, as we briefly interrupt their rural quiet.

Pulling more g again: the meter now shows 5. Up to 1,225m – 4,000ft – we climb in seconds, up and up through broken cloud, up and over, over and hurtling down, then turning hard left. This is no longer about being twisted and torn by g-forces, this is an aerobatic ballet danced on a spherical stage.

We swing up and over. As we roll around the sky I fancy that we've rented the space for the afternoon as our private pleasure dome. We dive to make a low pass above the runway and I see the knots recorded by the airspeed indicator rise above 400. At 420kt I'm suddenly distracted by a flapping bird, but the Wing Co. has already taken avoiding action, a delicate touch on the control column altering our global position and flight path, and almost before I spot it, the bird has passed harmlessly overhead. We pass over the line at Scampton, the Hawks parked there looking like little red lapel badges, then on and over the hangars that once housed the Lancaster bombers of Guy Gibson's Dam Busters squadron.

We practise a controlled glide towards the runway, simulating an engine failure by gliding down towards the runway. This, the Wing Co. explained later, is an important safety technique the Red Arrows regularly practise. If the engine failed in mid-display, there is little danger that the aircraft would plummet to the ground, killing its pilot, or hurtle into the crowd. Energy is still being created by the flow of air around the wing, and the

Pages 28-29 The radio selection panel on the port side of the BAE Hawk cockpit.

Pages 32-33 The smoke trail is turned on and off by a two-position smoke control switch in the front cockpit of the Hawk.

pilot harnesses it to change the aircraft's direction and bring it down on a controlled path in a safe place. We brush the runway gently, then hurtle up again on full power and turn into a roll to fly inverted for a few seconds. Some dirt, perhaps from someone else's boots, falls to rest on the inside of the canopy roof; beyond it spread the brown winter fields around Scampton.

More and more g. My ears crackle inside my tight helmet, releasing pressure. Then up to 1,225m – 4,000ft – in a few seconds. Up and up we climb, then down we push, level off and turn hard into more g. All the while, the silence is uncannily eerie.

The clock tells the Wing Co. that our 30 minutes is up. I'm horribly aware that if I'm to be ill, it will be soon. Now. Once your eyes tell the balance mechanism in your inner ear that you're no longer being tossed around like a lettuce leaf in a salad spinner, the contents of your stomach may rise to your throat. I'm still worrying about this as we touch down. On the taxiway, trivial conversation helps break my back-seat tension. A routine wave to those silhouetted in the Control Tower. I mention football. Bill says his beloved Chelsea drew and we laugh about the squippers kidding me that he follows Arsenal. I replace my seat pin in its hole, so my seat is no longer live.

We reach the stand, and the lineys – the maintenance team – approach with steps. I still feel pink and there's no hint of nausea. I undo my bindings and once I've disconnected my PSP (with great care so as not to initiate an emergency search and rescue) I'm allowed to stand up and leave the jet. I clear my spluttering ears. The spinning earth suddenly leaves me behind and I totter on one leg as the other counterbalances. For a few moments I feel drunk and reach out and clasp Bill's gloved hand, leather crackling against leather. I grip hard to show my appreciation for his having shared my experience, as if we were fellow survivors of an alien abduction. I've seen others do it – holding on as if it were a polite, if pointless, gesture by a wannabe kindred spirit. This flight was special to me, my first time.

"I'm not a jet virgin any more. Thank you."

"That's all right." He's already striding away, but he turns back. "Too long ago for me to remember my first time." And he ambles off for a cuppa.

I wobble off, feeling like a space cadet. In the squips' room, Corporal Paul Horrocks looks worried. He might think he's in for a mucky cleaning chore just as his shift ends. And I let him think just that. After all, I had passed!

RAF Scampton Air Traffic Controllers preside over the take offs and landings from the base on Reunion Day for former members of the Red Arrows and their families.

The charity fund-raisers of the Cyprus-based RAF Association may have been the smallest crowd to watch a Red Arrows display during the anniversary season, when they were treated to the full programme at the Princess Mary Hospital, RAF Akrotiri.

Peter Chadburn was a propulsion engineer, or sootie, with the Red Arrows from 1965-67, their first two years. He looked after the Bristol Orpheus engine that powered the team's first jet trainer, the Folland Gnat. Here, he photographs a sortie on Reunion Day.

The Red Arrows have performed at Southend-on-Sea, Essex, every year since 1986, when an air show was first held there. An estimated 300,000 people turned up to watch their display at the 19th annual show.

Southend Airshow
30th and 31st MAY
Do Not
Obstruct Steps
Or Footway

Flight Lieutenant Steve Underwood's commentaries on the Red Arrows' performances entertained thousands during the 2004 and 2005 display seasons. Here, parked on the cliffs at RAF Akrotiri, Cyprus, he watches the first sortie of SpringHawk – the Red Arrows' pre-season training.

"So the Red Arrows cost a lot of money. So what? They give pleasure to millions. They're British and they couldn't do better. At Trooping the Colour you think, 'Where are the Red Arrows?'"
A spectator at the Farnborough Air Show.

Reds 6 and 7, the Synchro Pair, draw a heart with their smoke above Weymouth.

With the Northumberland landscape as their backdrop, these speakers relay to the public Flight Lieutenant Steve Underwood's commentary on the Red Arrows' display at the Kielder Forest Air Show. Nearby, three spectators follow every manoeuvre.

Seafront, Weston-super-Mare, Somerset.

DONKEYS £1.50
CARRIAGES £1

Grand Pier, Weston-super-Mare, Somerset.

AEROBATICS

It's 16:30 hours on an August afternoon and I'm strapped into the rear seat of Red 1, the team leader's or Boss's Hawk, which heads the Red Arrows' formation. We're lined up on the Scampton runway, our engine idling, waiting for the other eight Hawks to form up behind. Pilots and Hawks have just had a ten-day respite from their punishing display schedule and this is an In-Season Practice (ISP) they'll fit in before they rejoin the display trail.

The Boss and I seem to read each other's minds, because his voice, eerily disembodied by the mike, suddenly says: "Look at that! Isn't that great?" He's looking skywards. Through my darkened green visor I'm also looking up through the Miniature Detonation Cord (MDC) that zigzags around our canopy, at a blue gap that's opening up directly above us, between veils of high cloud. But I'm thinking the cloud is too heavy for us to practise a full display. "You're kidding, right?" I hear my voice say. "No, no! It's fantastic," calls the Boss. "The ceiling is over 4,000 feet. We'll have so much room..."

We dance into the first formation of the 2004 sequence: Big Vixen Arrival Roll. Our nine jets seem to roll in unison as if tied together. The air speed indicator touches 360kt and we're shifting references into Delta for the next pass. From Delta we metamorphose into Concorde...Short Diamond Loop...Gripen Bend...in a seamless transition of reference points.

Passing from Concorde into Short Diamond during a loop, I'm pinned by the load-bearing straps that grip my thighs and shoulders, but there's no gut-tearing drama to our slow, deliberate roll. The horizon rotates round the canopy as if we're static and the skies are moving round us. I remember the same feeling from my touchline view in the BAE Hawk simulator at RAF Valley, earlier in the year. Then I was warned, when the aircraft rolls I may keel over as the landscape tilts, my brain empathizing with the revolving horizon. But today, as we glide upside down along our curling path, the motion seems lazily gentle and I feel no different, not even lighter.

From my vantage point in Red 1, I see Red 3 on the left and Red 2 on the right change their position in orderly fashion, their jets hovering and settling. Beyond my field of vision, the pilots of Red 5 and Red 4 are enduring far more g than the Boss and I in our cosy central spot in the formation. I almost hear them grunt, mumble and pant as they fight the onset of g, while fine-tuning their own space in the sky.

The spectators below watch us pass by and then return a few minutes later, but from inside the formation every moment is squeezed, tunnel-like,

Opposite Three Hawks streak across the summer sky above Eye, Suffolk.

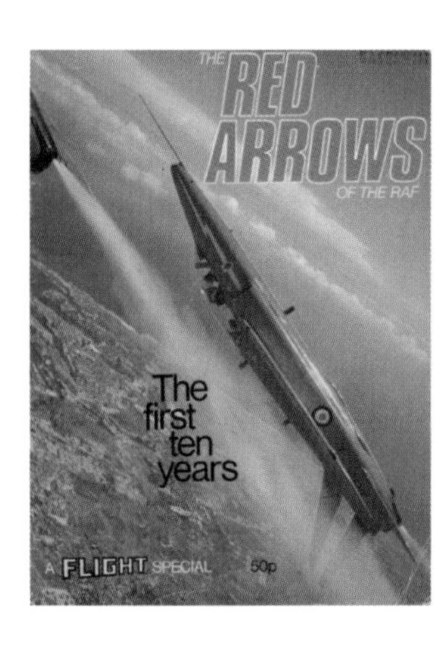

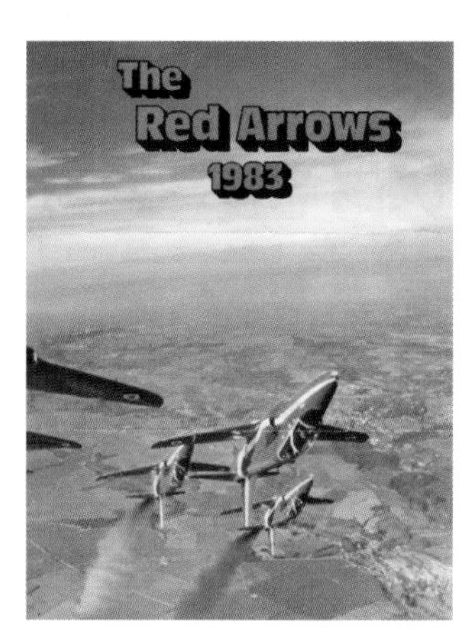

into momentum and activity, as pattern blends into pattern, Quarter Clover into the 5/4 Split. Our neighbours alongside and behind pull up with us past a hazy horizon that now dips out of sight. As we arc over the loop's apex, a dazzling sun and its shadows travel across the artificial horizon instrument on the panel in front of me.

All the time Reds 6 and 7, the Synchro Pair, have been out of sight behind us, but after the Champagne Split, which marks the end of the display's first half, they break away from the formation for their two-ship performance. We progress independently until Synchro rejoin at the end of the show, but they're so far away that I see nothing of their Carousels and Cubans.

We drive down the straight for the Goose, where we lead the five jets of Enid section, Reds 1–5, approaching from crowd right: Red 1 on the top of an inverted V-shape, with the other four spaced below us. The Boss alerts me to expect oncoming smoke and I catch sight of a blue ribbon streaming back from a tiny red projectile that's streaking towards us. It's Red 8, Flight Lieutenant Jez Griggs, but by the time I've caught sight of him, he's upon us…gone beneath our smoke pod…cutting between the other four. He's a daytime meteorite, his vaporized smoke trail following him on its silent trajectory. "Nice one, Jez," says the Boss. But by the time we're shifting our positions into the Twizzle, he's not so pleased: "C'mon boys, you're late." he mutters.

Going into the Twizzle, the view from Red 1 as the Boss leads Enid on the inside is of clear sky, then we're suddenly heading back down towards the runway leaving coloured smoke trails. The Boss calls "Smoke off Go" and we're beyond the runway, moving into Battle and turning back towards the runway. Reds 2–5 behind us reform into line astern and we're on the climb 'up the hill' for the Caterpillar. The Boss's hand seems to pull back on the stick forever and I'm reminded of the journey into space in an express elevator to the top of New York's Empire State Building. At last we reach the ceiling (at 2,000m or 6,500ft on this clear day), trailed by the rest of the formation, with Red 5 at the back hanging on to the underbelly of Red 4. And now, Red 2 from our right and Red 3 from the left come corkscrewing in beautiful arcs around us as we fly straight, just above the ground for the Rollbacks…and they're gone…

All too soon we're climbing, looping and diving into the breathtaking Vertical Break. Reds 3 and 2, our neighbours to left and right, fill my vision, then shrink to rolling specks in the haze as we bottom out and fly straight,

Above left A *Flight* magazine special edition from 1975 marked the 10th anniversary of the Red Arrows Aerobatic Team flying the Folland Gnat.

Above right The Reds' 1983 brochure shows the team flying the British Aerospace Hawk trainer.

away from the crowd to regroup for the Vixen Loop. Just as Synchro finish their Opposition Barrel Rolls and vacate our space, we're back, flying at right-angles to the runway, our landing lights blazing at the crowd. We climb sharply into the clear sky, just short of the runway edge (a point 230m or about 750ft in front of the crowd – to pass it would breach safety regulations). The *whoosh* of the Hawks' wings as they overcome gravity during the Vixen Break signals the end of the show.

Out of sight of the crowd, the scattered aircraft re-form as a nine, run through the pre-landing checks and head back towards the runway in Big Battle formation, ready for the break to land. I know what pain is imminent. "G coming on," confirms the Boss. Hands and camera tight down on thighs, away from stick. Halfway along the runway we pitch up violently and bank hard 90°, rolling right. We buck and turn...and...turn ...it feels like we're in a centrifuge. We seem to be bolted to this 7g turn for an eternity, but it's only about five seconds. I strain. Emptied of blood, my face sags. I see shimmering black and white, the stripy static you might see on an old TV set after you yank out the aerial plug. My camera weighs an extra 7kg or about 15lb, and I'm pressing down into my seat with the force of 400kg or 880lb.

Then it's as if an internal tuner returns me to normal vision and flushes away the pressure in my head. The practice is over. We fly level again, backtracking to begin the slow turn to final approach. Each jet in order brushes the threshold with a short yelp of rubber. Our speed falls off and the Boss's boots touch the pedals for smooth ground steering and braking. We sit stationary on the runway, engine idling, as the others roll up behind.

"All aboard!" Red 9, Squadron Leader John Green, calls from the back, meaning they're all down safely. We taxi back in close formation, as perfectly aligned on the ground as in the air.

•

As the nine pilots attend the debrief that follows this and every practice display, I compare this ride with Red 1 with earlier ISPs I've flown in Hawks positioned on the outer fringes of the patterns in the display. This one felt effortless by comparison: the Boss endures relatively little g. He's occupied with flying smoothly and consistently, massages the display according to wind strength, timing and the appearance of unforeseen obstacles such as low cloud. As leader, he's the in-flight choreographer, monitoring every aspect of the display from his front-row seat.

In their 2004 display, the Red Arrows flew some 25 manoeuvres each lasting 24 minutes (depending on factors such as cloud conditions). The new Boss for 2005, Squadron Leader Dicky Patounas, decided to shorten the display by two to four minutes. "The 24 minutes inevitably crept up to 25 or more and that made the display feel a bit samey. I've watched displays that nose up towards the half hour and they really seem to go on for too long. It's better to leave the public wishing they'd seen one more manoeuvre than losing interest before the end."

To make the cuts, Dicky Patounas and Red 6, the Synchro Leader, had to work on the timings. Shaving off just five seconds between each manoeuvre can save two minutes through the whole display. Then, to cut it to around the 20-minute mark, the Boss axed the Twizzle, a manoeuvre in which Enid fly individual loops, following the leader. The Twizzle headed the list of possible cuts. "It's very unforgiving," explained the Boss. "We strive time after time to fly a display that looks perfect all the way through, but the smallest error in the Twizzle is always obvious, even to the untrained eye." To balance the display, the Synchro Pair cut one of the manoeuvres they flew during the second half – the Opposition Loop or the Ellipse.

The age of the Red Arrows' Hawk jet trainers made a big contribution to the Boss's decision to shorten the display. Even the youngest aircraft in the fleet are over 20 years old. "The longer they're in the air, the more fatigue we put on them," explains Patounas. "Shortening the show is a way of managing fatigue so they can go on for longer."

Cutting back the 2005 display reverses a 40-year trend. The first Red Arrows display in 1965 lasted just 15 minutes, and the tradition has been to add new manoeuvres each year. While the display retains a number of 1965 manoeuvres, the impression is that the two shows are completely different.

The 1965 display consisted mainly of a succession of gentle formations. There was an arrow, a rhombus (a seven-jet precursor of Diamond Nine), and Big and Little T formations (flown by seven and five jets respectively). The emphasis in today's displays is on being dynamic. "Overall," says Flight Lieutenant Dan Simmons, "the number of nice gentle shapes has decreased and the number of dynamic manoeuvres has increased considerably."

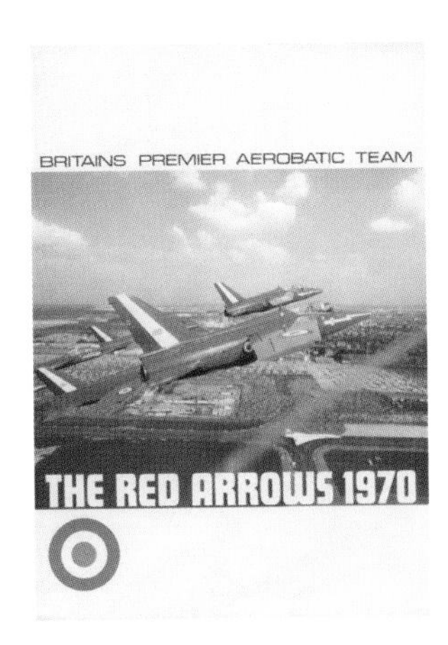

The Vixen formation of 1965 (named after a 1960s jet fighter) evolved into the spectacular Vixen Loop and Vixen Break, which now end the display.

Every aircraft handles in a different manner, so the type a team flies influences the generic shapes that make up its display. The first Red Arrows team, which operated the compact, nimble Folland Gnat from 1965 to 1979, developed its core formations such as the Diamond Nine, Vixen, Viggen and Concorde. Viggen, a nine-ship formation in the shape of a famous air-defence fighter, has transmuted into the Typhoon. The two jets that fly the formation on either side and slightly behind Red 1 represent the small canard winglets fitted to both the Saab 37 Viggen and the Eurofighter Typhoon. Early manoeuvres included the photogenic Cascade (a seven-ship dive and pass across the runway) and the Join-Up Loop into the Parasol Break finale – the precursor of the Vixen Loop into the Vixen Break.

Dan Simmons, who joined the Red Arrows in October 2002, flew as Red 7 in 2003-04 and became Red 6, Synchro Leader, in October 2004, explained how this works. "We flew the Swan in my first year with the Reds and we aim to fly it again this year. But we didn't fly it in my second year, so our second-year guys may never have seen the Swan and certainly haven't flown it. Even the new Boss didn't fly the Swan when he was first on the team (Dicky Patounas did his first tour with the Reds in 1997-99), so only third-year pilots like me know how to fly it and we have to teach everyone else." The Swan featured as a simple swan-shaped pattern in the 1965 display; and around the early 1980s it developed into a more dynamic manoeuvre, the Swan Roll. It may change again: "They may not like the way we flew it in 2003," says Dan Simmons, "and if not, they might alter it here and there to make it look better." And so the display evolves.

Rarely do the Reds count any manoeuvre out for good. The historic Twinkle Roll, a manoeuvre of the 1960s when the Red Arrows flew the Folland Gnat, can't be flown in the Hawk. The Gnat was famous for its ability to roll at more than 360° per second and in the Twinkle Roll, every aircraft in the formation rotated at over 300° per second, but this manoeuvre was axed after 1972. Roulette, a crossover manoeuvre involving a split-second decision on which side two approaching Reds should cross, was permanently struck from the display after a collision killed four pilots and wrote off two Gnats in 1971. But these are rare examples of manoeuvres that may have gone for ever.

So the fatigue-accelerating 1990s Twizzle may be cherry-picked at any

Above left Reds flying the Folland Gnat are shown in formation on the cover of their 1970 display brochure. Ray Hanna, the now-legendary leader of the Red Arrows from 1966 to 1969, famously answered 'Both, please' when asked which he would go for if offered a choice between a Spitfire and a Gnat.

Pages 58-59 Flight Lieutenant David Slow going through his six-month emergency drill at the BAE Systems simulator facility at the RAF's fast-jet flying training centre in Anglesey.

DANGER
PARACHUTE ASSY.
SERIAL No.
PART No.
REF. No.
DATE OF MANUFACTURE
ISSUE
MODIFICATIONS

DANGER
SEAT

time from a full catalogue of formations and manoeuvres that every team can draw on for inspiration, to reappear, in updated form, in a future Red Arrows display.

•

Those pilots who strapped themselves into the canvas-and-wire flying machines of early aviation inevitably became the heroes of their day, showing off at pre-World War I airfields in front of astonished voyeurs. In August 1913 Lieutenant Pyotr Nikolaevich Nesterov of the Imperial Russian Air Service first looped the loop – and was arrested for his pains. A month later, a French stuntman, Adolphe Pégoud, repeated the feat to great acclaim. He practised inverted flight by tying his aircraft upside down in its hangar. That November, Lieutenant Bentfield Hucks of the Royal Flying Club Special Reserve was the first British pilot to loop the loop, and by 1914 the numbers of aerobatic pilots who had performed this feat were enough to warrant the formation of a club in London for such clearly mad gentlemen. The Upside Down Club dinner started with coffee and ended with soup; and was accompanied by a singer who stood on his head while performing.

Today's Red Arrows' displays reflect the development of aerobatics from these early years of aviation, much of that evolution having been forged by military pilots. It was a British naval pilot, Lieutenant Wilfred Park, who on 23 August 1912 became, by instinct or pure luck, the first pilot to recover from a spin by applying rudder control.

Formation flying began during World War I as a way of protecting fighters on reconnaissance flights. Turns and rolls developed as aerial combat techniques. Consequently, aerobatics played a prominent part in the Royal Air Force from its foundation in 1918. It attracted new recruits; was an essential part of pilot training, and, not least in the early years, of winning prestige when Britain's newest service was fighting for independence from the army and navy. Today, RAF instructors teach some formation flying and aerobatics to student fighter pilots. They're good practice for flying in convoy and in aerial combat – and for displaying new military aircraft – and they develop the trainees' belief in themselves and their reactions, their understanding of their aeroplanes, their teamwork, and mutual trust.

Above left Since the Red Arrows were formed in 1965, the squadron has had a major role in recruiting new pilots into the RAF. This advertisement appeared in their 1970 brochure.

The Royal Air Force staged the earliest public military air displays in the UK. In 1920, the first annual RAF pageant was held at a small grass airfield at Hendon, outside London. Veteran World War I pilots demonstrated turns and dives to a crowd of 40,000; and staged dogfights in biplane bombers and fighters, with smoke trails to make their hits look realistic.

The Red Arrows are officially the Royal Air Force Aerobatic Team (RAFAT), a squadron under the command of the RAF's Central Flying School (CFS), whose role today is to train and monitor the service's flying instructors. The CFS was the world's first military flying training school. It was founded in 1912 to train pilots for the naval and military wings of the Royal Flying Corps, the first air arm of the British military forces. In 1920 the CFS formed the world's first specialized aerobatic team, which flew five Sopwith Snipe fighter defence aircraft. At the 1921 Royal Air Force Pageant at Hendon, the CFS team demonstrated formation flying.

RAF flying schools and squadrons took turns to appoint an official aerobatic team to display at its Hendon pageants of the 1920s and 1930s. The 1929 team of two Gloster Grebes from No.22 Squadron flew a synchronized display while trailing coloured smoke from a sky-writing device. The 1930s displays featured aircraft tied together by the wing tips with breakable cord. Squadrons equipped with the new Hawker Furies spectacularly demonstrated synchronized loops, rolls and turns while changing formation, and rolled whole formations as one unit. Prolonged inverted flight was the speciality of the 1933 CFS team's five Avro Tutors.

The RAF needed new pilots after World War II to replace the many who had demobbed, so it continued the tradition, selecting top aerobatic teams from operational fighter squadrons. Celebrity veteran Wing Commander Don Kingaby led teams from Nos.54, 72 and 247 squadrons in 1948–50, flying Vampires in Battle of Britain displays around the UK. The 1948 official team, the 'Odiham wing', flew the first nine-jet close formation; No.54 Squadron's six-ship team toured North America in 1948. By 1952 there was even a display team with an official name: a team from the CFS flying three of the first British jet fighters, the Meteor T.7, was billed as 'The Meteorites'.

Up there at the apex of the Red Arrows' distinguished family tree are the RAF display teams of the 1950s, capable of high-speed aerobatics in their new subsonic jets. The best known are the team the French called 'Les Flèches Noires' or 'Black Arrows', inspired by the spectacular flying skills

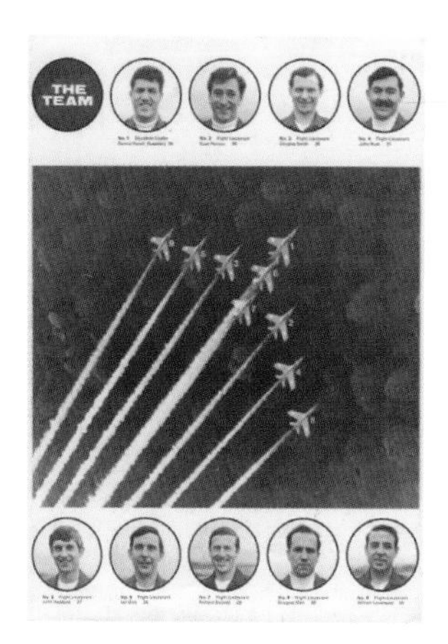

Above left The Red Arrows' official 1970 brochure (*right*) showed the team and their Gnats in Nine Arrow formation. The 1983 brochure (*left*) included a group photograph of the squadron's 80 Blues engineers, plus drawings of the BAE Hawk in Red Arrows livery.

of the team from No.111 Squadron and by its Hunter Hawker jets painted glossy jet black, the squadron's colour.

'Treble One' Squadron's team of four Hunters became the RAF's premier aerobatic team from 1957, expanded rapidly into a five-jet team – then unique in Europe – and won celebrity status, making TV appearances and sending out signed photographs of the team and its formations. From 1955 to 1958 the Black Arrows' Boss was the celebrated World War II veteran Squadron Leader Roger Topp, and it was in 1958 that the Black Arrows team joined by Hunters from other RAF squadrons performed a synchronized loop of 22 Hunters in Pterodactyl formation. It still stands as the world record for the greatest number of aircraft ever looped in formation.

By 1960, the Black Arrows had set the style to be followed by all their successors down to the Red Arrows. They introduced new formations and named them: Wine Glass, a shape flown by the Red Arrows at their maiden 1965 display, is one example. They enhanced bomb bursts with smoke trails; stationed a pilot on the ground as commentator to the crowd; and tripled the number of displays flown annually by the team at home and abroad to 59.

The futuristic English Electric Lightning supersonic fighter was scheduled to wow the crowds at 1960s displays, but by 1962, the Tigers aerobatic team from No.74 Squadron was finding this jet not ideal for flying tight formations at low altitudes. It was hard to keep the high-speed manoeuvres in the crowd's vision; low-level aerobatics were prematurely aging the RAF's pricey Lightnings; and they were far from cheap to run. Furthermore, Fighter Command was nailbiting about maintaining operational readiness when its front-line interceptor squadrons were fielding three of the RAF's official display teams.

The Red Pelicans, a Flying Training School (FTS) team flying Jet Provosts, looked like a cheaper solution, and the RAF chose them as the premier team for 1964. But after the sweptback Lightnings, the Provosts looked slow and *out of date*. They were even outshone by their supporting team from the FTS, the Yellowjacks. This part-time team of five instructors led by a former Black Arrows pilot, Flight Lieutenant Lee Jones, was impressing the crowds at air shows. They were flying fun new advanced jet trainers: fast, sweptwing Folland Gnats, painted all-over bright yellow.

The Red Arrows began as they were to continue: in a climate of economic cutbacks. Maintaining multiple display teams, each flying between five and nine jets, was costly – in 1960 the RAF had presented fifteen official teams. In 1964, the MoD cut back. The Yellowjacks were allocated more pilots and seven fast, manoeuvrable Folland Gnats, and in 1965 they became the RAF's only full-time aerobatic display team. Their Gnats were repainted red and as a salute to the Red Pelicans and the spectacular Black Arrows, the team was renamed the Red Arrows.

The first Red Arrows' air display was a modest event for the aviation press that took place in poor weather on 6 May 1965 at Little Rissington RAF base, near Cirencester. The first show for the public came three days later, in France, when the Reds displayed at the French National Air Day at Clermont Ferrand. With hindsight, both seem little more than dress rehearsals for the big appearance: the third Biggin Hill International Air Travel Fair on 13–16 May, held to raise the popularity of aviation with the public. There was little fanfare: the display merited 40 words in *Flight* magazine. The 7-Gnat team led by Lee Jones put on a "fine sequence", it reported, to a crowd of about 150,000. "...Very impressive was the team's downward bomb-burst with smoke, on which two aircraft then superimposed an upward burst."

By the end of the 1965 season, the Red Arrows had flown 65 displays at home and in France, Italy, Holland, Belgium and Germany. The MoD then enlarged the team by two and made it the RAF's permanent, nine-ship air display team, with a mission to fly an average of 95 shows a season at home and abroad. The fast climb, dive and roll rates of the Folland Gnat were a revelation and a new design tool in the hands of Britain's finest aerobatic pilots. The Red Arrows developed their display with this aircraft until 1979, when fatigue took its toll of the fleet. On 15 September 1979, the Reds flew their Gnats from RAF bases at Abingdon, St. Athan and Valley, to commemorate the Battle of Britain, before switching to the Hawker Siddeley Hawk (*see* pp212-241).

By the end of the 40th anniversary season, Red Arrows' teams had flown more than 3,000 displays in 52 countries – in 1995 they flew a record 136. And there's no way of counting the millions of people who've been thrilled by the elegant Cygnet Roll, the heart-stopping Gypo Pass and the dramatic Opposition Loop. Today, no British air display seems complete without the patriotic smoke that drifts away after the Red Arrows passed by.

Lake Windermere, Cumbria.

Clacton-on-Sea, Essex.

The Wreck datum point, RAF Akrotiri.

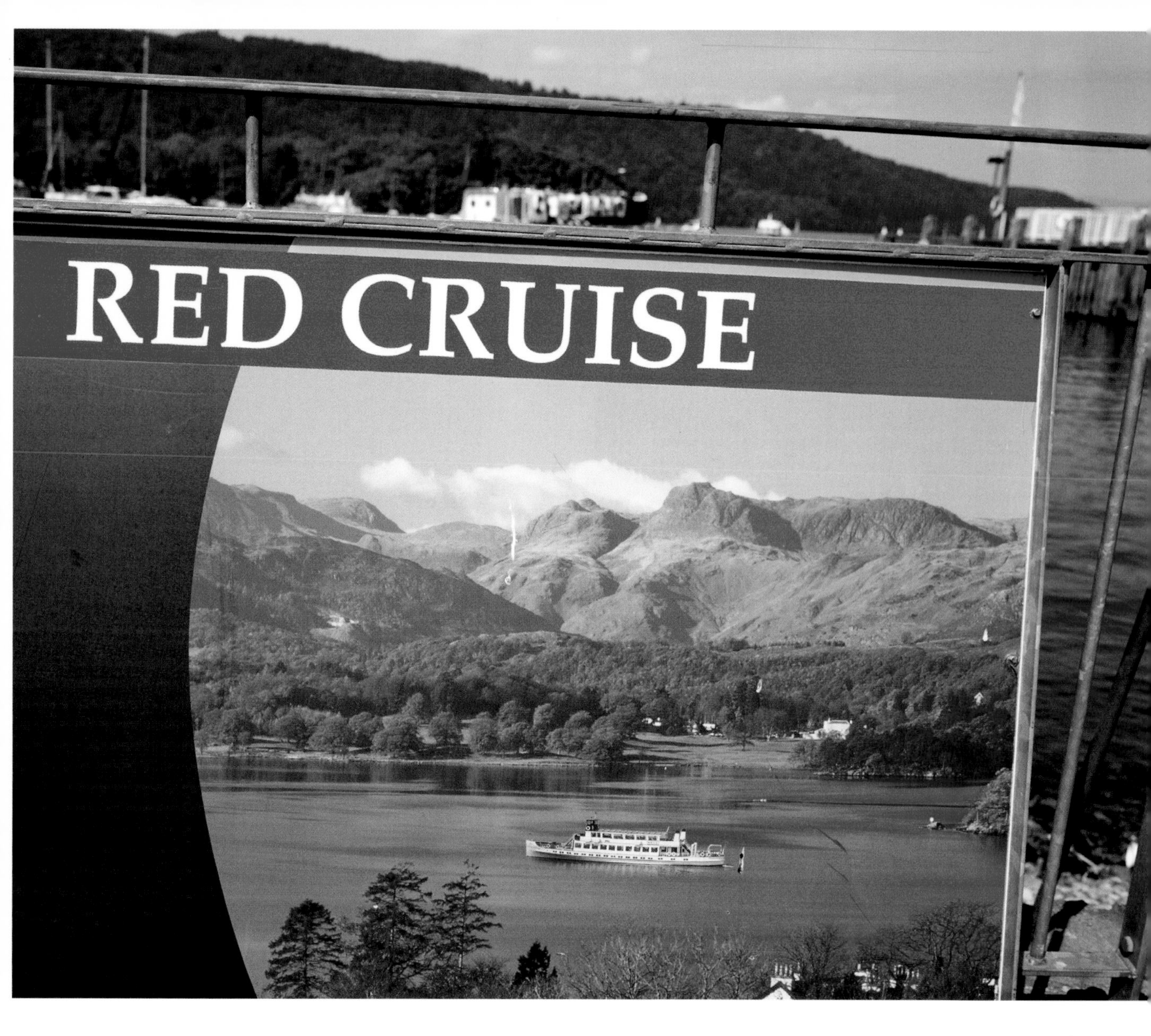

Lake Windermere, Cumbria.

Squadron Leader Dunc Mason and Flight Lieutenant David
Slow sign autographs at Airbourne Eastbourne, East Sussex.

St Peter Port harbour wall, Guernsey.

Thames Estuary, Southend-on-Sea, Essex.

1101

"All ships! Between 14.00 and 16.30 on Sunday 1st August, the RAF will be providing an air display centred on Belle Isle and focused on Bowness."
Windermere Lake Wardens' radio transmission.

Kielder Forest, Northumberland.

BFC

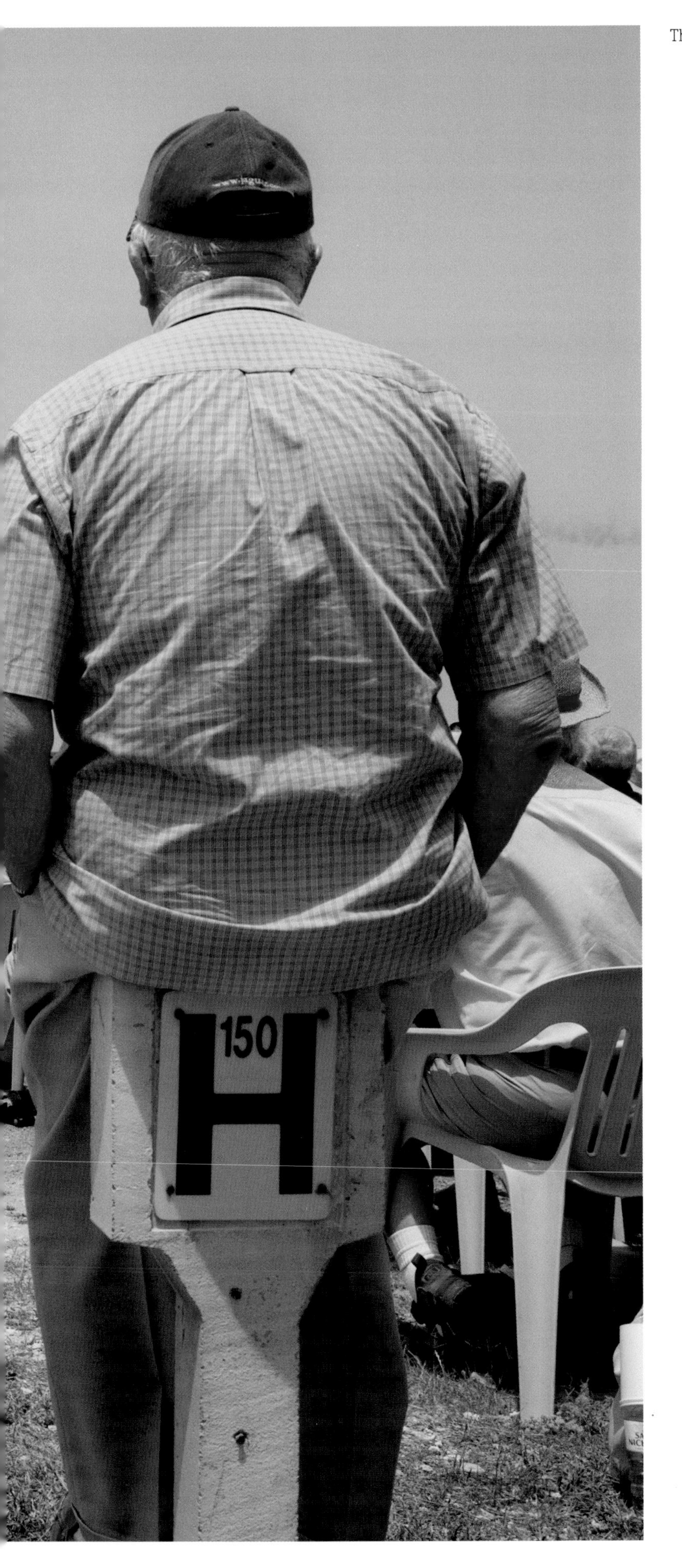

The Princess Mary Hospital, RAF Akrotiri.

ROYAL
2
3
5

Opposite The first official nine-ship portrait.

On the first working Monday of January 2004, I nervously entered the gate of RAF Scampton, the Red Arrows' HQ. Walking into their inner sanctum is like entering a trophy room. Team portraits taken every year since 1965 line the long, narrow corridor that runs past the Reds' offices – peaked caps in the 1960s, moustaches in the 1970s, and those timeless red flying suits. I could see the current team crowded in a room at one end; I ventured along the red carpet towards them, feeling as if I was walking the plank.

Would they be wary of me? Like all celebrities, the Red Arrows often find themselves misunderstood and even manipulated by the press. Would they take me seriously? Here was I, a technophobe padded out with bluffer's jargon, wanting to talk to them about flying, engineering and maintenance. Would I feel inadequate?

And what was I going to call them all?

As a photographer, I was in a privileged position. The Red Arrows receive hundreds of requests from aerophiles pleading for a chance to fly with them as passengers. For reasons ranging from Health and Safety regulations to RAF policy, only those on the 'approved' list will be accommodated. Offers of £100,000 to a charity in exchange for a trip have been rejected. A visiting Air Commodore may be offered a back seat on a practice sortie; a request from a doctor researching into the effects of g may be accepted; and applicants for the team's yearly intake of two or three new pilots who have amassed fifteen hundred-plus flying hours on Tornados, Jaguars or Harriers may be offered a trial flight in the back seat of a Hawk jet during winter training. Then there are photographers and journalists who apply to the RAF for the go-ahead to carry out an assignment.

The crew room at the end of the corridor is a serviceable canteen/meeting room/visitors' lounge. Behind a counter gurgles a venerable coffee machine and an overworked toaster is frequently cranked up. The fridge is full of the home-made salads the pilots bring in for lunch, the cupboards crammed with bottles of squash. Pilots crowd in and out, often followed by Public Relations Officer Rachel Huxford leading groups of visitors and introducing them. The Reds mill around drinking coffee, chatting to visitors or holding impromptu discussions.

Impressive décor and excessive comfort do not generally feature in RAF facilities, and the Red Arrows' HQ is no exception to this rule. The style is institutional; the upholstery brown mock leather. But the windowsills, side

Above left Display commentator and Red 10, Flight Lieutenant Steve Underwood, sips tea on the Esplanade at Southend-on-Sea before the show.

tables and the walls above the visitors' chairs are crowded with trophies and shields commemorating past aerobatic glories; here a mascot captured from a rival team, there a row of model aeroplanes – Gnats, Hawks, Concordes – mementos donated by admiring hosts at home and abroad.

Here on that first morning I judged an ordinary day's business in progress. Surging around in high humour were a gaggle of pilots who, when they spied me offered intense eye contact over warm handshakes, a fine mug of coffee (from the Team Leader) and the promise of interesting times ahead.

I quickly noticed how they communicate: through rapid exchanges as they nudge past each other in confined spaces, as if transmitting radio messages from their cockpits during high-speed passes. The reason for their clipped sentences and compressed language became clear: the Red Arrows are governed by the clock. They operate in what must be a nirvana for a time and motion expert, with every programmed minute accounted for and rarely a second lost or wasted.

As an outsider whose day is controlled by factors other than a flying schedule, I found this super-punctuality alarming. If I fell just one step behind the gathering pace of adding ticks to the to-do list, I'd be left behind or in the wrong place, coming to the awful realisation that I'd missed the moment. I also learned to be a slave to the clock.

Seconds after I was handed my coffee, a clang on a ship's bell hanging outside the Flight Planning office along the corridor, summoned a bunch of pilots to the briefing room, whose door closed firmly but politely behind them.

The chat among those of us left in the crew room was light but purposeful. If something's worth saying, it's listened to and frank views are given in return. We ranged across news from Iraq, Defence White Papers, RAF cuts, haircuts, X-box games and a lot of banter. Volunteer a personal view and you may become the brunt of their collective humour.

Behind the frivolous repartee and relaxing chatter, signs of the gnawing worries associated with a steeply rising learning curve whose summit is out of sight occasionally surface. But it takes time to learn to make the diagnosis.

As for names, at first I tried calling the higher-ranking squadron members 'sir'. But there were howls of protest, so I settled on first names. Then, after I was introduced to Squadron Leader Spike Jepson, the team leader, I called him what everyone else calls him: 'Boss'.

Every moment of the months I spent with them was a chance to learn more about how this team of people do what they do - how they train new pilots to fly a perfect Diamond Nine and whether their displays are as good as they're said to be. How do the Red Arrows rate among the world's aerobatic teams? Here's some of what I learned in those months.

NEW SEASON

The last display of the summer, which is usually scheduled towards the end of September, marks the end of each Red Arrows' year. The very next day, red flying suits are folded away and may be auctioned off for charity and the Reds and the Blues are all back in green suits. "Taking off the red suit after the last display is like shedding your skin," recalls Spike Jepson.

Just as one year ends, preparations for the next commence. "The team quickly disintegrates," remembers Spike, "but it rapidly reforms within a day as the outgoing boys are replaced by the new boys." The return to Scampton after the season's last display is the finale of their tour for the third-year pilots and there are end-of-season dinners to organize; while the new pilots, usually called 'new boys' and often 'F.N.G.s' ('F...... New Guys'), arrive. Before officially moving into their second or third years, the five or six pilots who will stay on are due some leave. So are many of the Blues who accompany the team on the display circuit to carry out inspections and minor repairs. Some of the younger Blues may be leaving. Their replacements arrive and pitch in.

For the senior ranks there are deskfuls of end-of-season paperwork to get stuck into and the forward planning for the new year to start on. The Road Manager will be off visiting and surveying possible sites for the next season's shows, because already, applications will have been arriving by the sack-load. They're sent in by organisations and individuals who want the Red Arrows to fly a display or a fly-past at their local event next year.

It's already time to get on with the winter training schedule. On the day after the team return at the end of the summer display season, usually before October has ended, at 08:40 on the dot, a new Red Arrow's year is under way.

ON TOUR

But sometimes, usually every three years or so, the display season may be shortened because a team of 11 Hawks, their pilots, engineers and a back-up team make a foreign tour. Their last one took place in September 2003, when the team flew off on a goodwill tour taking in several Gulf states, Egypt,

Thailand, India and Malaysia, returning to Scampton at the end of October.

One of their longest tours began in October 1995, when the team displayed in the Gulf States and South Africa, then went off on an Australasian tour, performing in Malaysia in December and in Indonesia, Brunei, the Philippines, Singapore and Australia in January.

Normally, October is the first of about seven months of intensive graft, when the Red Arrows lick themselves into shape in preparation for the crucial test, usually held in the first or second week of May, for their Public Display Authority (PDA) or official permit to fly the summer's air shows. To achieve this goal, team members give themselves about five months to make any changes to the display, train up the new pilots and practise to the point where they can fly as a 'nine-ship' – all nine pilots fly in formation together. The tour meant that the intake of new pilots in 1995–96 had to compress their preparatory training into three months instead of five.

The only option was to train the new pilots while on tour. On their return to Scampton in January, the Reds had to practise even more intensively than usual for their first nine-ship. This flight is special to every year's team because it marks the point from which they can start polishing their performance for the all-important PDA test. The strategy worked: the team flew a successful nine-ship in spring 1996 and it was business as usual for the Red Arrows on PDA Day 1996.

Opposite Senior commanders watch the PDA display on 12 May. From left to right: Air Commodore Glenn Edge, Flying Training; Group Captain Jon Fynes, Commandant Central Flying School (CFS); and Air Marshal Sir Joe French, Commander-in-Chief, RAF Personnel and Training Command.

SHAPING UP

For new recruits, the two or three pilots who join each year are extraordinarily well qualified. They're all commissioned officers with front-line, fast-jet backgrounds and all have combat experience. To give just two examples, Flight Lieutenants Simon Stevens and David Slow flew Tornado F3s and Harriers respectively on missions over the former Yugoslavia before joining the Reds in October 2003; and Flt. Lts. Martin Higgins and Jim Turner, who joined in October 2004, flew Tornado F3s, Jaguars and Harriers respectively on operational missions over Iraq.

Despite their impressive CVs, the new pilots have to work up their concentration skills. They learn the display and their role in it, but most people who see the Red Arrows perform don't realize that there are three versions to a show. The team can only fly their full display when the cloud base is at least 1,400m or 4,500ft and the loops can be flown to a height of

Above left Squadron Leader Spike Jepson addresses the assembled Blues, all dressed for the first time in their blue overalls, on PDA Day.

1,850m or 6,000ft; their 'rolling' display, for days when the cloud base is at least 750m or 2,500ft, cuts out the high loops; and for days when there's low cloud cover of at least 300m or 1,000ft, they have a third, 'flat' display.

The recruits must first learn their role in every manoeuvre in all three displays, and then how to change from one display to another at any point on a call from the Boss. For example, when flying their flat display, the Boss will be alert to a break in the cloud cover big enough to allow the team to fly the higher rolling or even full display. Once he decides a change is feasible, he radios a command and the pilots flying behind him all move seamlessly into the manoeuvre he's called for.

New guys also have hundreds of commands and other details to memorize. They need to know at what points in the display their smoke is switched on and off, the command to listen out for: 'Smoke on Go'; and the right responses to give. And they must get it right – they don't want to leave a gap in the team's smoke trail or be trailing smoke when their neighbours aren't; and they must never hit the blue button in error when they're on the red side of the smoke trail.

They have to know what the Boss's beeps mean. Radio time has to be apportioned between the Boss and the Synchro Pair, Reds 6 and 7, who need control at different points in the display. For example, when Synchro are flying towards each other in Opposition Loop or Carousel, they have to talk on the radio. At these moments it is vital that they have exclusive use. The other seven jets are elsewhere, repositioning, and if the Boss in Red 1 needs to communicate with them, he'll radio a tone. The whole team can hear the tone, including Synchro, because it briefly interrupts the radio without cutting out any conversation being transmitted. A whole language of tones has evolved. A tone at one point says 'I'm coming right'; at another 'Now move into Big Battle formation'; and at another point there could be two tones, one to signal a turn and the second to confirm that the turn has ended. New pilots have to learn what the tones mean at the various points in the display, remember them all and execute the correct action at every beep.

"It's not that they've never encountered anything like this before," explains the Boss. "On every front line you have code words to tell people to do certain things. But the new guys have to learn all our beeps." It's the learning curve that's so demanding. Every day there's something new to know and the curve is pretty vertical for several months."

Trainee military pilots learn basic formation flying, an essential skill when aircraft have to fly in convoy. To maintain their position in the formation they must stay a certain distance from their neighbours. To do that, they pick a couple of points on neighbouring aircraft and try to stay at the apex of an imaginary triangle formed between the two reference points and the pilot's eye – "just points in space," as Spike Jepson puts it.

Aerobatic formation flying is far more complex. The formation changes constantly as it performs various manoeuvres, splits and re-forms, so the references change with it. Every aerobatic team has its own system based on the aircraft they fly and how far apart the aircraft must be. The Red Arrows generally fly at 3–3.6m or 10–12ft distance. This is a safe distance, but much closer than most new Reds ever flew in formation with their front-line squadrons. The distances vary to some extent in different formations. In Apollo formation, for example, they fly about 2.5m or 8ft apart.

Squadron Leader John Green, Executive Officer and Red 9 explains how the new guys learn accurate referencing: "We take them to a Hawk parked on the line and put a helmet on the ground so they see how to check that reference. Then we move the helmet 30cm or 1ft forward, as they might move in their aircraft, and get them to check it again; then we move the helmet the same distance back from the original point. That shows the pilots that they can move inside an area the size of a beach ball and stay on-reference, but if they go outside that distance, they're off-reference. Then in the air they sense where the aircraft needs to be to maintain accurate alignment."

In the Red Arrows, each pilot has a numbered position in the formation. The Boss is Red 1, the lead aircraft, with Reds 3, 5 and 9 on his left and Reds 2, 4 and 8 on his right. The year's new pilots fly beside the Leader in Reds 3 and 2; the most experienced pilots fly at the back in Reds 9 and 8. Directly behind the leader, in the centre of the formation and at the tail are the Synchro Pair: Reds 6 (Synchro Leader) and 7. In the formation they're also called the 'stem'. They occupy the least active positions in the formation, but their name comes from their role in the second half of the display, when they split away to fly a series of dynamic synchronized manoeuvres.

Each pilot learns the references for his position all through the display. The new pilots in Reds 2 and 3 formate on the leader just ahead and above them. They need hours of flying time checking references. It's tricky, and

Above left Squadron Leader John Green, Team Executive and Red 9, takes short-listed candidates to join the Red Arrows out to a Hawk parked on the line to explain how to achieve accurate referencing when flying in formation.

optical illusions sometimes make it more so. If the light is bright, it can confuse the eye, so the pilots have to make themselves look very carefully. And gusts of wind can blow a jet off-reference.

Accurate referencing depends on all pilots being roughly in the same position in the cockpit. The seat restraints hold the pilot against the seat, but it's possible for one pilot to sit a bit farther forward than the others. "That pilot will keep on finding an error and having to fudge (make a correction)," explains John Green. "If you move just forward of your primary reference (the leading edge of the wing, perhaps) the secondary reference (the trailing edge of the tailplane, say) won't work. That means that you're probably looking at the angles incorrectly and you're off-reference."

The struggle to stay accurately on-reference while moving through the complex aerobatic manoeuvres at speeds of 420kt or more is one of the key challenges that make the learning curve so steep in the first few weeks of flying with the Red Arrows.

The start of a new Red Arrows year may be like musical chairs for those pilots who have moved into their second or third year and may have changed flying position. Squadron Leader Dunc Mason flew Red 5 during the 2004 season, his second year, and moved to Red 9 and the position of Executive Officer for 2005. Flight Lieutenant Dan Simmons flew Red 7 – Synchro 2 – for the 2003-04 season and moved on to Red 6, Synchro Leader; while Simon Stevens, who flew Red 3 in 2003-04, his first season, took over Red 7. Up to six veteran pilots may change position in any year and some have to relearn the display patterns from a new perspective.

However often a year's new pilots are overheard wondering whether they'll make it to the nine-ship, winter training is tried and tested and scarcely any new recruit fails to make the grade – despite the confidence-testing that results from the relentless criticism. While the public's favourite questions to the Red Arrows are 'How fast do you fly?' and 'How high do you go?', the question the Reds must ask most often is: 'Can I hack it?' They need to give and take support, which is why they must be able to bond quickly and deal with the occasional personality clashes that are an inevitable part of working in such a fast-moving environment.

Above left The Reds fly a winter training sortie over Brattleby Hill, just outside the Scampton airfield perimeter fence.

Right En route from the UK to Cyprus, the Red Arrows wait in their Hawks for start-up permission from Air Traffic Control at the US Naval Air Station in Sicily.

WINTERHAWK

Flashes of red wings tearing through winter sunlight is a daily sight for commuters along the busy A15 highway from Lincoln as the Red Arrows piece together their display. Craning locals can spot if it's a good day or a bad one for them. "The Arrows are like a flock of birds that appear in the autumn," observes Brattleby villager Roy Thornhill. "I associate winter with the sight of them. There's an emptiness when they fly off to Cyprus."

In January or February the Reds, with their engineers in the back seats of their Hawk jets, fly off to RAF Akrotiri in Cyprus for 'Exercise WinterHawk', the phase of winter training in which the team practise flying in the milder Mediterranean climate. At Scampton, Synchro have been practising together the manoeuvres they fly in the display, so there have been few opportunities for all nine pilots to fly in formation. Transiting in formation, the Hawks, followed one hour later by an RAF Hercules C-130 transport carrying repair equipment, spares and a back-up team of Blues, take two days to fly to RAF Akrotiri.

An overnight stop is usually made at the Italian Air Force base in Brindisi, but in 2004 it was at the US Naval Air Station Sigonella in Sicily at the foot of bubbling Mount Etna. Early the next morning, in the astonishingly clear air beside the volcano, the team were strapped in and ready to go, with a Blue standing by to assist the pilots at start up and take off. But all the best-laid plans go awry. The local Air Traffic Control, perhaps unfamiliar with the procedure for dealing with a team of red jets all wanting to start up and take off at once, were not ready for them.

Fingers clad in leather flying gloves drummed on still-open canopies. After ten minutes (an eternity for the super-punctual Reds), all the canopies closed simultaneously and all the engines started up together. The attendant Blues carried out pre-taxi checks ('undercarriage clear, air brakes good…') and, on command, all marched away, turned, and stood to attention, giving the thumbs up to their pilots. The jets began to taxi in numerical order and tight formation, the Boss leading and the Hawk belonging to Red 11, the Wing Commander, bringing up the rear.

The Red Arrows have their ways of doing things and newcomers find themselves having to observe thousands of tiny details known to no other squadron. "When you come here fresh, it takes a while to see what it's all about and it's a year before you understand it," comments Corporal Mark

Above left Chief Technician Kerry Griffiths helps to load Albert, the C-130 Hercules transport, before the two-day flight to RAF Akrotiri.

Gage, Airframe Technician. "You often hear things like 'it's always been done that way' and you may try to change it, but then you go back to the way it's always been done. You realize it works."

RAF Akrotiri, south of Larnaca, is inside one of Britain's two sovereign military base areas on Cyprus and the largest RAF facility outside Britain. But why travel there to practise? Just arranging it all takes weeks. Corporal Andrew Haynes, Supplier, handles some 23 tons of freight, including about 12 tons of personal effects, which have to be sent ahead by sea. The remainder is loaded into the Hercules C-130 transport on the day before departure, taking about two hours.

Meanwhile, Flight Planning have been getting to grips with the flight details. Starting weeks before departure, they've produced a skeleton flight plan and submitted it with maps to the pilot in charge of navigation for approval, made the resulting adjustments, and made hundreds of other arrangements. Flight Planning track details from fuel and oxygen supplies to diplomatic clearances and booking facilities at the en route bases. It's their job to ensure that the team have all the tools to arrive at the precise location exactly at the planned time. "We check all weather conditions en route," explains Corporal Alex Stockbridge; "Prior to departure we phone up every airfield on the way to find out what kind of weather they're having, and relay it to the team."

Flight planning doesn't end when the team take off. "We work remotely," says Alex Stockbridge. "Anything they need – a weather update, a revised ETA because of a delay – wherever they are day or night, we're always here to check," she explains.

The weather is the reason for training in Cyprus. February in Lincolnshire means limited flying time. Even on a good day flying is possible only between 08:30 and 15:30 hours and many slots and days are lost to low cloud base, rain, sleet, snow, or fog. The skies above Akrotiri are cold, but they're almost always clear for full display practice.

Above left Red 7's helmet is temporarily stored in his Hawk's open canopy, waiting for its owner to return for his next sortie.

Opposite Squadron Leader Spike Jepson, complete with red helmet, is plunged into the Mediterranean for a Wet Drill during spring training in Cyprus. The aim of the exercise is to practise a helicopter recovery after an ejection over the sea.

SPRINGHAWK

After four weeks, the team leaves Akrotiri for Scampton. A month later, they will be ready to fly their first nine-ship of the year. This is symbolic: a successful nine-ship is proof that the new year's team is in business after months of relentless learning and practice. "I had a lump in my throat," admitted Spike Jepson, after he'd led his first nine-ship into the air. So did everyone else in the squadron. The symmetry of the formation had reappeared and the flying was nearly perfect.

A successful nine-ship also marks the start of a new phase of training; the team hits another gear and demands more from each performance. It brings the next important date, PDA Day in May, into focus. Without a Public Display Authority, the Red Arrows could not fly their display in public, so within a month of their first nine-ship, the team are back in Cyprus for 'Exercise SpringHawk': six weeks of intensive practice before their PDA test. The quality of their formation flying needs to improve dramatically.

Akrotiri slots start and finish early and with few visitors to entertain, the pilots focus on flying, including parachute drills and survival skills. Ejection and recovery drill takes place early in SpringHawk. Rather than dunk those expensively trained bodies in the icy North Sea off the Lincolnshire coast, the Reds, along with their regular passengers, the Circus Blues, are thrown from a Royal Navy boat into the drink to practise an ejection-over-sea ditching and recovery by helicopter. This annual wet drill isn't popular, RAF types being naturally more comfortable in the air than in the still-chilly Med.

One important aspect of training is learning to stay 'on datum'. The Boss plans the display to ensure that the formations are never too high or so far left or right that the crowd can't see them from the correct perspective. Since the Red Arrows fly at dozens of air shows, each with its own quirks of geography, Flight Lieutenant Steve Underwood, Red 10 and Road Manager, accompanied by the Synchro Leader, Red 6, establish a datum point at each one during their winter and spring inspections of the proposed display sites. Datum will be a point 230m or 750ft in front of the crowd at an air show, or a pier or cliff on a coast, which will be the axis or central focus of the team's display. As long as the point is accurate and the Red Arrows fly 'on datum', the crowd will see the whole display from the best perspective.

In Cyprus, the Boss selects a datum in five or six different locations for practice. The sandstone cliffs at the southern end of the island are used most

often, followed by the Wreck (a coastal shipwreck), a coastal lighthouse and the 'Trig point' on the cliffs. On practice sorties the Boss chooses a datum according to the wind direction.

Above left Flight Lieutenant Antony Parkinson, Red 2, contributes to the banter at the Reds' accommodation block, RAF Akrotiri.

Right The RAFAT Executive Officer and Red 9, Squadron Leader John Green, walks out to his Hawk for the transit from RAF Akrotiri to Marka in Jordan.

PASSING OUT

"Are they all red rockets?" Spike Jepson asked Junior Engineering Officer or JEngO Simon Race about the state of the Hawks during morning briefing in the crew room. It was his third PDA Day as Boss and his sixth as a Red Arrows pilot. The pressure to gain the PDA tells on the team. Over the last 5 weeks in Cyprus, they have flown some 60 sorties totalling about 30 hours. The strain shows up as uncharacteristic long silences and curt replies to enquiries about how things are going. No one wants to let the side down.

To an outsider, a PDA Day may look like any other Akrotiri practice day: after the met. brief, the team take off to fly practice slots. Yet an insider would spot that the Hawks are so polished they sparkle; that the eyes on the ground, watching every practice and noting every detail, belong to the big brass; and that while the rest of the base goes about its business, the RAFAT people are grouped on the cliffs watching the flying.

To gain their PDA, the Red Arrows must fly their display in line with the exceptional standards expected of the RAF's official aerobatic team, while maintaining the highest standards of safety in accordance to the RAFAT's Mission Statement. They begin the day with a practice sortie, then fly the display for the judge. If they failed their exam sortie, it would be back to the drawing board for the team. But that *never* happens.

On the morning of PDA Day, the Boss led the Red Arrows into the air at 08:00 and, using the Akrotiri cliffs as the datum point, flew a practice slot, then landed and debriefed. At 10:00 the team took off on a second slot. On this PDA Day, the judge, Air Marshal Sir Joe French, Commander-in-Chief of RAF Personnel and Training Command was the judge, accompanied by Air Commodore Glenn Edge, Flying Training; and Group Captain Jon Fynes, Commandant Central Flying School (CFS). The Commander-in-Chief declared himself satisfied after the second display, and issued the PDA after they landed. You could almost hear the sound of stress lifting.

Once the PDA has been granted, the team can officially shed their olive green off-season wear and metamorphose into Reds and Blues. Back in their respective locker rooms, evaporating tension results in high jinks among

the pilots and engineers as they change into their new uniforms before reappearing for the celebrations. "It's a proud moment when you put the red suit on for the first time," remembers Flight Lieutenant Antony Parkinson. "It's bigger than getting your wings, and that's pretty special."

Outside in the sun, official pictures are taken to record the day. The judge and other senior officers are photographed shaking hands with the pilots. The Reds and the Blues, resplendent in their primary colours, kneel in formation on the line and stand in front of the Boss's Hawk; along its wings. And the Champagne flows.

PDA Day marks the official opening of the display season, and barely two days later the first public display takes place over RAF Akrotiri, watched by RAF personnel and their families on the base. This open day immediately after PDA is the first time those red suits are seen in public and it makes an indelible impression on the wearers. His first steps out into the crowd are still imprinted in Flight Lieutenant Simon Stevens's mind: "You feel very honoured – it was one of the proudest moments of my life. Yet you don't feel as if you've earned it when the season has barely begun."

The first public display makes the Blues feel especially proud. Ten of the Blues are selected from a group of volunteers and then assigned special responsibilities for one of the Hawks and its pilots, and they're collectively known as the 'Circus'. The Circus Blues fly with the Reds to Cyprus and accompany them to most displays, travelling in the Hawks' back seats. Joined by the back-up team who flew over in the Hercules C-130, they take part in the PDA celebrations and they pre-flight (prepare) the jets for the Akrotiri display. "It's a great moment on the first display in Cyprus," recalls rigger Senior Aircraftman (SAC) Richard Adams, one of the back-up team of Blues. "We're responsible for filling all the smoke pods with the derv and the dye. If the display has been shown on TV, I watch it at home afterwards and think, 'yep, that's my smoke'."

"When we returned after PDA last year," remembers Airframe Technician Mark Gage, "I flew in the back of Red 7, with Squadron Leader David Thomas at the controls. We flew in formation above Scampton and we looped and dived. That was a big moment, my family were waiting down below. We'd been away for perhaps five weeks and this was the first time we were flying as the Red Arrows."

Above left It's PDA Day and Squadron Leader Spike Jepson is warily opening his locker door to get his new red flying suit. It's a Reds tradition that the pilots hide in each others' lockers and leap out as the door opens, making as much noise as they can.

Right Flight Lieutenant Jez Griggs in characteristic good humour slides down the banister of the squadron building at RAF Akrotiri.

Above left A gaggle of geese pass Ground Safety Officer Flight Lieutenant Steve Underwood as he makes his important pre-take-off brief to the Boss. The Red Arrows are about to display at the agricultural community show at Eye, Suffolk.

FORWARD PLANNING

After PDA, the team faced a schedule of 127 displays and fly-pasts in just under 6 months, an average of 6 a week. The season had to start bang on time since the calendar had long since been set in stone. Promotional literature and schedules were printed well before the team returned from Cyprus.

Scarcely were the previous summer's displays over than air show organizers and individuals were sending in their requests for the Red Arrows to fly at local, national and international events planned for the next summer. The team receive so many bids that they ask for them to be in before September. The RAF's Participation Committee (PC) at Strike Command in High Wycombe, which plans flying display schedules, received 172 requests for full displays and 1,000 applications for fly-pasts. This was whittled down to 83 displays, 7 formal fly-pasts and 37 en route fly-pasts (carried out while flying from one event to another without deviating from the flight plan).

Merit and safety are the basis for their first short list: those applicants who will receive a site survey visit from a Red Arrows' representative. That person is Red 10, the Road Manager and Ground Safety Officer, who also commentates on the team's displays to the crowds. Flight Lieutenant Steve Underwood has been Red 10 and Road Manager since the 2001-02 season. Every winter he's away for a fortnight at a time, surveying sites where the team have not displayed before or haven't displayed for some years.

Steve Underwood manages to visit most sites himself and, whenever possible, he takes Red 6, the Synchro Leader, along with him to be certain that the site is suitable for the dynamic manoeuvres. "We look for hazards," he explains, "cranes, high tower blocks, industrial hazards." He will look for a datum point and, where there's no runway, a suitable display line – a line along which the Reds can fly, parallel to the crowd and the regulation 230m or about 750ft from the forward crowd line. "And at sites where there are lots of people and cliffs around, like Sunderland or where we displayed at the end of the Great North Run on 26 September, we make sure the planned route is legal – that it complies with CAA requirements."

The Civil Aviation Authority (CAA) publishes CAP 403, a set of rules for air displays and fly-pasts; and the military issues a Joint Service Publication (JSP). The Red Arrows follow the rules set out in those documents to the letter. "We wouldn't dream of transgressing those," says Steve Underwood. "They're the limits and you can't massage them in any way."

Many of the Red Arrows' display fixtures are regulars: the Royal International Air Tattoo (RIAT) at Fairford, Gloucestershire, and the Farnborough Air Show in Hampshire. Others are planned by professional impresarios, many of whom hold regular air displays. But the Red Arrows also consider applications from individuals and amateur organisations. Wing Commander Bill Ramsey recalls an occasion when, asked to visit a site in place of Red 10, found himself meeting a prospective organizer in the front room of a private house in Penzance:

> "I arrived at the front door and glimpsed a gentleman looking out from a window. I introduced myself and he explained that his wife, the prospective show organizer, was not there. She was upstairs getting ready for the meeting, so we chatted until she came down. We discussed the show and I asked where she thought datum should be. She hadn't thought about datum, so we had a nice cup of tea and a cream cake, then we drove out to see where datum might be. On the way I pointed out that it would cost £7,000 for a display and she said she had only raised £400. I told her she didn't have very long to raise the rest, but wished her good luck because the Red Arrows would love to display there. Unfortunately, she was unable to raise more for that year. However, we persuaded the Participation Committee to keep that venue in, and the team went to Penzance."

Applicants always have a long wait to be informed of their acceptance or rejection. Mike James, Director of the Caernarfon Air Show in Wales, plans his event around the Reds: "We apply for the Red Arrows to be at our show in September, but we don't hear until March. They're billed on our tickets, car passes and brochures, so we have to plan for a yes." By the end of March the organizers have all been notified and a provisional schedule published.

WHAM

"People ask why we need a 'Mange', when there's already a Red 10 on the ground acting as Road Manager," reports Squadron Leader Sally Varley, the Team Manager. 'Mange' is the affectionate title inherited by all who undertake the daunting task of chaperoning the Red Arrows.

In fact, until 1998 there was only one Team Manager: Red 10. He

Above left Team Leader Sally Varley, Public Relations Officer Rachel Huxford and photographer Corporal Chris Ward plan a meet and greet event before the Reds' arrival by helicopter at RAF Waddington.

dealt with *everything* during the display season: applications from show organizers; visiting display sites; working out the display calendar; organizing accommodation and transport; flying the team's spare Hawk to off-base venues; commentating on the displays to the crowds; and meeting and greeting visitors. By the 1990s the Red Arrows had grown so much in popularity and size that he was finding it tough to fit everything in and maintain the excellent standard of organizational support the team needs.

It was decided to split the job into three. Responsibility for getting the pilots and the back-up team to the right place at the right time was given to the Mange and the job of dealing with visitors, the press, charities and promotional materials was given to a civilian Public Relations Officer. Red 10 kept charge of display coordination, acting as Road Manager, Ground Safety Officer, show commentator and flying the spare Hawk to venues.

The Mange heads the planning and organization behind the scenes: the timetables, transport, accommodation and catering for all Red Arrows events, year round. Sally Varley's grasp of logistics makes her the perfect guardian of the team's on-road programme. She is, as she puts it, "on a conveyor belt of information." From the beginning to the end of the season, the broad outlines of every team outing flow to her from the administrative staff of the Adjutant, and her job is to organize those outings and transmit the details to those who are travelling.

She does this by issuing a WHAM or 'What's Happening Manager?'. This is just a few pages of instructions for an aerobatic team on the go, an apparently unexceptional document. Yet if there's one reason why nine red jets appear bang on time at every event for which they're booked, the WHAM is that reason, because each time the team leave Scampton, the WHAM is their best and worst friend. The planning begins months before the event and it's vetted by everyone down the chain of command. Yet "the WHAM is a live document," the Mange insists; and being live, it's naturally subject to last-minute changes. "We replan in minutes and use local rather than Zulu times (GMT)."

The Red Arrows' team of more than 50 people travel from display to display through the season, often in separate convoys. It's a miracle of organization. But the RAF prides itself on efficiency, so whenever Red 10 addresses an expectant crowd over a PA system with the following words: "If you look to your right-hand side, to your 2 o'clock, you can see the nose lights of … the Red Arrows…" the Mange is already planning her next

WHAMs. During one season she issued 22. "In my pocket are the next two documents that I keep working on. And I keep a notebook by my bed in case I wake up in the night thinking of something I've missed."

Above left Ground Safety Officer and display commentator Flight Lieutenant Steve Underwood checks cloud levels over South Shields as he approaches the show datum by Squirrel helicopter. He's preparing for the last display of the season: the Great North Run.

ON-ROAD PROGRAMME

The Red Arrows generally take ten aircraft to a show: Reds 1–9 flying their jets, plus Red 10 as the spare. Every day on the road begins with a morning met. brief, which includes information about the weather en route and at the display site or sites, since on some days the team displays at more than one venue. The Boss updates the WHAM and the PR Officer elaborates on the WHIPR (*see* p125).

The Road Manager arrives at the site at least 90 minutes before the scheduled display time, landing there in the spare Hawk, or transported by a Squirrel helicopter from Central Flying School (CFS). He liaises with the show organizers, gauges the weather, notes the cloud base height and phones a report to the Boss before take-off time.

As Ground Safety Officer, he checks for flight hazards. TV people often set up 'cherrypickers' at air shows so they can raise their cameras high above the crowd. Red 10 needs to find out where they are and whether they might be a hazard during the display. If he judges that they will be and they can't be moved, the display won't be flown. He will assess the numbers of birds around and, if necessary, he'll warn the Boss of a high bird strike rating and advise Synchro to wear double visors for extra protection.

Red 10 has to ensure that every display is videoed, primarily for debriefing and analyzing, but also should anything go wrong they have a record of the incident to study and, if necessary, send to the CAA. The team photographer needs to arrive in time to find the best vantage point at datum, so the video will give the team the most accurate record possible of the display for the debrief. There must be no shaking and the picture must be clear.

The lighthouse in the harbour wall was identified as the ideal spot from which to video the team's display over Guernsey. The Harbour Master ferried Corporal Chris Ward, the photographer, in his outboard just before the team was due to appear – only to find some 50 spectators occupying the spot. They'd been there for hours. "Sorry, Ladies and Gentlemen, you've found the perfect place to watch the Red Arrows and that's why I'm having to move you," Chris Ward announced spontaneously, and explained that if he couldn't film the display, the Ground Safety Officer couldn't let the Red Arrows fly. Those very understanding spectators quickly moved away; but at Clacton-on-Sea in August, Chris had found it hard to dissuade a few lads from jumping in front of the camera, despite warning them that the display might be cancelled. This is a recurring problem for the photographers.

Half an hour before the Red Arrows arrive, Red 10 goes to his stand, which is located as close as possible to datum. He checks that the organizers are ready and confirms the wind velocity and atmospheric pressure readings, and he radios the Boss to advise whether it's safe to fly the display. During the show he keeps an eye on the sky and, just before Synchro fly the Heart *(see* pp44-45), he'll radio to advise on the most visible smoke colour – red or white.

He prepares to commentate, but he also keeps his Ground Safety Officer's hat on and his eyes are peeled for hazards. At Eastbourne, the Reds were ending the first half of their display when a lone light aircraft made a leisurely flight right over the beach in front of the crowd, heading over the pier. Its altitude was about 30m or 100ft – just the height above ground that the Reds level out to for some of their low passes.

For safety reasons, Steve Underwood stopped the show. "The pilot should be prosecuted," he announced, appealing for film or still footage from the crowd. No pilot is allowed into the air space when the Red Arrows are flying and afterwards, a Council spokesperson confirmed to the Boss that the pilot had been given no clearance to be there. "I've had to deal with twenty incidents of this type in my two and a half years as Ground Safety Officer," he said afterwards. "It's very frustrating, being unable to fly a full show and disappointing the crowd."

Giving his commentary is the part of each show that Steve Underwood likes best. "I try to make it intimate. The shows I like best are small ones such as Chichester, or the Goodwood Festival of Speed. There's a crowd of 60,000 people just a couple of paces away from me. I introduce the Red Arrows and all applaud. When I say, 'look to your left-hand side' all the heads go left; and when I say 'look to your right' they all turn right, so I know they're all watching and interested." Crowds at other shows respond in different ways. Some don't make a sound until the end. At others they clap and whoop at every manoeuvre.

Opposite Top left Squadron Leader Spike Jepson pumps Flight Lieutenant David Slow's hand after the first successful nine-ship.
Top right The Reds are greeted by pilots of the Italian Frecce Tricolori aerobatic team at Air 04 in Payerne, Switzerland.
Bottom left Red 10, Flight Lieutenant Steve Underwood thanks the RAF Sea King helicopter crew for their help during a day's ferrying over the Channel Islands for the Jersey International Air Display.
Bottom right Wing Commander Bill Ramsey progresses down the line on PDA Day. Here he offers his congratulations to Squadron Leader Dunc Mason.

Above left The Synchro Pair, Flight Lieutenant Dan Simmons and Squadron Leader David Thomas, brief for their sortie outside the squadron building at RAF Akrotiri.

ARRIVAL

Taking a cue from the weather reports and updates relayed by Red 10, the Boss will decide as the Red Arrows arrive whether they should fly their flat display (for when the cloud base is above 300m or 1,000ft) or rolling display, or if the cloud base is high enough for the full display (at least 1,400m or 4,500ft). The Boss has to think ahead, calling the pilots flying behind him to get into position.

All through the display, the Reds flying behind the Boss strive to stay on-reference, so that the shape of the formation they're flying doesn't waver. The Boss must fly smoothly and accurately, because if he jerks out of true and then corrects, the eight jets following him will repeat the error. To the watching crowd, a wave will seem to pass through the formation.

Flying on-reference in formation feels unnatural at first because a pilot's instinct when flying a fast jet at 400kt is to look directly ahead, not at a neighbouring jet. Learning trust is a major part of the training, and the Boss mustn't forget for a second that eight pairs of hands are repeating his every move and eight pairs of ears are alert for every command. "I must make my mouth match my hands," says Squadron Leader Dicky Patounas, who took over as Red 1 in October 2004 – meaning that he can't make any new move without barking his intentions into the mike. "I have to think in multiples – of everyone behind me and what they're going to do. I'll say: 'Going full', or 'Going flat' and I'm flying into the first manoeuvre as we've practised 1,000 times. But I'm putting that bit of my brain on autopilot and working the rest of it to capacity to sift through all the information that's coming in, and work out what's coming up: how I'm going to get us from this point to the next."

For example, through every manoeuvre the Boss has to maintain safe distances from any obstacles that have been reported to him – and keep an eye open for any new obstacle that might obscure the display from the crowd or jeopardize safety. A thundercloud, for example, might blow in very quickly. If the Boss is leading the Reds through a manoeuvre, he's concentrating on engine power, the angle of bank and the amount of g. Keeping an eye on the height, he is attentive to every instrument and control.

"At the same time," he explains, "I'm heading over the other side of the airfield towards a point 30 seconds' flying time distant and I'm thinking, 'There's that tall office block over there, so I need to be at this sort of angle to move into that manoeuvre, and there's a cloud in the way. We're going to have to make a change at that particular point, and I've got to tell the guys now so they know to position themselves'. My brain's working hard, so that when I get to the key point I give the right command and the boys behind will follow."

SYNCHRO

'The crowds go wild at the Synchro Pair/With their dangerous stunts in the air…' begins a poem written and sent to the Red Arrows by six-year-old Dean Harman. The Synchro Pair are so called because halfway through the display they split off and fly a series of synchronized manoeuvres, in some of which they cross, apparently so close they appear almost to collide. But Synchro are showmen and tricksters, for as the crowd 'Oooh' and 'Aaah' with wonder, they're demonstrating an illusion they call 'fudging', a *trompe l'oeil* that has us believe, through ground-based perspective, that we see two jets pass within centimetres or inches, whereas for safety the margins are far greater.

Maintaining the highest standards of safety is a key Red Arrows' objective, as is evidenced by the squadron's low accident record. Since 1980, when they began flying the Hawk, no pilots have been lost in accidents. CAA regulations for safety at air shows, which prohibit pilots from flying over or too close to the crowd, are important. But the Red Arrows attribute their excellent safety record to their own rules and vigilance. Their pilots have at least ten years' experience of flying fast jets and they study their mistakes. They also analyze accidents such as the mid-air collision during an aerobatic display by the Italian team, the Frecce Tricolori, at the Ramstein Air Show in Germany in 1988, which killed 70 people, and they work out how to prevent a repetition. Then they teach what they learn to all their new pilots.

On top of all that, they develop internal safety systems. For example, the Cyclone, a new manoeuvre, has been checked out at many levels. At the start of winter practice, Dan Simmons, the new Synchro Leader, took the idea to Squadron Leader Dicky Patounas, who cleared it with the Wing Commander, who put it before the Commandant of the CFS. All studied it in depth. "We consider what happens at various points of the routine if, say, the canopy explodes or the engine fails," Patounas enlarges. "We come up with many such scenarios and the answers to those questions. We must always have an escape." If a 'danger point' is found, the manoeuvre is modified to eliminate it, or an escape is worked out.

Above left Young Red Arrows fans wave an anniversary flag on Jersey sea front.

Opposite Commentator Flight Lieutenant Steve Underwood and spectators at Hoylake, Wirral.

The outcome of the analysis was that the Cyclone was approved for the display. "At that stage," declares Dicky Patounas, "only ill-discipline or bad luck could cause an accident. And since we eliminate any discipline problems by recruiting the right pilots and supervising them, the only remaining problem is bad luck."

EVENTS

Few state occasions seem complete without a fly-past by the Red Arrows. The 2004 team proudly recall flying down the Mall in London with red, white and blue 'Smoke On Go', just as Olympic champ Steve Redgrave dashed along it bearing the Olympic flame. Shortly afterwards, on 14 July, France's Bastille Day, the Reds were invited to close the military parade with a pass over central Paris. The BBC reported that their fly-past from La Défense, over the Arc de Triomphe to the Louvre 'stole the show'.

Every year the team fly two or three displays in Europe and these are often spectacular. Air 04 was a three-day air show in Payerne, Switzerland, to celebrate the 40th anniversary of the Patrouille Suisse, the Swiss aerobatic team, the 15th anniversary of the Swiss PC7 aerobatic team, and the 90th anniversary of Swiss military aviation. For the finale on 4 September, the Red Arrows joined the Switzerland's foremost aerobatic team, the Patrouille Suisse, the Frecce Tricolori of Italy and Spain's Patrulla Aguila in an impressive 40-aircraft fly-past.

Unpredictable English summers made it necessary for past Red Arrows teams to develop their flat and rolling displays so as not to disappoint crowds of thousands who turn out to see them fly. But the weather sometimes stops even the Reds from flying. At the Airbourne Eastbourne International Show, with a low cloud base and huge down-draughts of air rolling off the South Downs on to Beachy Head (a phenomenon called 'rotor-streaming'), the Reds could only fly half a show.

The biggest crowds congregate at the seaside shows. The squadron count themselves as a public service, so they love displaying to the many families who find the cost of train tickets and entry fees to the bigger shows prohibitive. The Harwich International Port sponsors the Red Arrows' display at the Clacton Air Show, Essex, and the show along Weston-super-Mare sea front in Somerset was sponsored by the organization that runs the Grand Pier, which was celebrating its 100th birthday.

Having the Red Arrows display for 24 minutes over Weston-super-Mare each summer fulfils all the expectations of Rachel Marsh, Tourism and Marketing Officer for North Somerset Council. "It's impossible to gauge exactly how much revenue the Red Arrows bring into our resort," she said. "The press coverage alone pays for staging the event. We appeared on GMTV and were mentioned on the BBC, HTV and ITN." On the sea front the crowd was 120,000 and, she estimated, "most of them were day visitors."

But the big crowds at the family events can sometimes be hard to control. "We've had kids swearing at us, jumping in our way," groan the photographers, "and because you're a member of the Red Arrows you must only ask them politely to move. But they just stand there, hurling abuse, with their parents looking on, doing nothing."

In high summer, the team are away for days at the Royal International Air Tattoo (RIAT) at Fairford, Gloucestershire, and the Farnborough Air Show in Hampshire, which occur close together in July. At these bigger shows, the Reds whirl around the hospitality tents and shake hands, surrounded by adoring fans or just the curious. Perhaps because they wear the Union Flag on their flying suits and fly their jets for UK plc, they're always under pressure to sign their names and to answer incessant questions about themselves, the squadron, their jets and their flying.

Less prestigious than Farnborough but more homely and more fun is the 100-year-old agricultural community show at Eye, Suffolk, in late August. The crowd, clad in corduroys, tweeds and green wellies, mill around the traction engines on display. Steve Underwood, who arrived there by helicopter ahead of the display, was busy phoning his report to the Boss when he found himself surrounded by a flock of racing sheep belonging to the lady winner of the 'One Man and his Dog' TV programme.

August ended with two displays flown on Bank Holiday Monday. At 12:30, the Reds performed at Caernarfon, Wales; then at 16:30 they arrived at Hoylake on the Wirral sea front. Just up the coast, cockle-pickers stayed bent over their baskets as the Red Arrows hurtled overhead after the show.

SEASON'S END

On 27 September, a small crowd of Red Arrows' families and friends gathered on the grass at Scampton as 11 jets passed low over their squadron building in true RAFAT tradition, then broke to land. Champagne flutes

Above left Hawk models on sale at the RAF Akrotiri families air show.

clinked, for this was the last landing after the last show of the season and, for a few, the last day as a Red Arrow.

Since the beginning of winter training 2003, they had flown 4,182 sorties together, logging 3,225 hours and 15 minutes in the air. They had consumed 4,118,866.7 litres or 905,245.44 gallons of fuel and used the last barrel of 32,760 litres or 7,200 gallons of dye the day before over South Shields.

Spike Jepson climbed down from XX227, grabbed the hands of each team member and hugged his wife, Helen. "That's the end of the 2004 season, one of the most demanding we've had to face," he declared.

"I've just climbed out of the aeroplane, still in my g-suit, and it feels like it's part of me," he confided later on. "Everybody puts so much work into the Red Arrows to achieve RAFAT standards. It's probably one of the greatest privileges you can have. Then at the end of the year you just walk away from it and start again...I'll have a last look around the hangar and a nostalgic sniff around, and watch it being closed."

"It's like the end of term," the Wing Commander muttered as he walked out to his BMW at the end of his last season in office. He clutched a framed picture under one arm. Just inside the open hangar, dead leaves were already rustling; summer seemed to have slipped away.

Antony Parkinson had left the team once before, only to return six months later to take over from Flight Lieutenant Matt Jarvis, who had resigned due to illness. So he, uniquely, has twice experienced the pain nearly all third-year Red Arrows pilots have to go through, of being almost surgically removed from team membership. "You drift in the day after you've officially left and your picture's gone. There's another bloke in your slot and they've changed it for his. And there's someone else's flying helmet in your box."

Next morning, 28 September, the new 2005 Team Leader, Dicky Patounas, zipped through Scampton's main gate with a roar on his Kawasaki ZX10R motorbike, ready to take the reins and get another Red Arrows team into the air in eight months. The 2005 season was on its way.

So are the Red Arrows the world's best aerobatic display team? As I watched their last display after the Great North Run on 26 September I considered the last of the questions I'd asked myself on my first day with the team.

I remembered finding the patterns of Italy's Frecce Tricolori display at Kemble Air Day in June confusing to watch. And a report by the Editor of

Diamond Nine, the Red Arrows' fanzine, of a late start and repetitive flying at one display by the US Navy's Blue Angels, came to mind. Yet Daljit Heer, an airframe engineer at Heathrow, found the Red Arrows' Farnborough display "a bit conservative, though I know crowd safety is paramount. Still, you don't get the same excitement as when they're tightly packed together, like the Thunderbirds." The USAF aerobatic team, the Thunderbirds, fly only 30-40cm or 12-18in apart in some manoeuvres. John Green, who flew Red 9 until the end of 2004, thinks that this focus on accuracy restricts what can be done aerobatically, so that in fact, the displays of teams that fly in such close formation lack punch.

Where the Red Arrows shine on the air display circuit is in presenting a full entertainment package, polished in every detail from the faultless flying to the ground-based commentary. They never make their public wait; and they fly in weather that would daunt teams from countries with balmier climates. And if anything causes a glitch in the performance, the soothing voice of ringmaster Red 10 loses no time in giving the crowd a full explanation.

The Red Arrows have a mission to fulfil: 'To maintain public support for the Royal Air Force ...stimulate recruitment...contribute to wider national interests' reads their mission statement, and they achieve these objectives spectacularly well. Their displays are public-service flying and broadcasting from the team with a rich RAF tradition to uphold, along with an unshakeable sense of the importance of consistency and responsibility to their public.

Right The warm, dry squadron building at RAF Scampton beckons Senior Aircraftman Michael Evans, an avionics specialist, as he walks back from the line at the Red Arrows' Lincolnshire HQ.

ROYAL AIR

JOB DESCRIPTION

During winter training, some of the pilots who have applied to join the RAFAT are invited to Scampton to fly as back-seaters in the Hawks while their potential is assessed for next year's team intake. The candidates selected will typically be A1 achievers of outstanding pedigree, like Flight Lieutenant Dan Simmons, who was awarded his Private Pilot's Licence aged 17.

About 40 pilots a year apply to be posted to the Red Arrows. The minimum qualification is 1,500 flying hours, but those chosen are still more highly qualified. Seven of the 2003-04 team were qualified flying instructors (QFIs). Red Arrows pilots come from many different flying backgrounds and have varying degrees of operational front-line experience, so they're mainly in their thirties. Several have been display pilots: Flight Lieutenant David Slow displayed the Harrier in 2002-03, and Flt. Lts. Simon Stevens and Antony Parkinson were Tornado F3 demonstration pilots in 1999 and 2000 respectively. Antony Parkinson won an award for a display at the Royal International Air Tattoo 2000.

Yet above-average service records and flying pedigrees are just the thin end of the wedge. Outstanding qualifications are not enough to satisfy those officers on the prowl for the most likely candidates. The applicants may be leaders and instructors used to giving orders, but they must be able to show that they're fast learners and prepared to work on the concentration needed for aerobatic formation flying. Stamina is essential. During the three-year tour, a Red will fly more sorties and pull more sustained g-forces than any other operational pilot. RAFAT recruits have to fly at least three sorties a day during winter training. Then, not only must they be prepared to work to exhaustion but they must also be happy to stay on after flying hours, shaking visitors' hands warmly and answering interminable questions. PR is a major part of the job and the type of person who'll be RAFAT material will feel as grumpy as the rest of us on a bad day, but will never let it show.

All the team meet the short-listed candidates and have a say in which two or three are chosen. Anyone who can't bond with his or her potential team-mates isn't Red Arrows material. "They need to fit into the mould and become friends," said Squadron Leader John Green, Red 9 and also Team Executive. "But they can't be the sort of people who'll try to force friendships, because they'll have to take criticism on the chin and they'll need to be equally hard on the others."

Right Flying the flag and promoting the UK is as big a part of a pilot's job in the Red Arrows as is flying a show. Flight Lieutenant David Slow autographs one of 60,000 brochures the squadron has printed each season.

Pages 116-121 Facsimiles of the Airmen Selection Test (AST) from the 'Joining the RAF' careers brochure. These multiple-choice questions help assess applicants' potential. Answers are on page 259.

SOCIAL SKILLS

The short-listed eight or nine visit the Reds at RAF Akrotiri in April. Over seven days they're tested to see if they have the mettle of a Red Arrows pilot. They ride as passengers in every formation position. They're interviewed. Then they're pushed to their *social* limits, just to see if flying and after-hours partying can compromise their flying skills. The crews who will be flying in the morning forgo the party and are in bed by 21:30, while the others keep the new guys up late. Reluctant to be first to retire, they always fall for the trick. They're taken go-karting and golfing to check out all their driving skills. The idea is to strain their affability to the limits using sleep deprivation and an accumulation of hangovers. "When we choose new pilots, we push them to the limit in Cyprus. We put cracks in their armour to see if they can cope with our hard life," says Team Manager Sally Varley.

Flight Lieutenant Simon Kilby of No.20 Harrier Squadron is one who, despite making the final short list of nine, wasn't invited to join the team for the 2004-05 season. "I instructed on the Hawk at RAF Valley in Anglesey for three years. On my visit to Scampton I flew six slots between 07:30 and 16:30. What I found hardest was flying upside down close to the ground. In the Harrier we experience about 4g but in the Hawk we pulled nearly 7 and by the end I felt like a wrung-out sock."

Some candidates get a form of Repetitive Strain Injury (RSI) just from prolonged gripping of the stick. "You notice it when you land," says Flight Lieutenant Martin Higgins, from No.43 (F) Tornado Squadron, one of the three new pilots who joined the Red Arrows in October 2004. "Your hand's blue, your tendons have strained. While you're flying, you notice that the aeroplane becomes a twitchy little monkey, which you don't want. You try to be smooth with your motor skills, but it's counter-productive. The more tense you feel, the worse the results."

The Boss takes each short-listed candidate up for a formation flying test, which includes two successive loops and barrel rolls. Then, in the weeks following Cyprus, the pilots themselves hold frank meetings to settle on the final two or three candidates, their future team mates, who are then invited to join the team. The announcement of the new team – new guys and new positions – is made in Jersey in September by the Squadron Leader, and the RAFAT issues a press release. The recruits will leave their units in summer for a Hawk refresher course at RAF Valley on the Hawk trainer. Then in August they join the Reds for the remainder of the display season.

"Only new guys? No girls?" I ask. "Watch this space," says PR Officer Rachel Huxford, indicating the photographs of the current team on the wall of the Scampton visitors' reception...

DAVE SLOW
RAF AEROBATIC TEAM
THE RED ARROWS

SPATIAL REASONING

This is a test of your ability to work with shapes and objects.
There are two parts to this test.

Spatial Reasoning Part 1

Part 1 tests how well you can fit shapes together.

In each question you will be shown either three or four shapes. You have to imagine what they will look like when they are joined together.

All of the shapes have at least one side that is labelled with a letter (either x, y or z).
You have to place the sides with the same labels next to each other to form a **new shape**.
For example:

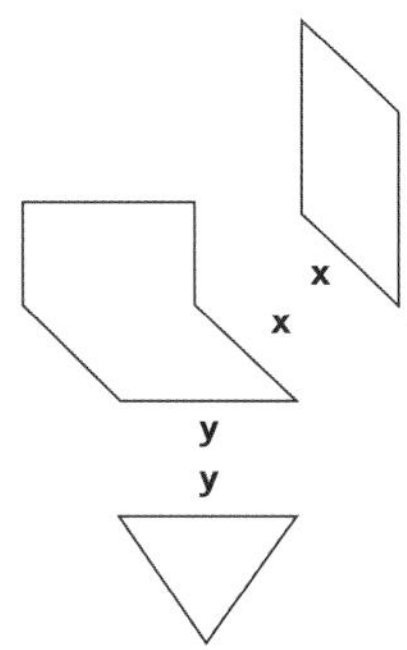

When joined together the above three shapes will look as follows:

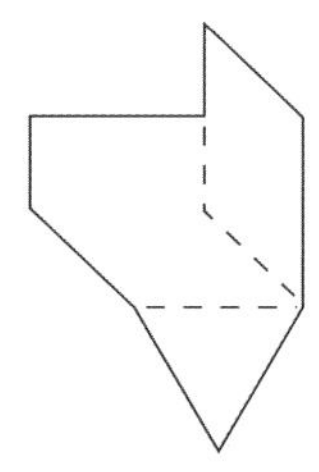

In each question you will be given five options (labelled A–E) for what the **new shape** will look like. You have to decide which one is correct.In the real test you will have four minutes to answer 10 questions. You will need to mark your answers on the separate answer sheet, in the space headed
SPATIAL REASONING (SR) PART 1.

On the facing page are some examples of the type of questions you will be given in the real test. Mark your answers on the detachable answer sheet provided.

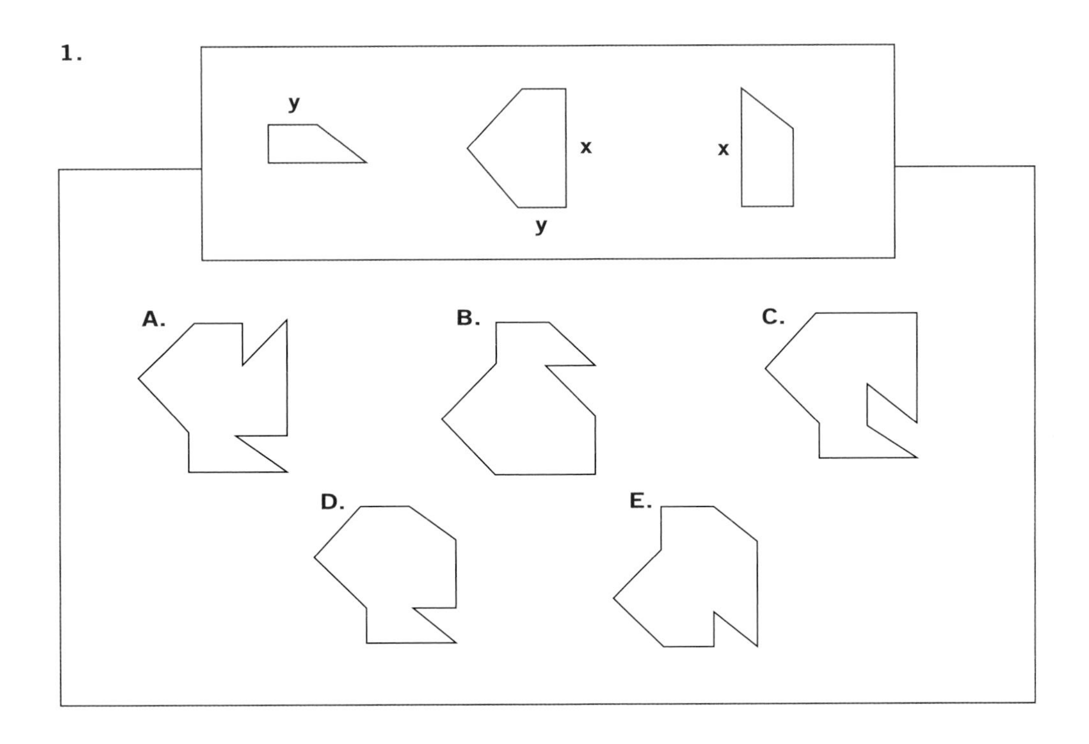
1.
y
x
x
y
A.
B.
C.
D.
E.

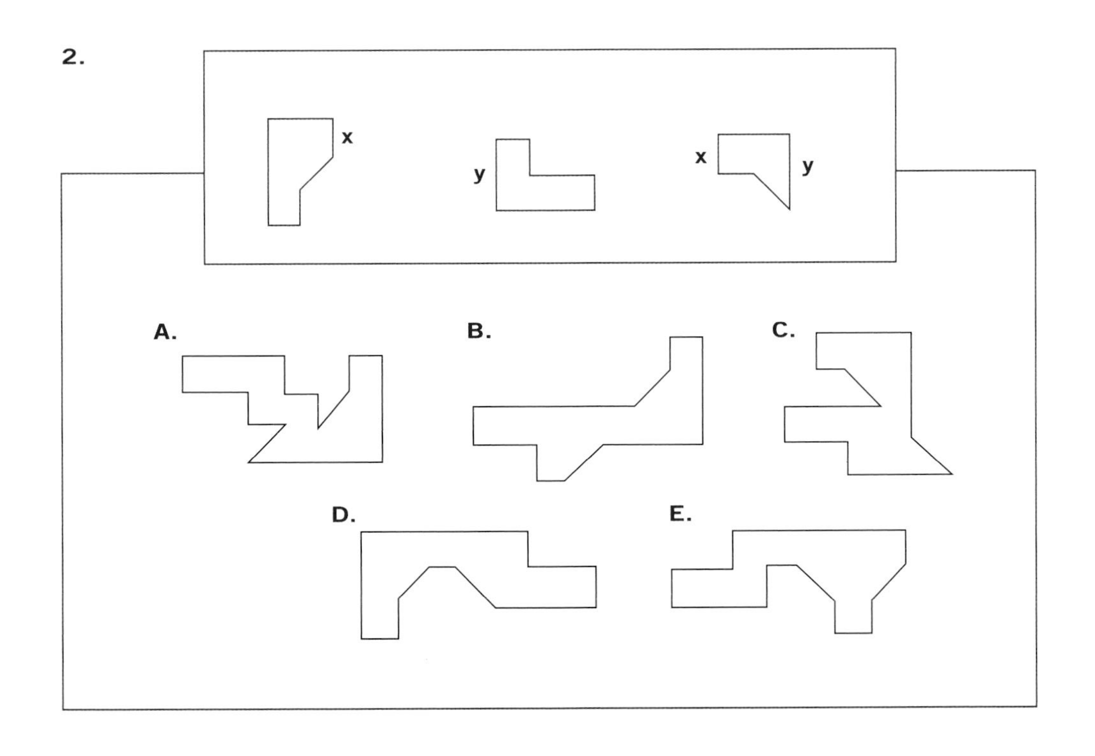
2.
x
y
x
y
A.
B.
C.
D.
E.

ELECTRICAL COMPREHENSION

This is a test of your ability to work with electrical concepts.

In the real test you will have 11 minutes to answer 21 questions. You will need to mark your answers on the separate answer sheet, in the space headed ELECTRICAL COMPREHENSION (EC).

Below are some examples of the type of questions you will be given in the real test. Mark your answers on the detachable answer sheet provided.

1. Anode is to positive as ... is to negative

A. Diode
B. Electrode
C. Terminal
D. Cathode
E. Triode

2. Which of the following substances is the worst electrical conductor?

A. Tin
B. Copper
C. Rubber
D. Air
E. Water

3. Ammeters measure the amount of current in a circuit. In the circuit below both the ammeters are identical. If Ammeter 1 (A1) reads 0.8A, what will Ammeter 2 (A2) read?

A. 0.8A
B. 0.4A
C. 1.6A
D. 0.2A
E. 0.6A

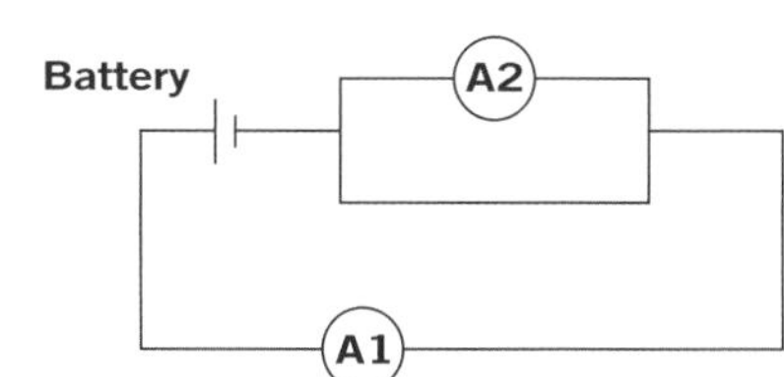

4. In the circuit shown below, what will happen when the switch is open?

A. Bulbs A, B and C will be lit
B. Bulbs B and C will be lit
C. Bulb A will be lit
D. Bulbs A and B will be lit
E. Bulb C will be lit

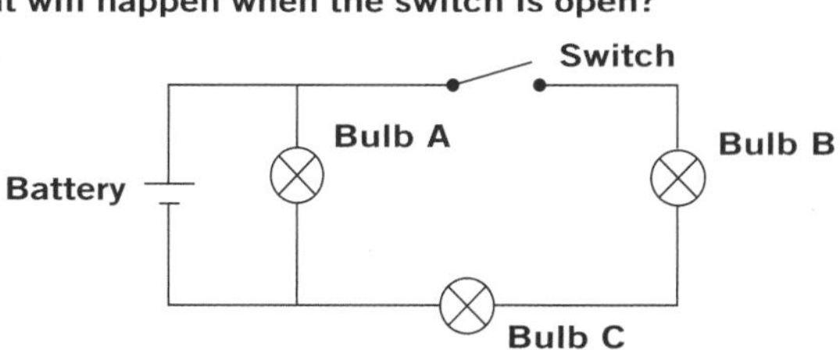

MECHANICAL COMPREHENSION

This is a test of your ability to work with mechanical concepts.

In the real test you will have 10 minutes to answer 20 questions. You will need to mark your answers on the separate answer sheet, in the space headed MECHANICAL COMPREHENSION (MC).

Below are some examples of the type of questions you will be given in the real test. Mark your answers on the detachable answer sheet provided.

1. In the diagram below if A is the drive wheel turning clockwise, what directions will B, C and D travel?

- **A.** B clockwise, C clockwise and D clockwise
- **B.** B anticlockwise, C anticlockwise and D anticlockwise
- **C.** B anticlockwise, C clockwise and D anticlockwise
- **D.** B clockwise, C anticlockwise and D clockwise
- **E.** B anticlockwise, C clockwise and D clockwise

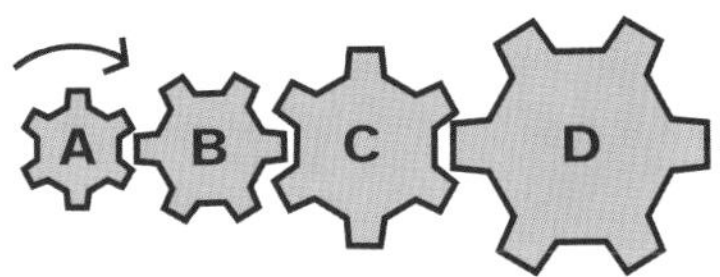

2. If an engineering drawing is not drawn to full size the scale of the drawing will be stated on the bottom of the page. What does 'Scale 1:4' indicate?

- **A.** 1 cm on the drawing represents 4 cm on the component
- **B.** 4 cm on the drawing represents 1 cm on the component
- **C.** 4 cm on the drawing represents 1 m on the component
- **D.** 1 cm on the drawing represents 4 m on the component
- **E.** The drawing is 4 times the size of a full-scale drawing

3. A ...... is usually used to tighten nuts and bolts?

- **A.** Screwdriver
- **B.** Spanner
- **C.** Hammer
- **D.** Pair of pliers
- **E.** Drill

4. What will be the effect on the pressure in the cylinder when the piston moves from position A to position B?

- **A.** The pressure will decrease by a quarter
- **B.** The pressure will increase by 4 times its original value
- **C.** The pressure will remain constant
- **D.** The pressure will double
- **E.** The pressure will halve

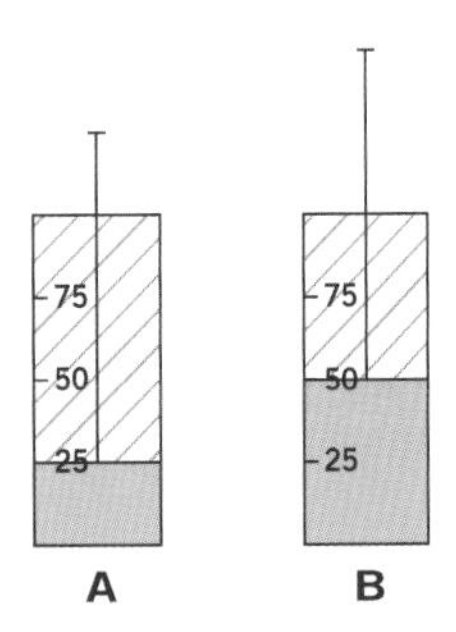

MEMORY

This is a test of your ability to remember patterns.

You will be shown a sequence of either two or three grids.

The grids will be shown one at a time.

Each grid will have a number of yellow squares, like the one below.

You have to remember where the yellow squares are in each grid.

Then you have to imagine what the grid would look like if all the grids were 'added together'.

You will then be shown four possible answers (labelled A–D).

You have to decide which one represents the 'added' grid.

For example, if the sequence of grids shown was:

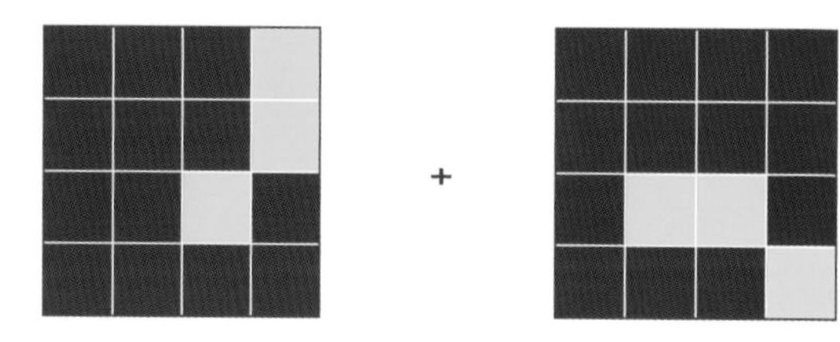

Which grid (labelled A–D) represents the 'added' grid?

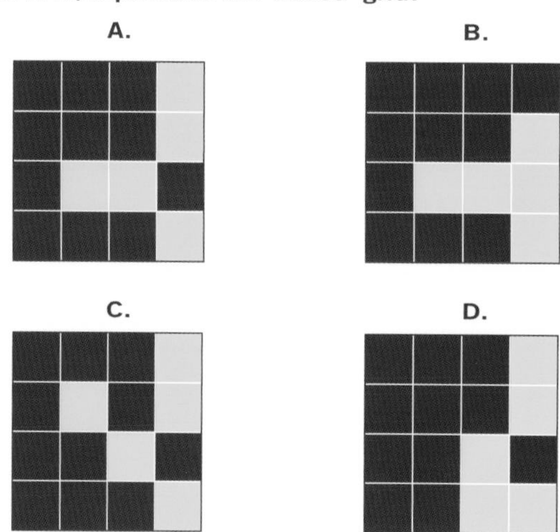

The correct answer is **A.**

Question 1

Study the following sequence of grids and then answer the question. Remember, in the real test the grids will be shown one at a time.

If the sequence of grids shown was:

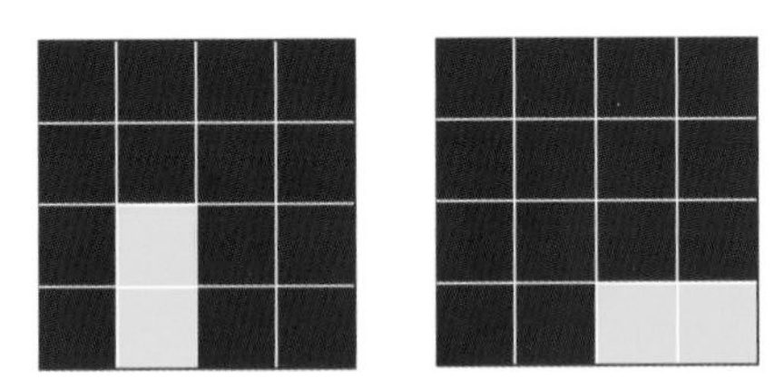

Which grid (labelled A–D) represents the 'added' grid?

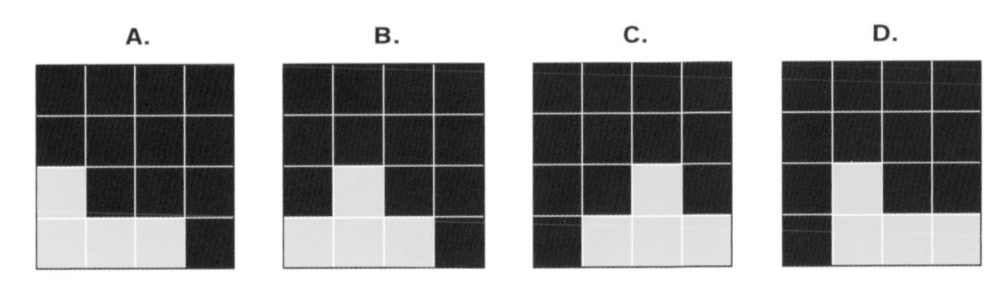

Question 2

Study the following sequence of grids and then answer the question. Remember, in the real test the grids will be shown one at a time.

If the sequence of grids shown was:

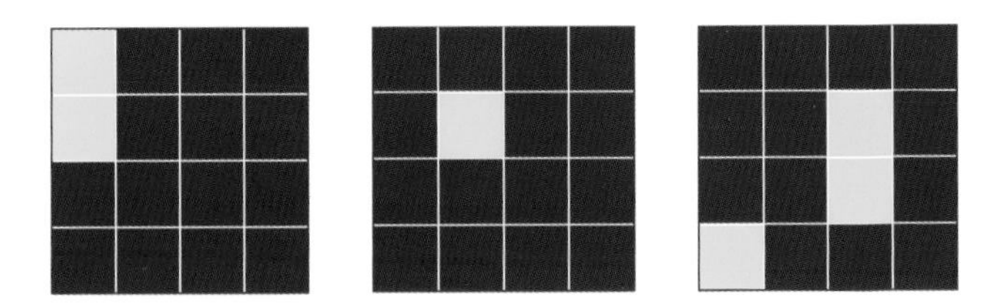

Which grid (labelled A–D) represents the 'added' grid?

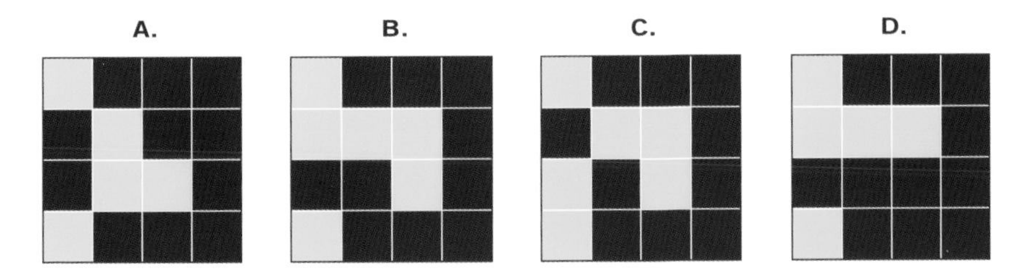

DAY AT THE OFFICE

Dressed in greens for winter training, the Reds roll up at their Scampton HQ before 08:00 in an odd assortment of transport: a Porsche, a Land Rover, a Volvo, a Cherokee Jeep, an L-reg Primera and a 1930s Austin are lined up in the Scampton car park. The choice of wheels perhaps best describes their own interpretation of the 'Right Stuff' – that elusive mix of courage, grit, competence and fine judgement identified by American writer Tom Wolfe as the quality possessed by those pilots who make the A-list.

BRIEFING

In their room upstairs in the squadron building, the Reds kick off by tackling their in-trays; then before 08:30, they assemble in the briefing room. With seconds to spare, the glossy red door closes and what follows typifies the Red Arrows' obsession for punctuality. Let's face it, if you can't turn up on time for a chat about the weather, how can you be expected to be up to speed for a fly-past over the Queen's front porch? Latecomers stay outside.

Squadron Leader Spike Jepson barks the last few seconds: "Ten seconds. Five. Four. Three. Two. One. Hack!" At 08:40 and no seconds, the day's first brief commences with weather news from forecaster Dave Witherden via a live audio link with the Met. Office at RAF Cranwell, and weather profiles fill the briefing room's video screen.

Next, Flight Lieutenant Barrie Robinson of Scampton's Air Traffic Control briefs the team on current airfield operations: taxiways out of service, perhaps because of resurfacing, necessitating detours to and from the runway; landing lights needing replacement.

And last, Squadron Leader Sally Varley, Team Manager, and Public Relations Officer Rachel Huxford calmly detail the day's packed ground programme: the visiting groups of the public to be entertained; journalists and photographers who will want to ask questions and take photographs; visits from VIPs.

Right Squadron Leader Dunc Mason, Red 5, strides out to his waiting Hawk at RAF Scampton.

FLYING

The briefs end, the red door opens and the Reds crowd into their offices and into Flight Planning for more administrative chores. At 09:15, Flight Lieutenant Simon Stevens dings the Squadron bell outside the Flight Planning office to summon those detailed to fly the 09:45 sortie, and the pre-flight briefing. They have seconds to get inside the briefing room before the door closes.

After the briefing, the crew go downstairs to their lockers to don their g-pants, life vests, helmets and gloves. By the time they're ready and crowding round the corner into Line Control to sign the aircraft out, the Blues are doing last-minute visual checks on the waiting Hawks. The Line Controllers notify the pilots of any technical problems with their aircraft and at 09:30 the crew, in full flying kit, walk out to their waiting aircraft as the PA announces 'Crew Walking'.

And so begins the day's flying and entertaining; entertaining and flying. Weather permitting, there are daily slots from 08:30 to 15:00 to be prepared for and flown.

The Synchro Pair had their own early-morning briefings before flying the 08:30 slot and they've debriefed and are back in the crew room, discussing one of their manoeuvres. Their next slot will be at 11.00, and they'll fly three afternoon slots. From the start of the season until the first nine-ship in March, Synchro operate independently, planning their own sequences, and today they're practising the two crossovers they make in Carousel. Their two Hawks cross less than 3.5m or 12ft apart and 30m or 100ft above the runway, and the timing must be perfected.

For the rest of the team, the Boss plans each 30-minute 'chock to chock' (practice sortie) in minute detail. Within the timeframe available to him, he guides his team through every formation shape and manoeuvre in the display in preparation for the first nine-ship and, all too soon, the first public display.

DEBRIEFING

The pilots scheduled to fly the 09:45 sortie land at 10:15 and disappear without delay into the briefing room. Someone has collected the tape of the slot from the photographer who filmed it from the foot of the Control Tower. For the next 45 minutes or more, every second is played and replayed, frame by frame, to the watching team. A pilot frequently applies a ruler to the TV screen and scales up the millimetres between the aircraft on the screen to metres in the air, to check whether he was on-reference. Those guilty of errors readily offer self-criticism, however minor the fault, brief apologies and no excuses. It's a gentlemanly affair, very RAF from the days of deck chairs and handlebar moustaches, and it goes like this:

ROYAL AIR FORCE

XX227
DANGER
HOT AIR

Slot 3 debrief, 15 March 35kt gusts
"Late smoke 4."
"Short 2."
"Tight 6."
"Wide 7."
"Long 4."
"Apologies, Boss."
"Shallow 2."
"I saw you coming round the corner and I thought, oh my, this'll be exciting!"
"Down it 3."
"I kind of had a feeling I'd be back early, so I put another 4 seconds on the pattern."
"Behind it 4."

The Reds have to be hypercritical with each other – 'short' means that they're too far forward and 'long' that they're too far back; 'tight' is too close to the centre of the formation and 'wide' too far to the outside. There's a wide vocabulary of terms indicating formation position infringements – they may be 'shallow' (too high) or 'deep' (too low). The mistakes are argued in cordial tones as they relive in freeze-frame every moment of the display, from the roll down the runway to the break to land. Heads turn when someone speaks up and ears listen out to catch every syllable of the point that's being made.

When the wind's gusting and the flying's been pants-poor, faces may drop and shoulders sag. But not for long. The doors reopen and the pilots beam broad smiles as they greet the first visitors.

Opposite Flight Lieutenants David Slow and Steve Underwood and Squadron Leader Dunc Mason shelter under the tail of the team's full-scale model Hawk, Kemble Air Day.

ENTERTAINING

The crew room is full of the winners of an aviation magazine competition. Their prize is a day at Scampton with the Red Arrows. The crowd, accompanied by the magazine's editor are being shepherded around by Public Relations Officer Rachel Huxford and are chatting to the Wing Commander. The team join him and are immediately assailed by questions. This will be the first chance most of their visitors have ever had to talk to the pilots – but they're unlikely to ask any questions the Reds haven't been asked before.

After half an hour, the prizewinners are ushered off on a guided tour of the hangar. The Boss and four pilots make for the briefing room and the pre-flight briefing for their 12:20 sortie. Those remaining gather in twos and threes, talking over hitches that came up in the last sortie.

The Team Manager goes off to meet a group of corporate visitors. The RAFAT's mission statement declares that the Red Arrows exist to promote the excellence of the Royal Air Force and to enhance national prestige abroad, so they take care not to promote any specific commercial product or company in the UK. However, they do look out for opportunities to save money for the taxpayer, by accepting offers from carefully selected commercial companies to pay for appropriate aspects of their organization, such as their promotional literature. In return, representatives from the organization or company may be invited to Scampton for a day, for example.

At lunch time the prizewinners return to the crew room for sandwiches and make the most of half an hour of one-to-one with most of the team, who have also crowded in. At 13:30 a roar from two of the Hawks parked out on the line announces the next sortie. The visitors are bused out to the Control Tower to watch the flying practice. Later, wearing high-visibility vests for safety, they're guided out to the line for a close-up of five Hawks being pre-flighted for the 15:00 sortie, the last of the day.

As the winter dusk falls, trucks are driven out to the line to tow the Hawks, one by one, into the hangar. Upstairs, some of the crew are struggling to clear their in-trays, while others are rerunning the day's sorties on the video and making sketches and notes.

It's 18:00 and five of the crew are in a meeting with the Boss. They'll be finished in half an hour, but they may drift along to the offices down the corridor, where some of the staff are taking advantage of the quiet to catch up. Sally Varley is preparing the next morning's brief. Rachel Huxford sits at her computer answering some of the many emails she receives from the public, asking anything from 'Please can I have an autograph?' to 'How do you make the coloured dye?'

Rachel is well aware that everything the team does is PR and she sees herself as a kind of brand guardian. She is the author of her own programme, the WHIPR or 'What's Happening in PR?' which, during the display season, sets out the schedule and background information for the team during their public appearances. "We may not work seven days a week during winter training," she says, "but we don't just put our feet up. Today, the team have flown 6 sorties and we've received about 20 visitors. And every day we get tens of enquires from the media."

The Reds plan their displays by moving magnetic jet and runway shapes on a board in the briefing room at Scampton. Earlier generations of Red Arrows used a blackboard, chalk and duster.

ROLL RATE
1/4 close = BIG INPUT
Fire door
keep shut

The Boss for 2004, Squadron Leader Spike Jepson, explains the Corkscrew manoeuvre to the team and visiting RAF pilots seated behind.

After the day's flying, the briefing room is cleaned.

Team Leader Spike Jepson writes a speech after PDA, while Team Manager Sally Varley, packs crates for the return to Scampton in the squadron building at RAF Akrotiri.

Ashworth

Newly delivered red suits, embroidered with the names of their future owners, are lined up in the Team Manager's office ready for shipping to Cyprus in advance of PDA Day.

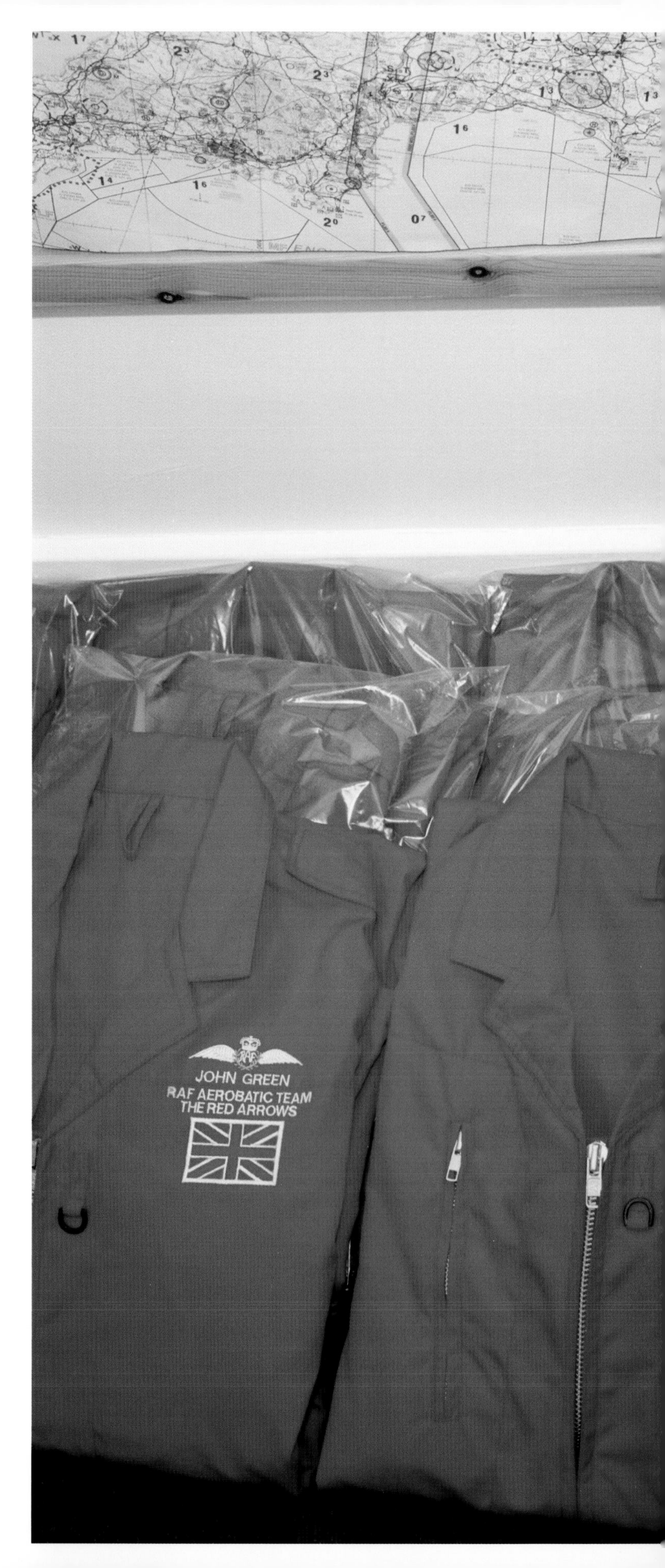

RICHARD CARLETON
RAF AEROBATIC TEAM
THE RED ARROWS
UNDERWOOD

Flight Lieutenant Antony Parkinson signs publicity material back at Scampton, after returning from the last display in which he will fly as a Red Arrow.

ANTONY PARKINSO
RAF AEROBATIC TEA
THE RED ARROWS
AVIATION WEEK
LINCOLN CATHEDRAL
2004
Red Arrows

Last of the few
ELEVEN

Flight Lieutenants Steve Underwood and Antony Parkinson, and Wing Commander Bill Ramsey discuss logistics beneath the emblems of long-disbanded fighter squadrons that decorate the squadron building at RAF Akrotiri.

“5-4-3-2-1-Hack!” The glossy red door of the briefing room at RAF Scampton shuts and the Reds begin a briefing. To the second.

STOP
DO NOT ENTER
BRIEFING IN PROGRESS

MANOEUVRES

By their 40th birthday in May 2005 the Red Arrows had flown almost 4,000 public displays, an average of 95 shows during each 5½-month season. Their 4,000th display will fall in August 2006, according to the calculations of Adjutant John May. The team have displayed in 52 countries on six continents. Their foreign tours advertise and promote the excellence of British industry by demonstrating the capabilities of its equipment and expertise. At home, where they fly more than 90% of their displays, they're billboard ambassadors for RAF recruitment.

The Red Arrows' main product, their flying display, is a world best-seller. Their audiences and their corporate pulling-power run into figures that would turn movie moguls green. In a typical month, 8 million browsers hit their web page. Indeed, according to publishers McGraw-Hill, the RAF mother site falls third in the top ten most-watched aviation addresses in cyberspace.

Aviation history has an important part in the display's present and its future. Today's air shows are as exciting to those who watch them as were the stunts flown by the Blériot kites to the crowds of the early 1900s. There is always an element of danger in flying fast jets and even at modern air shows serious crashes sometimes happen. Nevertheless, the Red Arrows' manoeuvres are less dangerous than those performed in the early days of aviation by stuntmen such as Eugène Lefebvre or Adolphe Pégoud, because pilots today know more about their jets than did those first aerobatic pilots, who flew their aeroplanes to their very limits. Today's professional pilots will want to do the utmost to show off the jets they fly, but will back off from the very extreme of their performance because today's spectators will be satisfied with the drama of fast and close formation flying.

The following pages show pictures of some of the formations and manoeuvres from the Red Arrows' 2004 displays. On pages 144–5 Synchro Leader tells in his own words the inside story of flying one of his most spectacular manoeuvres – Cubans to Opposition Barrel Rolls, No.23 in the 2005 display.

Opposite The Opposition Loop, RAF Akrotiri.

Concorde formation, RAF Akrotiri.

Big Vixen, RAF Akrotiri.

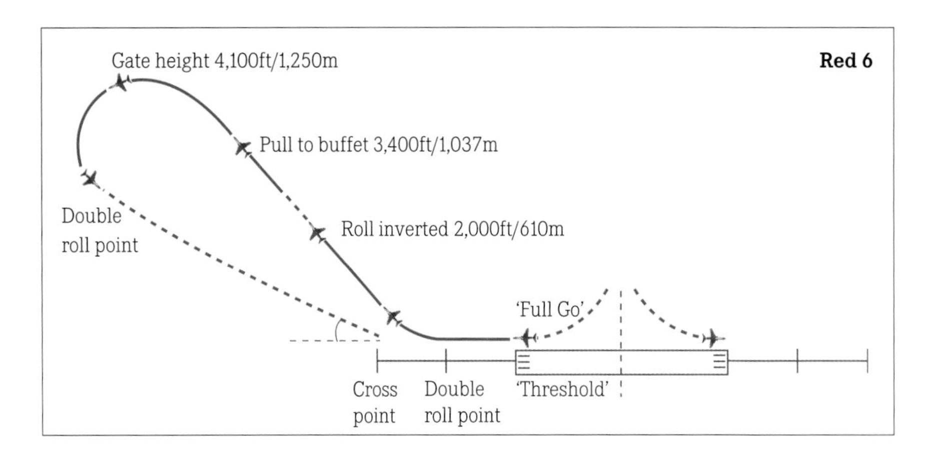

Trailing smoke, Synchro Leader (Red 6) flies his Half Cuban before flying into the Opposition Barrel Roll.

CUBANS TO OPPOSITION BARREL ROLLS

Towards the end of the display, the Synchro Pair both fly a Half Cuban, then they fly in, Red 6 from the left and Red 7 from the right, to perform the breathtaking Opposition Barrel Rolls. They cross over by barrel-rolling – spectacularly looping while rolling around each other and flying towards each other, making the cross in front of the crowd. Flight Lieutenant Dan Simmons, who has flown as Red 6 and Red 7, tells the inside story of this manoeuvre.

"As I come out of Carousel and fly down to 100 feet, I'm looking up at the weather and deciding for sure that we can go full. And I'm looking ahead for the double roll point we've chosen, where we'll pull up for the Cubans.

I radio 'Going full' and flick the switch to put the air brake out. I check the speed's not above 350 knots. And then I call 'Go' on the radio…pull back on the stick, feeling for the buffet, then holding the buffet all the way up, keeping the wings level…full power…until I get to 70° nose up…then I push forward on the stick and all the g comes off.

I watch the height going up…quite quickly…anticipate for 2,000 feet when I'm going to roll inverted. I pull the stick left, making sure not to pull back…rolling left…completely upside down…then pushing and pushing until I get to 3,400 feet…I'm anticipating…and then I'm pulling. My nose gets through to the horizon and I check I'm above 4,100 feet. This is my gate safety height – if I'm lower than 4,100 feet I can't pull back and go into the dive because I'd crash. And I'm keeping the buffet…holding the buffet…all the way over the top…at full power still…until my nose is pulled all the way through the vertical.

Now I'm looking towards the site again and I look for the double-roll point. Then I push forward on the stick to let all the g off and all the buffet off and I point absolutely at the double-roll point. I'm still at full power and watching the speed. As it comes up towards 330 knots I'm going to idle with the throttle and flick the air brake out. That's going to hold me wherever I am at 330 knots, just pointing down directly at the double roll point. And here I'm having to trust the gate safety height and the aeroplane, because I dive 4,000 feet in 19 seconds and all the way down it looks like I'm going to crash. I've hardly got any time.

I look up in the top of the canopy where I can see Red 7, who's coming down on the opposite side of the display site. I'm checking he's about the

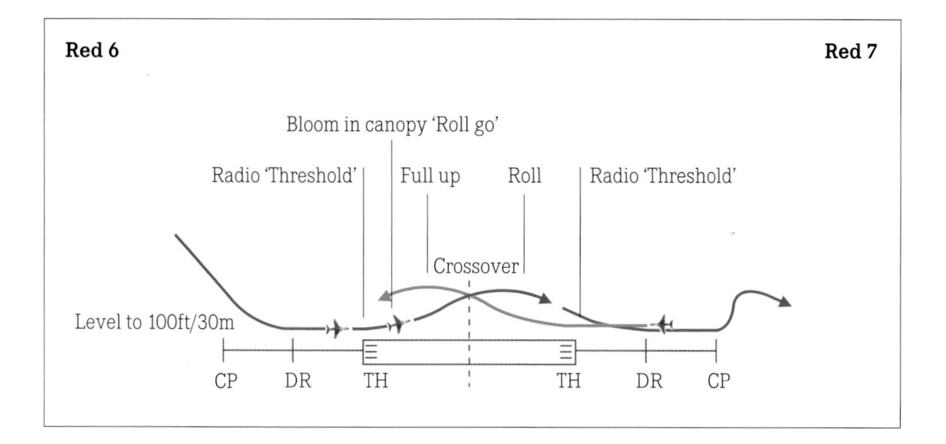

On completing their Half Cubans, Reds 6 and 7 fly towards each other to perform their Barrel Rolls.

same height as me. If he's a lot lower than me, we'll cross over on my side of datum; and if he's way, way up in the sky, I know I need to start slowing even more or we'll cross towards his side of the site. We want our double rolls, which come next, to happen right in front of the crowd. I'm starting to think about the ground rushing up towards me and I mustn't let it get up to 340 knots…so I'm checking that it's no faster than 330 knots… and I'm judging it…and now I pull on to the buffet again and level at 100 feet.

I've let the g off as I level and I'm looking at the display line and making sure I'm absolutely straight. I'm also checking that 7 has set up at the right spacing just out on my right-hand side, that he can see me and that we're not displaced. I'm looking for the threshold point and as soon I'm over the threshold – I see that my shoulder's gone right past it – I radio 'Threshold' and listen for 7's 'Threshold' call. If it comes well before mine, I know I'm effectively late into the manoeuvre and the cross is going to come my side of datum. If he's yet to call, I'm slowing down so we get the crossover right in the middle.

He calls 'Threshold'. Everything's fine and all I need to do now is wait until he starts blooming (the red image in the canopy, which first appeared small, gets bigger and bigger) and my judgement says it's time to roll. I press the radio transmit, I call 'Roll Go', and we both roll right…I'm watching him to make sure he's rolling with me. Then I'm just waiting for him to reverse his roll and I reverse mine with some left stick and left bank – I start pulling back with the stick and the g increases, and then I very quickly flick left by increasing the roll rate.

Now I'm watching 7 as he's coming up the other side. Once he pulls up, I can commit into my pull-up and we can make a nice high cross in front of the crowd. I wait until he goes right past the windscreen, 100 feet away, and from there we can commit into the roll. So I pull…right on to the buffet…full power…then get the nose down quite a lot…just as much as I can bear…until we get down to 100 feet. I level off again…wait for the cross point…take a deep breath and then I pitch, using the stick, just full back stick. At that point I turn the smoke off, and for me, the show's over.

And it all happens much quicker than you can possibly put into words."

"We were so close, they were about 100 feet off the ground, we could see the pilots' helmets but we didn't want to put them off." Beach lifeguard and volunteer datum marker, Phill Cotton, Hoylake, Wirrel.

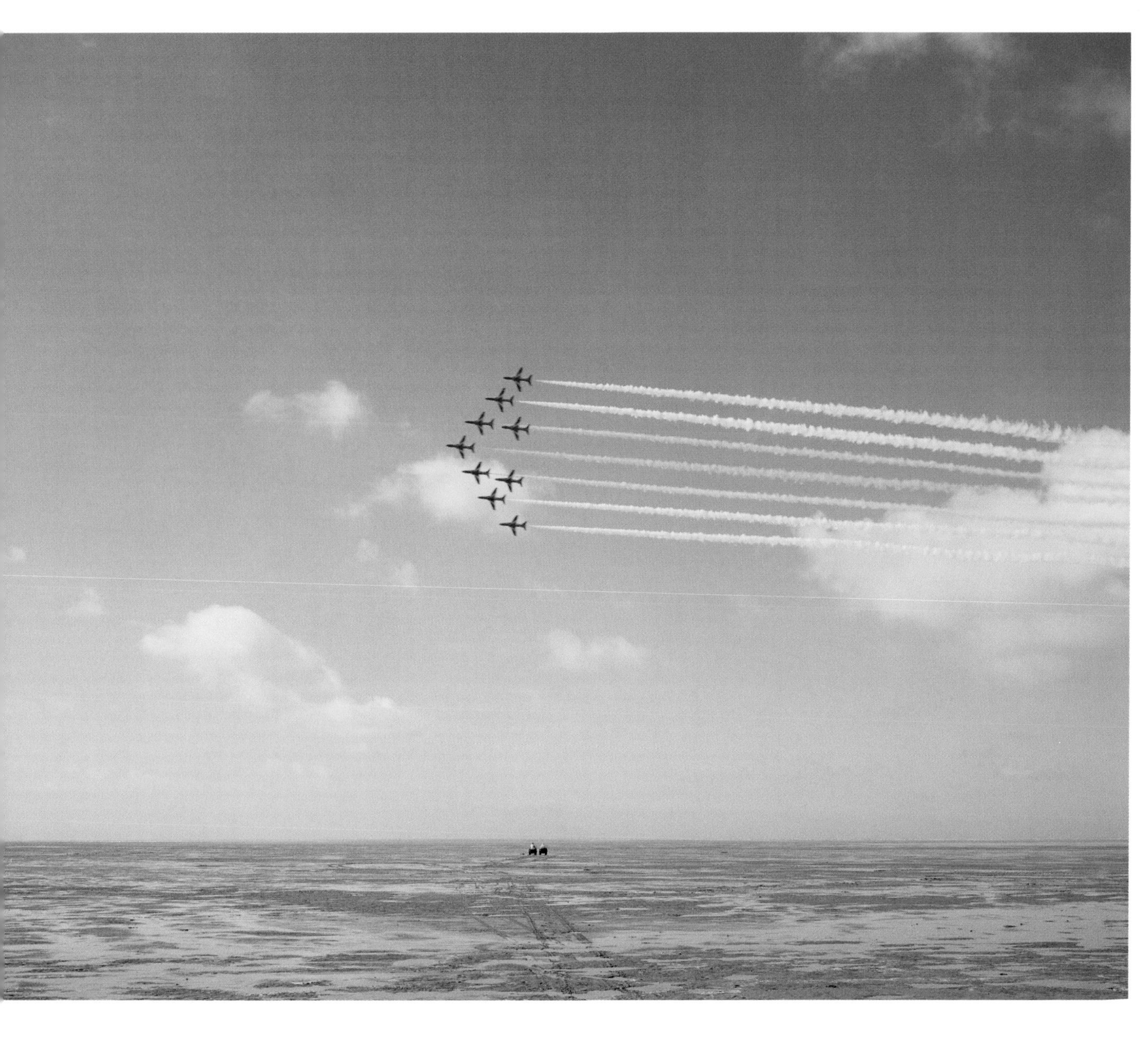

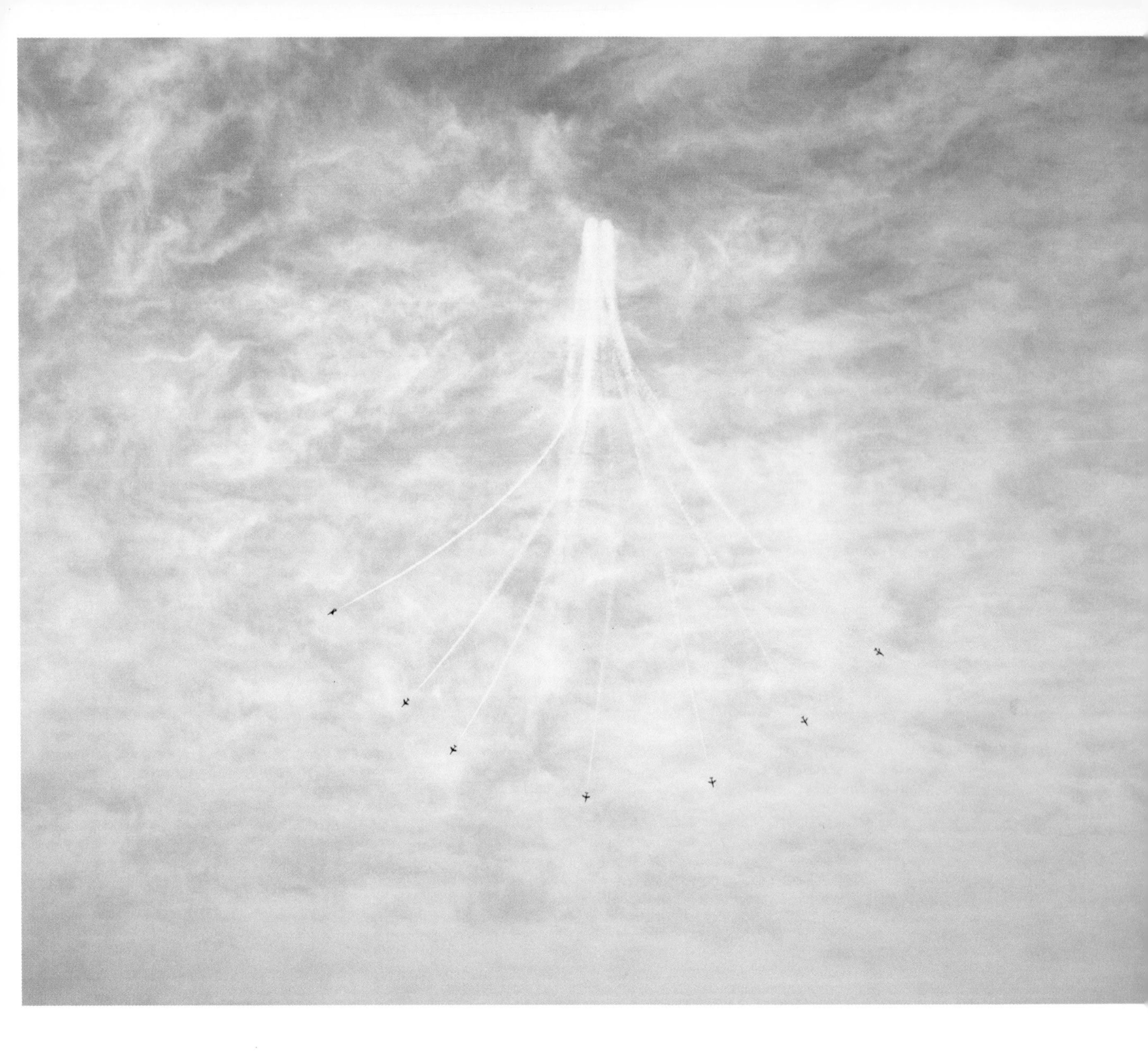

The Vertical Break, RAF Akrotiri.

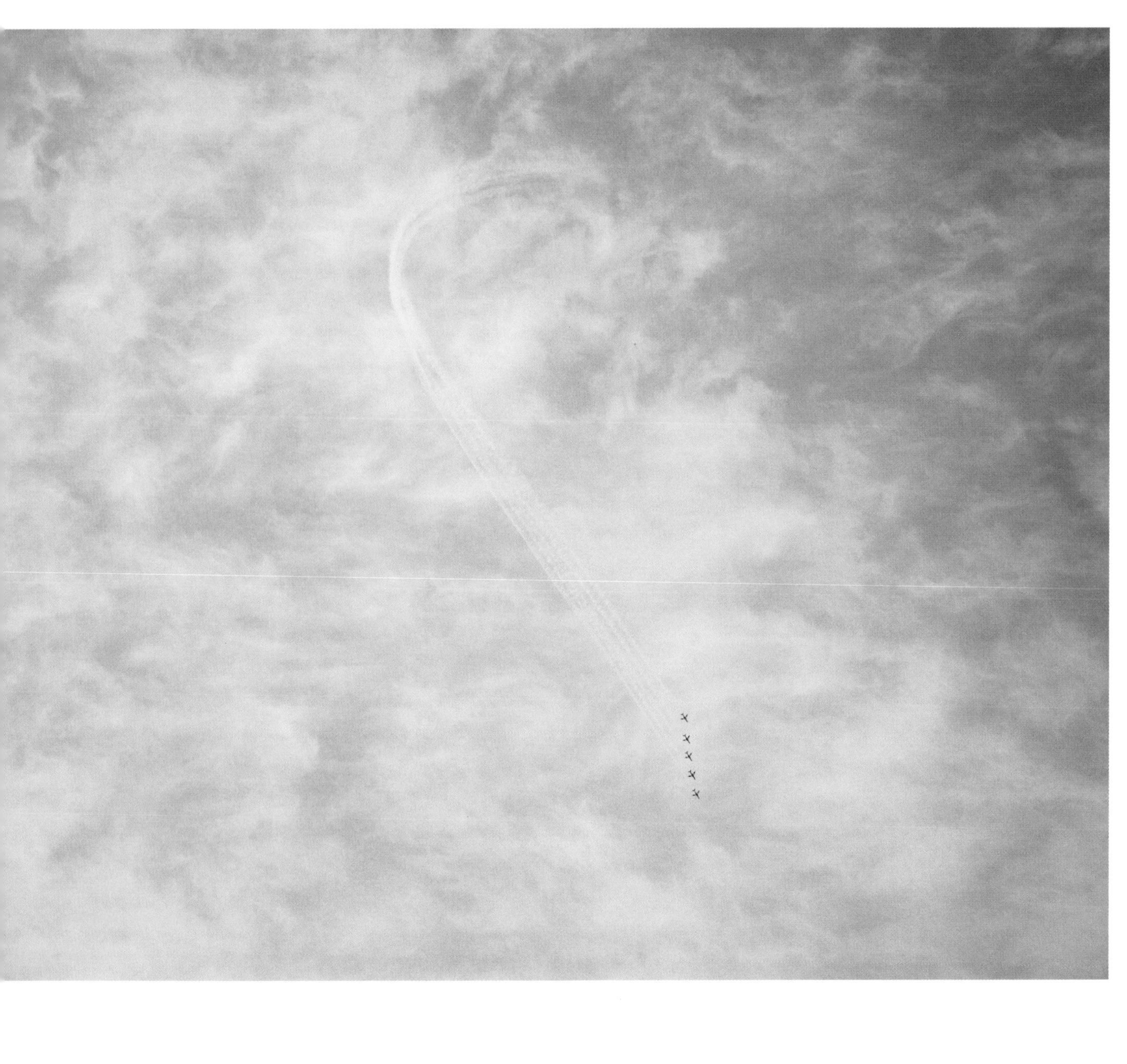

The Caterpillar, RAF Akrotiri.

THE RED ARROWS
40th ANNIVERSARY

¼ Clover Split and Cross

9-Arrow to Fred Pull-up

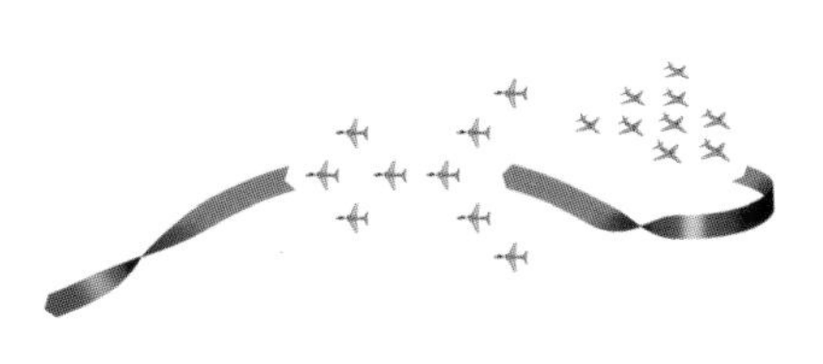

Apollo to Typhoon Roll

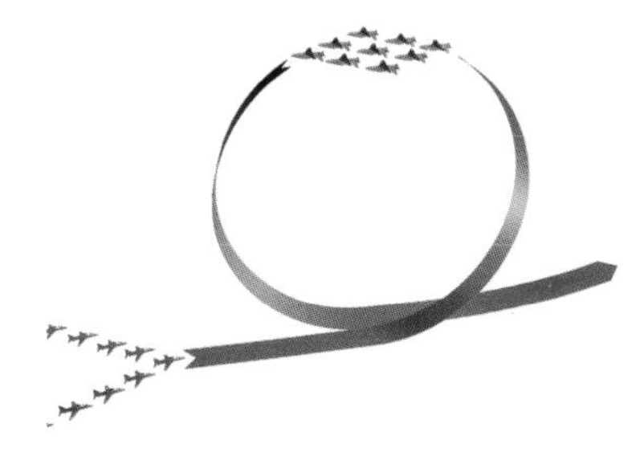

Big Battle to Short Diamond Loop

Big Vixen Roll

Carousel

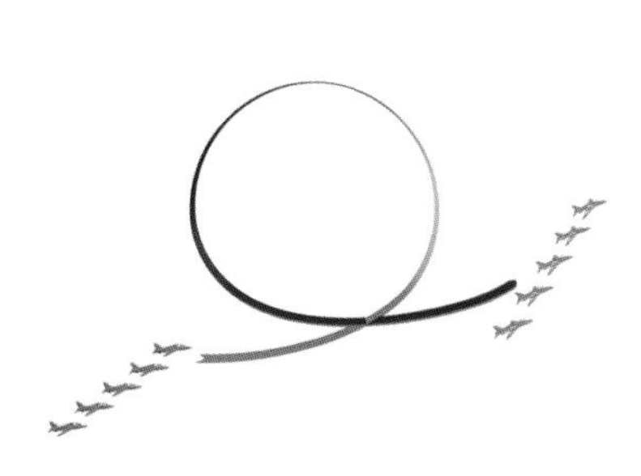

Caterpillar

Champagne Split

Concorde to Short Diamond Loop

Corkscrew

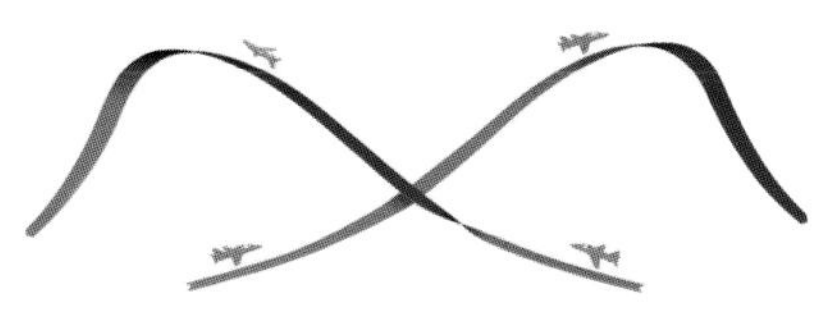

Cubans to Opposition Barrels

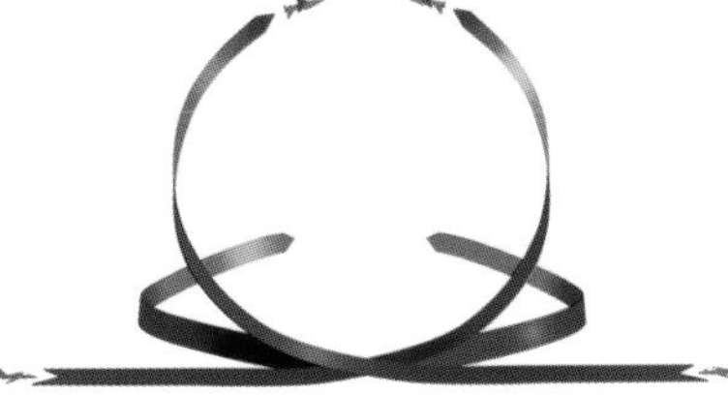

Cyclone

Delta Bend

Diamond 9 Arrival

Diamond to Swan Bend

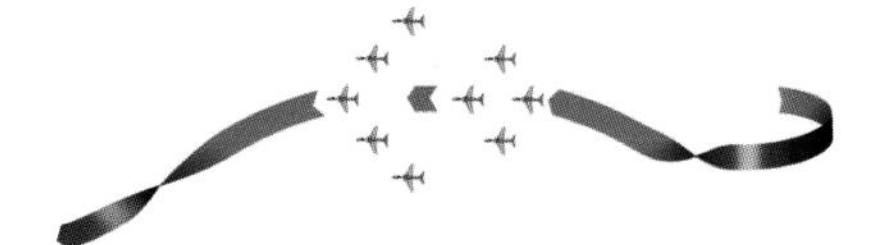

Double Diamond Roll

Double Rolls

Eagle to Chevron Roll

Goose to Steep Climb

Gripen Bend

Gypo Break to Opposition Loop

Gypo Mirror Roll

Gypo Pass

Heart

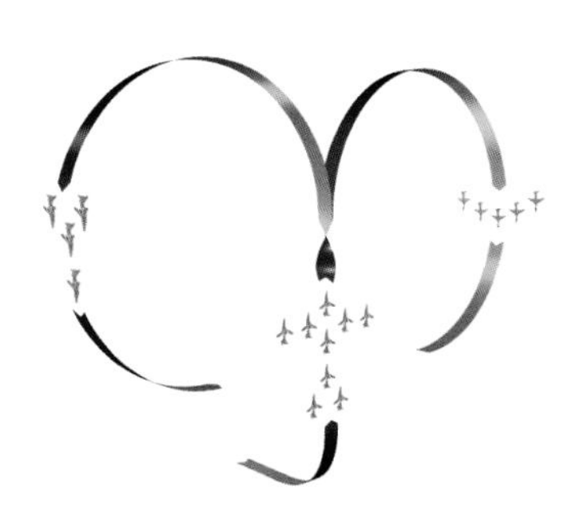

Lancaster ¼ Clover to 5-4 Split

Lancaster Pull Up

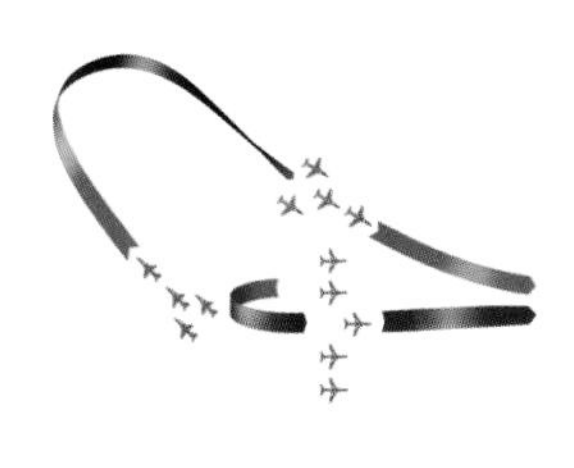

Leader's Benefit Bend/Gypo ½ Horizontal

Opposition Barrel Rolls

Rollbacks

Short Diamond to Eagle Bend

Swan to Apollo Roll

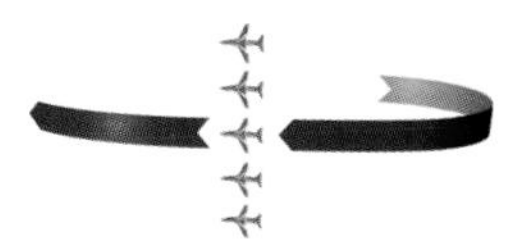

Tango Bend to Big Battle

Twizzle

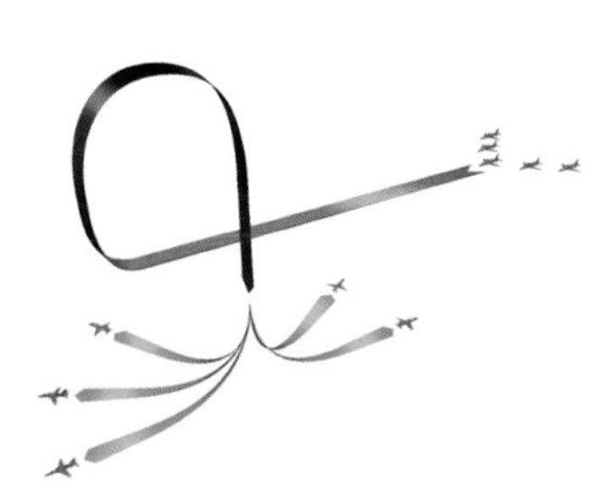

Vertical Break

Vixen Break

Vixen Loop

AIR FORCE

Pages 150-151 Diamond climbs above a naval 'Transit' marker, RAF Akrotiri.

Squadron Leader John Green and some of the Blues watch the display at Air 04, Payerne, Switzerland.

The Red Arrows squadron arrange themselves for their official portraits after being awarded the Public Display Authority (PDA), their version of a passing-out parade, at RAF Akrotiri.

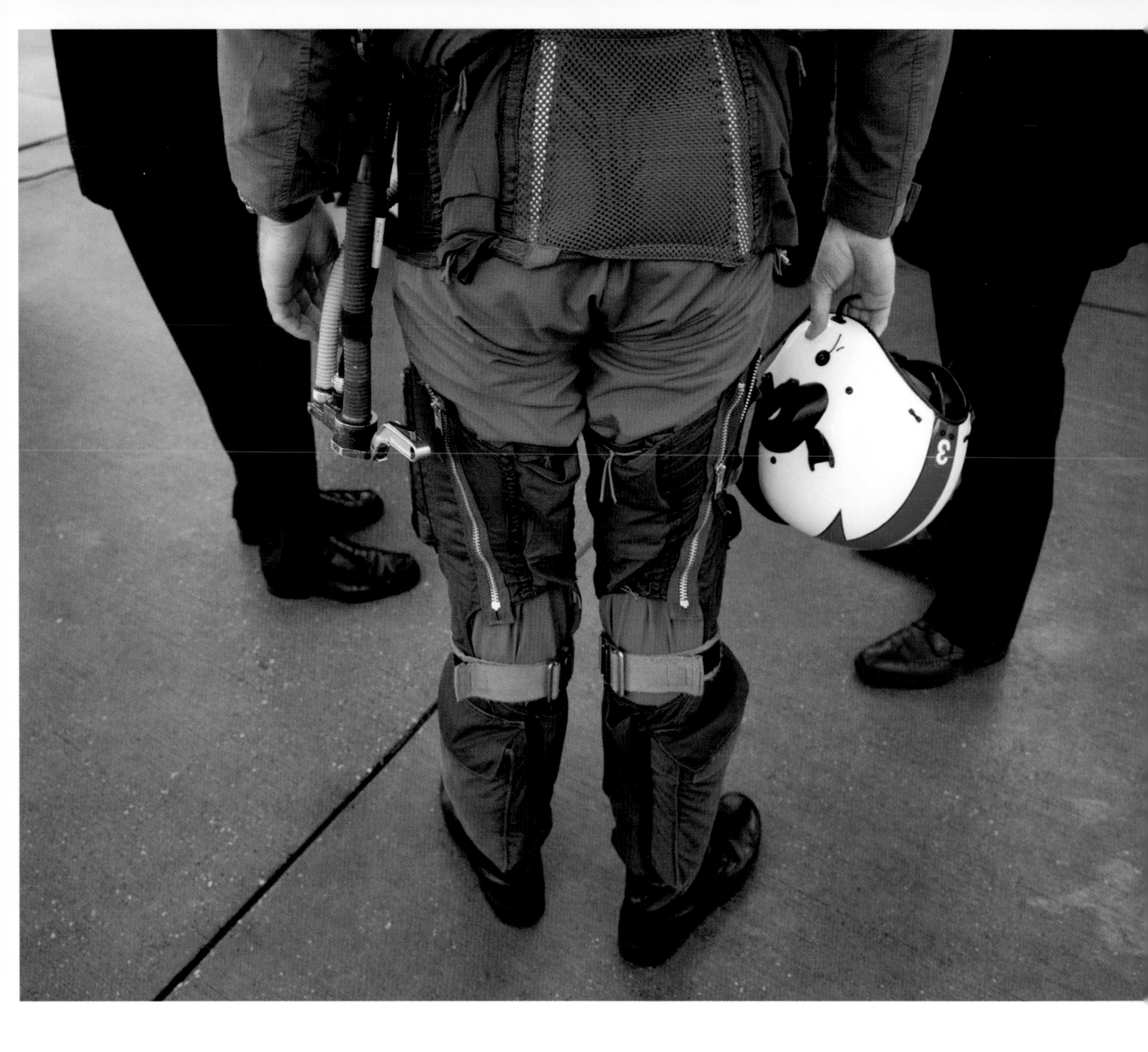

Flight Lieutenant Simon Stevens chats to corporate visitors at RAF Scampton.

The Reds line up during a speech by Jock Maitland, the organizer of the Biggin Hill air shows.

The Blues attending each aircraft march away in step before the jets taxi off, RAF Akrotiri.

Flight Lieutenant Steve Underwood and Squadron Leader John Green hold a conversation in the squadron building at RAF Akrotiri.

Always governed by the clock, Squadron Leader John Green and Flight Lieutenant Dan Simmons pace towards their respective aircraft before checking-in time is called from the Boss's radio. From that point the sortie is planned to the second.

Chocks are positioned during the on-the-wing briefing before the transit flight to Marka in Jordan.

Flight Lieutenant Dan Simmons zips up his g-pants before the transit flight to Marka in Jordan. Behind him, Synchro leader, Squadron Leader David Thomas, also prepares for departure from RAF Akrotiri.

61-PD
DANGER
DANGER

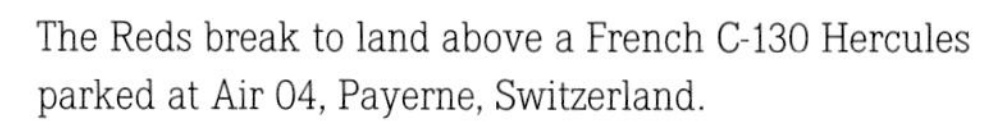

The Reds break to land above a French C-130 Hercules parked at Air 04, Payerne, Switzerland.

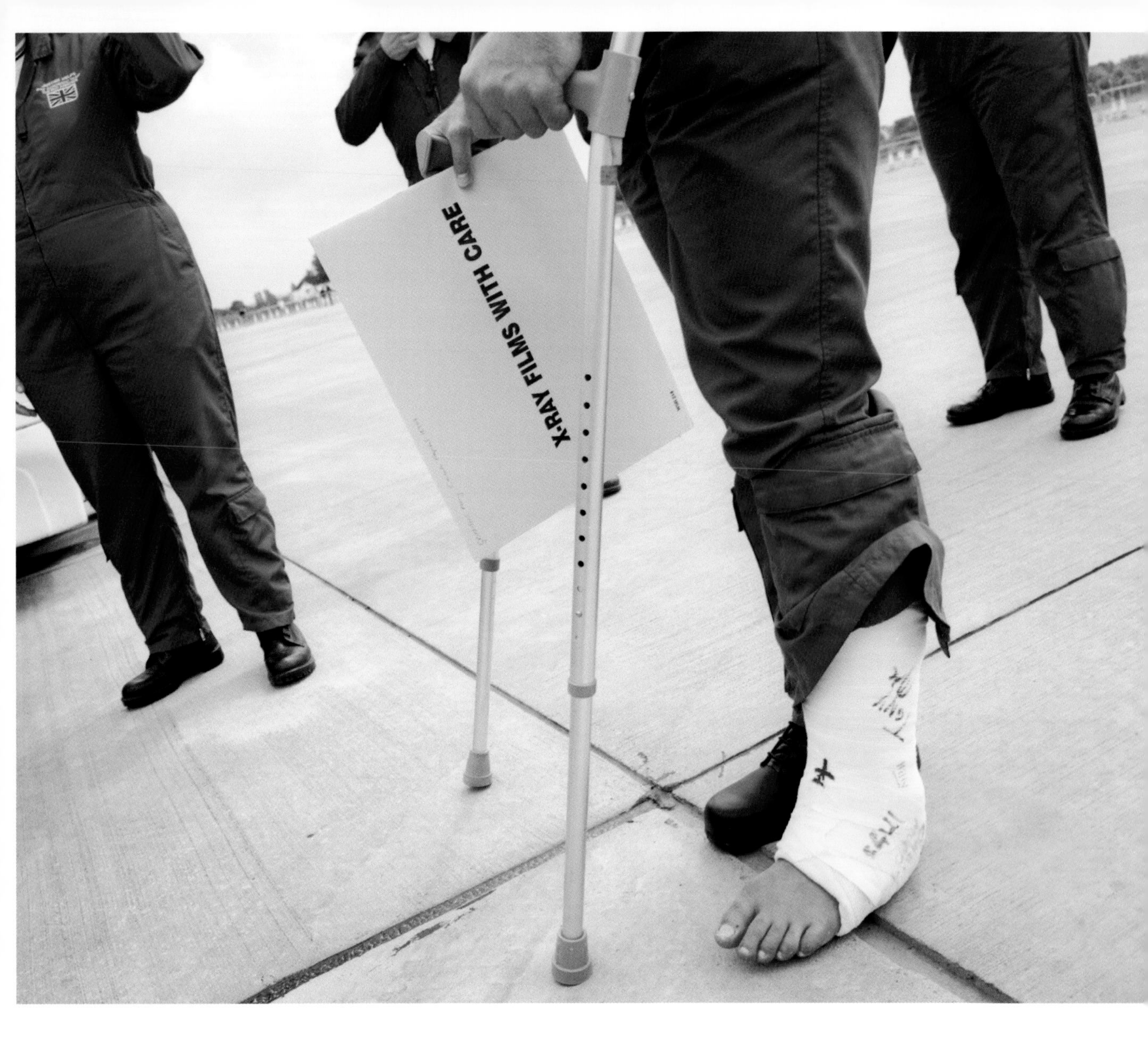

Chief Technician Kerry Griffiths returns from hospital at the Royal International Air Tattoo (RIAT), RAF Fairford.

Blue and red dye spills stain the line at RAF Scampton.

Members of the Reds walk to lunch after displaying at Air 04, Payerne, Switzerland.

BLUES

Opposite Junior Technician Darren Budziszewski examines a canopy for smears at RAF Akrotiri.

Scampton at dawn. A low rumbling sound breaks the silence as an earlybird engineer slides the giant hangar doors open on their runners. The orange glow gradually weakens as blue winter light edges over the building.

A Red Arrows' day begins when the first Blues, as the squadron's engineers and back-up staff are called, arrive to ready the Hawks for the day's flying. The night shift may already have ironed out any technical hitches, working until dawn if necessary to ensure that enough aircraft are available for the first slots, which crank up from 08:30. The day shift checks the aircraft over – fuel, tyre pressure, hydraulics.

The Blues are the Hawks' doctors and surgeons and the Reds' 85-strong technical back-up team. They normally operate behind the scenes, but they make appearances at the summer air shows where the Red Arrows are billed to fly. They're immediately recognizable in their bright blue overalls and you may spot them dodging under the wings of the ten Hawks parked on the tarmac, attending a fuel bowser, or climbing the toe-in steps to the high cockpit. They outnumber the pilots by 8:1 and without their many technical skills the Red Arrows couldn't fly.

All through the winter, the Blues dress in the RAF's standard-issue olive green overalls. Only during the summer display season do they wear the royal blue suits that make them stand out brightly against the landscape. Then, unlike the thousands of other RAF personnel and many of the other Blues, who work in anonymity, the Circus Blues appear in publicity and team shots and get into the public eye. "If you're with any other squadron and you get your picture taken by the press, it'll cost you a beer," reports Corporal Reg Davies, an electrician, "but when you're with the Red Arrows, you're always appearing in magazines and newspapers. You get used to it."

However, the limelight doesn't reach into every corner of every airfield during summer displays. "You can be on the far side of the airfield looking after the jets," says Reg Davies, "and it can be chucking it down, there are no toilets and there's nowhere to go and eat. You just have to eat when you can and make the best of it."

Drawn from 11 of the RAF's 60 trades, and all ranks from Senior Aircraftman (SAC) to Warrant Officer, the Blues are a mix of highly trained specialists with an in-depth knowledge of the BAE Hawk advanced trainer. Their list of job titles reflects their technical specialities – Propulsion Engineer, Airframe Specialist, Avionics Technician. Their brief is to keep

Above left The Blues prepare to refuel a Hawk between sorties at RAF Scampton.

as many as possible of the Red Arrows' 13 Hawk jets available to fly every day of the annual display season and, when that's over, every moment of winter training. They're the cream of the RAF's trades.

•

It's November and the Red Arrows are in the throes of winter training. They're flying six slots a day, five days a week. The Lincolnshire winters are raw and unforgiving, and although the really biting weather doesn't usually sweep in until after Christmas, a muscle-tearing wind is now howling off the Lincolnshire fens and across Scampton.

Rather like doing an MOT on road vehicles, each of the 13 available aircraft has to be serviced before every flight. The servicing team is in by 06.30 and the jets out on the line by 08:15, when the air crew turn up. As the first, Reds 6 and 7, the Synchro Pair, leave the building in full flying kit, the servicing team are carrying out last-minute visual checks on the Hawks. Prompt at 08:30, Synchro are taking off for their half-hour slot, and by 09:00 their Hawks are back on the line to be re-serviced ready for their second sortie.

Servicing the jets is the job of the dedicated army of Blues who work the line. These are the lineys, who operate in all conditions to pre-flight the jets (prepare them for the next slot). While the Synchro Pair fly the first sortie of the day, the lineys have half an hour to grab a cup of tea. But by 09:00 they're out on the line again for the next pre-flight, readying the jets for Reds 1 to 5 and 8 and 9 to fly the 09:45 slot. At the same time, they're checking 6 and 7's Hawks for damage to the airframe and engine, refuelling, replenishing the diesel and dye levels in the smoke pod and cleaning and polishing. One of them is Corporal Lance Did-Dell, an armourer: "You can pretty much be out there all day with only the odd quick break in between. You have to have lots of layers and keep moving."

Polishing the Hawks, particularly those flown by Reds 2–9, can be a six-or-more-times-a-day chore for the lineys. The jets behind the Leader's get dirtiest because they're often in the slipstream. Diesel and dye from the smoke pod become smeared all over the leading edges and have to be cleaned off after every training flight and display, winter and summer.

One thing that separates Blues with a trade imported from a previous RAF life from their colleagues in other squadrons is that their hard-won,

Above left Junior Technician and sootie, Craig Allan demonstrates that emptying the pressurized tanks in the smoke pod can sometimes cause dye to spurt out.

highly prized qualifications and skills are not always put to the use they'd imagined when they applied to join the Red Arrows. The squadron needs people with weapons training to deal with the explosive cartridges that power the ejection seats in an emergency, but looking after its 26 ejection seats is not a full-time job for its 7 armourers, who tend to be pressed into helping out with servicing the jets' other components. For this reason, before he joined the RAFAT, Corporal Mal Faulder envisaged life in the Reds as an easy one. "I couldn't have been more wrong," he says, "we work really hard." But when Lance Did-Dell arrived, he wondered what he'd got himself into: "Having no weapons to work on was the hardest thing to get used to at first, and having to work as a liney, servicing aircraft."

The lineys need special waterproofs and gloves for protection against more than their fair share of discomforts: electrical discharges, engine oil spills, coloured dyes splattering from the smoke pod, and the rain and cold.

Corporal Chris Ward also needs protection from the cold. Stationed beneath Scampton's Control Tower on a wintry November day, standing near-motionless for 30 minutes at a time, he videos a panorama of each wave for the pilots' debriefs – the postmortems they undergo after every sortie. An icy wind blows over the airfield, buffeting Chris Ward's elbow. Slowly, he stretches a locked arm straight, then returns it to the crooked position to cradle his preciously stable video camera, all the while hanging on to a steady panning shot of the formations. Seeing a singleton (single jet) 5km or 3 miles away and keeping it in the frame in winds up to 35kt, with rain pouring down the lens, is a skill he and his two fellow photographers have learned to perfect since they joined the Blues.

•

It's 16:30 on a February afternoon and dark outside, so the day's flying is over. The Hawks sit in their hangar, some swathed in engineering gantries and rigs, looking like Airfix models in plastic wrapping. The hangar is part-A&E department, part-strong room and part-museum. Aircraft components dot the floors and shelves looking like Victorian specimens from the golden age of powered flight. The Hawk has little by way of state-of-the-art computers, radar equipment or fly-by-wire systems on-board.

Sergeant Jim Rodgers, one of the Blues on night shift, walks me round

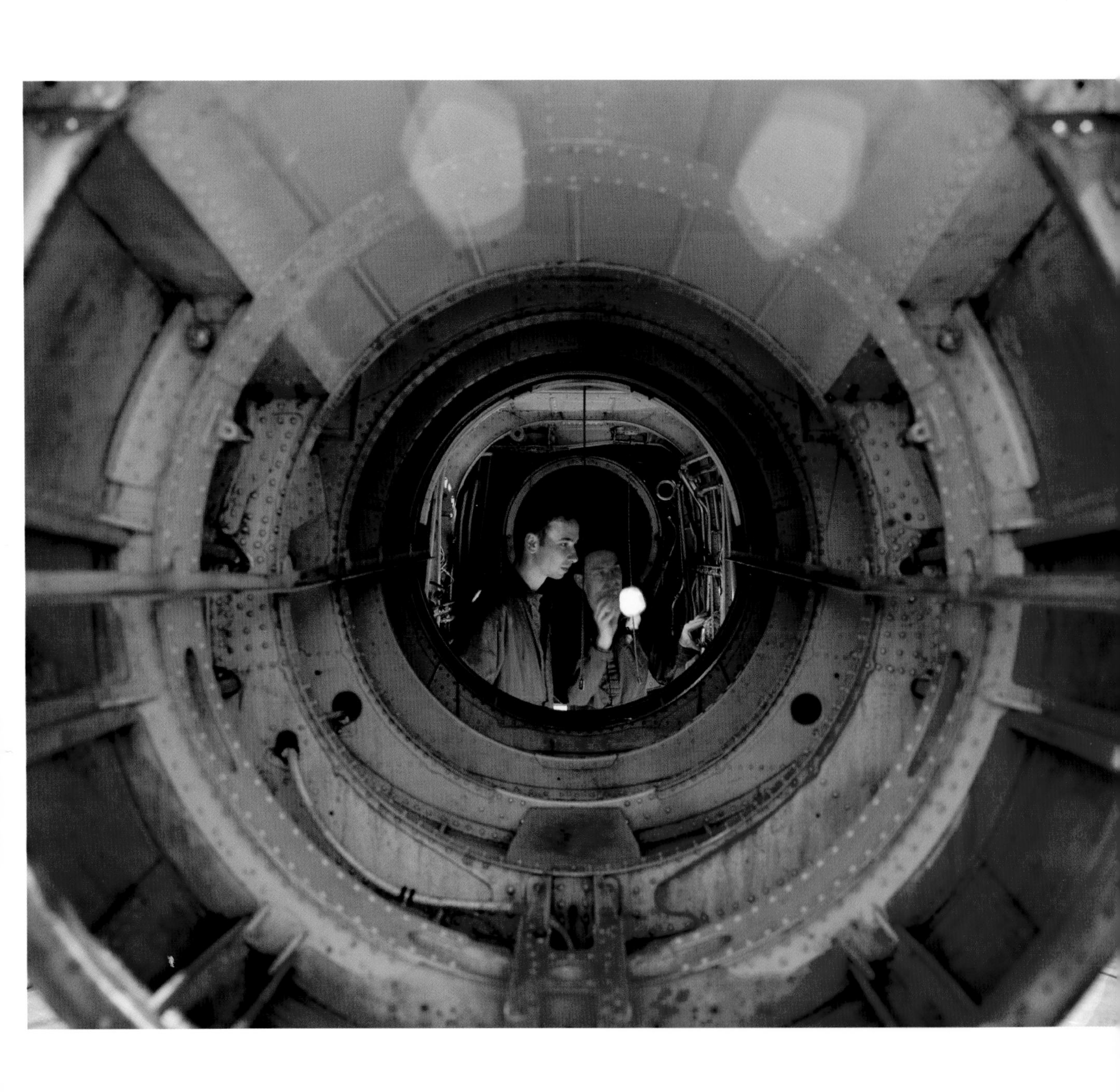

Hawk No.XX242, whose airframe bones are minus their panels, and whose weight is supported not by its undercarriage but by jacks. There's a gaping void where his beloved Adour turbofan engine should sit. XX242 joined the Red Arrows six months ago, and although it is a fully fledged Hawk, it won't be a Red Arrow until it has been modified to withstand the demands the Reds make of their hard-working jets.

The Blues recently measured and monitored the effects of these demands on XX260, a Hawk that had been flown for some time as one of the Synchro Pair and so subjected to high stresses. "XX242 is virtually a new aircraft from the rear cockpit back," proudly announces Jim Rodgers. "We put smoke pipes in, but because we've found that the high g causes a lot of cracking in the rear tail pipes, we strengthened the rear fuselage, padding out a 3in wedge between a support bracket and the rear cone."

In addition, I learn, XX242 had to have the wiring for its VOR (Very High Frequency Omni-Directional Range, a radio navigation system) changed because Red Arrow Hawks fly abroad, so they need better navigational aids than Hawks that fly only in UK air space.

While British aviation was fighting to impress in the early 1970s, many attributes and internal organs were shared by the Tornado, Hawk and Harrier, explains Jim Rodgers, an engineer whose experience on Tornados and Merlin helicopters over-qualifies him for work on the simpler Hawk T.Mk.1. For example, many of the flight controls hidden beneath the Hawk's roofing panels are clearly related to those on Harriers.

And he points out places on the Hawk that are inaccessible to the brawnier engineers on the team. Any Tornado man, I learn, will know about Zone 19. Its equivalent on the Hawk is Panel 121C, which the Blues call 'The Black Hole of Calcutta'. And I'm shown an open bay below the rear cockpit that does just what that name suggests: I see it swallow a man of slight build. As he stands up, his upper torso disappears inside what seems to be a storage bay for oxygen bottles, an emergency flap-lowering system and brake-control valves. "A man with a beer belly," observes Jim, "couldn't get in there." Every aircraft has its Black Hole.

Sergeant Pete Smith, who's been listening in, holds up two Mohammed Ali-sized knuckles and muses, "I have problems reaching igniter leads (like spark plugs) through the engine bay roof." He takes me beneath 242's wing and invites me to slip my hand up alongside a mass of wiring to touch

Above left The Blues operate a 24-hour shift system at the Scampton HQ. Here, Junior Technician and rigger Barry Pritchard straddles the rear fuselage to change the Ram Air Turbine (RAT) jack.

Opposite Leckies (electricians) inspect the wiring inside an empty engine bay.

a connector. I can feel it, but I can't imagine doing anything more than brush my skin against its sharp edges. "You need far daintier hands than mine to get in there, so I get armourer Mal Faulder to do the inside jobs," jokes Pete Smith.

Jim and Pete are both propulsion technicians, called 'sooties' in the RAF. Looking after the squadron's 17 Rolls-Royce Adour Mk.151 power plants is a major part of their job. "This engine is unbelievable," says Jim, indicating with parental pride the gaping bay that normally houses XX242's single Adour engine. Sooties love oily engine-changes. The Adour can be removed and its replacement tested in the running pan over the far side of the airfield and mounted in its bay within four hours. A Harrier engine-change takes much longer because the overhead wings need to be removed. The Hawk is much more basic.

"But it's robust," loyally interposes Lance Did-Dell; "it copes really well with all those rough taxiways in the Middle East." He explains that the Reds don't always practise anti-FOD (foreign object) taxiing in a staggered formation, instead they often taxi nose-to-tail, about 4 metres or yards apart. Any loose debris on a taxiway could get blown up by the jet efflux (exhaust) towards the Adour's air intakes. The Adour also gets the occasional bird strike. The distance between the Hawk's air intakes and its engine is short, probably about one-third of that on the Tornado, so if a bird is sucked in, it's likely to cause damage, I'm told. Yet a bird that went down one of the air intakes the week before did very little damage. "The guys had a look inside – it made short work of that bird," said Lance Did-Dell.

Squadron Leader Simon Davies, Senior Engineering Officer (SEngO), actually a Red, oversees engine serviceability. "It might only take one bird strike to lose the one spare engine available to us when we travel abroad, and that might mean losing a spare aircraft."

Stripped down, the grounded Hawk before me appears undignified and ungainly as the Blues, with a commitment verging on obsession, return it to a state of airworthiness. Jim Rodgers takes me into the Stores. They remind me of those hardware shops that brown-overalled men in glasses used to assist in. "Here, look at this – you know about the landing light, don't you?" I confess I don't. He brings over two heavy light bulbs shaped like miniature flying saucers. At any air show, the landing lights of the Hawks as they hammer down low blaze as bright as UFOs against the haze, sending the Red Arrows' signature for miles beyond the crowds. They pierce brighter than

Above left Sergeant David Ablard and a fellow rigger get to grips with an air brake issue at the Royal International Air Tattoo (RIAT) at Fairford.

Opposite Three of the Blues working on a Hawk during one of its scheduled servicings in the RAF Scampton hangar.

RA 10
DANGER

the lights of a non-Red Arrows Hawk trainer because they have an extra-large light bulb. Their bulbs are 1,375mm or 5½in – in diameter, compared with the standard 1,060mm or 4¼in.

Engineers who've done time with heavyweight Harriers and Tornados are unstinting in their praise of the little Hawk. "When a Tornado lands, there'll most likely be something that doesn't work. It's such a complicated bit of kit, so it's the nature of the beast," says Lance Did-Dell. Some of these Hawks are 25 years old – XX227 was one of the first Hawks to join the Red Arrows in 1980 – yet they're all still flying aerobatic manoeuvres hundreds of times a year. Nevertheless, wiring and other small problems do appear and reappear, a sign of advancing age. For example, the lineys always have to keep an eye on the Accident Data Recorder (ADR), to make sure it's working.

"But," summarizes Reg Davies, "there's nowhere I've worked with such limited assets – just 13 aircraft, with one often on a scheduled service – yet we always produce 11 aircraft fit for every practice and every display. No other squadron can do that time after time." Of 4,182 sorties flown during the 2004 season, only two were classed as defective. That's a big tick for the aircraft and for the engineers who work on them.

Opposite Orange light spills from the Scampton hangar.

•

Each November a team of Blues is chosen by their JEngO and SEngO (Junior and Senior Engineering Officers, both of whom are Reds) to fly in Circus. That doesn't mean they start training to become trapeze artists. Each chosen Blue is allocated a jet and its pilot to look after through the flying season – cleaning, servicing and, when necessary, repairing the aircraft – and supply the pilot's technical needs around the summer flying circuit. All through the display season a Blue dressed in full flying gear, complete with a helmet with a red arrow symbol, travels to and from most venues in the rear cockpit seat of most of the Hawks. As many as ten or eleven may go because the nine main display jets are accompanied by one or two crewed jets as spares; but the back seat of Red 1 is always occupied by the JEngO.

Being in Circus is the most prestigious role for a Blue. The name may derive from some forgotten tradition of referring to the Blues who flew with the jets as the 'travelling circus.' Flying in the Hawks and sharing the pilots experience is one of the biggest buzzes and major attractions of the job.

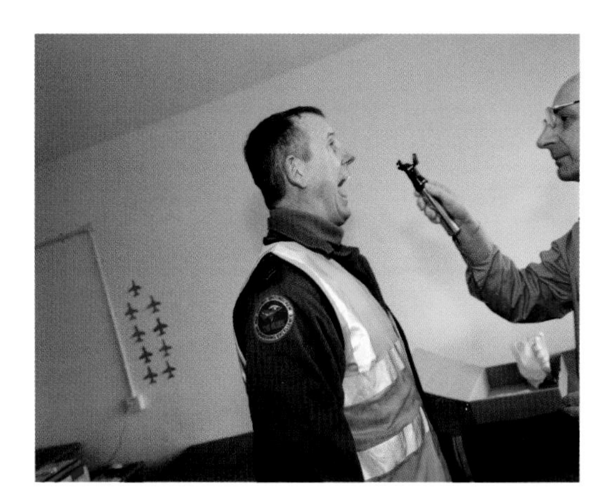

Circus members become the most visible representatives of the Blues. Competition is naturally fierce.

Although Circus members are selected each year and there's no guarantee that they may remain for longer, they may be chosen for the Circus for three or even four successive years. There's a rotation: during the year they join the Circus they're normally allocated to the more experienced pilots and they move progressively forward in successive years.

The special duties of the Blues chosen for the Circus really begin with their first overseas transit. That usually takes place in January or February, when they take off in the back seat of their respective Hawks to fly to RAF Akrotiri in Cyprus for WinterHawk – training in the longer daylight hours. But the Circus Blues alone couldn't service and repair the 11 Hawks for five weeks. They're accompanied by their support team of 55 Blues, who all fly out together in 'Albert'.

'Albert' is like a jolly uncle who gets drunk at Christmas and sings about all the women he's known. He is a fat but hardworking member of the RAF and an honorary member of the Reds' extended family. 'Albert' is the fond nickname of the RAF's huge C-130 Hercules, which, loaded with 10.8 tons of spares, dye and a miscellany of other freight, carries the Blues' support team to Akrotiri, and brings them back at the end of the Mediterranean practice.

In Cyprus in winter and again in spring, the Reds hone the aerobatic skills they practised at Scampton into the display routines they'll be performing through the season; and the Blues put their all into turning out faultless red rockets for them to fly. It's hard work out in the Med. During spring training, the Blues have to pre-flight the Hawks for perhaps as many as 36 waves a day in temperatures that hover around 30°C or 86°F. Circus people are the first in every day and they organize a night shift. Mosquitoes swarm in the jets' wheel wells. SpringHawk is notorious for giving the Blues insect bites and skin rashes, and swelling welts on exposed faces. Pale Anglo-Saxon skin reddens in the fierce heat. Patience can fray.

The pressure mounts relentlessly for five exhausting weeks. Everyone's mind is on the goal: PDA – the all-important permit to fly the summer displays and the culmination of everyone's work. The pilots make heavy demands on themselves to perform to perfection, and the Blues try to relieve some of the tension by always providing the requisite number of perfectly functioning, gleaming aircraft. "If they have to do extra slots for more

Above left Sergeant Chris Shaw, leader of the Circus Blues, is given an ear, nose and throat check by an RAF doctor before leaving for WinterHawk.

training, we don't complain," says Corporal Mark Gage, Airframe Technician. "You sense the mood building up."

The closer to PDA Day they get, the harder the Blues clean and polish the jets, so on the big day, the sunlight sparkles on a row of dazzling Hawks. After a 2003 post-season tour of the Middle East, the 2004 winter training commenced six weeks late and poor weather caused another two weeks of delays. "Our character has been tested all along the way," said Squadron Leader Spike Jepson to the lined-up Blues on PDA Day.

Like the pilots, the Blues change plumage when PDA is granted, discarding their now soiled and oily greens for their eponymous and perfectly fitting royal blue suits. As members of the Red Arrows team, the Blues take their blue suits very seriously. Despite the grubbiness of their work, their dress codes are as important as their safety procedures. "We never do hands in pockets," says Mark Gage. And the flap has to be tucked over to hide the long zip that runs from breastbone to groin. 'Zip violations' are taken very seriously. "We've got standards that the public expect to see."

The first public display, which traditionally takes place in May at RAF Akrotiri, is the starting gun for a schedule of some 90 displays and fly-pasts. They take place every week until late in September. The Circus Blues hop from one short flight to another, zigzagging across the UK and out to Europe as the air show calendar flicks ever-onwards through the summer. The support team travels by coach or, if overseas, on Albert to the air-show venues. For them, any summer weekend is a blur of road or air miles, hotel foyers and remote airfield ramps, well away from the public.

On or off Circus, the Blues find there's a price tag on their travels. Many have homes in Lincolnshire within commuting distance of Scampton, so during winter training they get home to read bedtime stories. But for about six months of the year, when they're on the road – longer in the years when they go on a foreign tour – they spend more time in each other's company than their families'. Despite being absent from their wives and children and deprived of regular meals, the Blues underpin the entire display season. They work long and hard, and they rarely get weekends off.

Armourer Corporal Mal Faulder is a Circus veteran who rides with Red 10 and operates the team video when there's no ground-based photographer at an event. "To apply for Circus is to be prepared to commit yourself to a summer of weekend working. I've got two children and I miss a huge chunk

Above left Circus Blues' families waiting to see their men off to SpringHawk training in Cyprus.

of their life. I feel very selfish." Mark Gage has reached the end of his second season in Circus and he looks weary. "I'm tired and looking forward to finishing. Now I have to decide if I want to apply again. I don't think the team could survive without the support of their wives and girlfriends. They hardly ever see you, and they get no free trips abroad."

Usually every two years the Red Arrows go on a foreign tour, which may extend the flying season. They may travel to North America (as in 2002, when they displayed in Canada) or to the Middle and Far East (as in 2003). They fly their display in front of diplomats, salespeople and a public that doesn't often get a chance to see the Red Arrows perform. Travelling to other continents to display is a bonus for the Blues who are chosen to go on tour.

Ask the Circus Blues about their highlights on tour and they will spill their memories: "On the way back from the Middle East tour, we crossed the Suez Canal from Saudi Arabia to Egypt and suddenly, there they were: the pyramids and the Sphinx. I ran out of film." "At the end of the flight into Kuala Lumpur in Malaysia we flew right by the Petronas Towers – level with the tips of their spires."

Even a 'transit' (a relatively brief journey to and from an air show in the UK) can have a special significance. Lance Did-Dell remembers: "We flew over Lake Windermere, and it looked crystal clear. Then we spotted two walkers on top of Scafell Pike. They'd probably taken all morning to get up there, and just as they reached the top they saw us fly over. They waved up at us and the Boss called 'Smoke on Go!' and then 'Off.' For me that was the highlight of the year."

Opposite Members of the Blues await the departure of their jets from RAF Akrotiri for Marka in Jordan.

TRADES

The 85 Blues are selected from the cream of the RAF's trade and administrative expertise. Typically, an engineering graduate or admin assistant will join up shortly after leaving school and apply to be posted to the Red Arrows during his or her first year of training. The wait can be long. Unlike the Reds, the Blues are not on short-term contracts – they can stay with the Red Arrows for up to five years. The Blues' are drawn from 11 trades. They are:

TWENTY EIGHT AIRFRAME SPECIALISTS

There are more 'riggers' on the team than any other trade, because the airframe is the fuselage, canopy, flying controls, brakes and undercarriage and that's most of the aircraft. "Take out the engine, the electronics and the ejection seat and every other part of the aircraft is my trade," says Corporal Richard Adams, who waited for about ten years before being posted. "At the shows, we're responsible for the checks and replacement parts. Servicing goes on year-round, so there's always a team in the hangar." "Everything you see is what we riggers fix," says Junior Technician Barry Pritchard, who worked as a technician at a ten-pin-bowling company before finding his niche with the RAF in 1997. "The timescales for completing jobs are the hardest thing to adjust to," he's found. "They say: 'we want this jet flying by the morning,' and we have to work into the early hours to make that happen."

TEN PROPULSION ENGINEERS

The 'sooties' are the engine men. Their main job is to check, monitor, test, change and service the Hawk's single Rolls-Royce Adour engine. They're often found in the engine pan on the Scampton airfield running an engine to check for faults. Corporal Glenn King applied to the Red Arrows in 1993 – but he worked on Nimrods and Harriers, and on Wessex, Puma and Chinook helicopters before he was posted in 2003. Now he specializes in the Hawk's engine and fuel system. But "working with the Red Arrows isn't just about engines," he says. "We get involved in dozens of other jobs on the Hawk."

NINE AVIONICS TECHNICIANS

The avionics technicians' job in the Reds is to maintain and rectify faults in the Hawk's radio and navigation equipment. The Reds call avionics men 'fairies', but no one really knows why. Senior Aircraftman (SAC) Mike Evans was posted to the RAFAT two years after he joined up. His skills are in flight systems but his knowledge of radar, VOR and tactical navigation aren't used by the Red Arrows. "Avionics technicians specialize in communications, radar and flight systems, attitude, heading and reference systems, navigation, landing, IFF (air traffic recognition) and Friend or Foe (identifying friendly aircraft in combat situations)," he explains. "But the Hawk's avionics are fairly basic and there's no radar. The Red Arrows have one unique system: in-flight video camcorders to record TV footage. They designed it themselves."

NINE ELECTRICIANS

The 'leckies' are engineers who specialize in aviation and service the Hawk's electrical systems. These include flight instruments such as the airspeed and altitude indicators. Corporal Reg Davies worked on Harriers for almost eight years at RAF Laarbruch and Cottesmore before applying to the RAFAT in the mid-1980s, and he waited almost ten years to be posted. He describes his job simply: "If there's anything powered by electricity, leckies have something to do with it – lights, batteries, electrical distribution, instruments. The Hawk's so simple that we often deal with easy faults like a loose earth. But it has no built-in test equipment, no computer you can fire up to ask what's wrong. So you have to get back to basics and prod about with multimeters to find faults."

SEVEN ARMOURERS

The armourers all come from squadrons flying combat aircraft such as Harriers and Tornados. The Hawk carries no armaments, but armourers are needed to arm and maintain the rocket-propelled ejection seats and the explosive cartridges that shatter the canopy when activated. The Red Arrows' armourers also handle the flaps and undercarriage.

Corporal Lance Did-Dell trained as a weapons expert on the Tornado GR4 at RAF Marham and Lossiemouth, but applied to the Red Arrows because "it was something to aspire to." He didn't enjoy his first six months at all, but looking back, he sees that it has been a good grounding. The Hawk's ejection seat is much simpler than the Tornado's, "But the challenge is that we can never do a functional test on a seat, we know it works only when it gets used."

FIVE DRIVERS

Military transport (MT) drivers deliver back-up kit and fuel to the travelling team; and they transport the Blues support team from air show to air show through the summer season. During winter training they fuel the jets. SAC Dave Dyche is a military transport driver, who used to deliver parachutes for the army. "We never stop during the season and even during winter practice it's all go, go, go for us." Dave Greaves (cruelly nicknamed 'Whiplash') served 24 years in the RAF as a propulsion engineer. He's now a civilian, who joined the Blues as a driver six years ago: "I know about aircraft handling, so I was ideal for the job of driving the team. A few years ago we did 100 days of road-pushes between May and September, but because of cuts we now do about 70."

THREE SURVIVAL EQUIPMENT TECHNICIANS

From their ordered office, the squips supply, maintain and repair the Reds' and Blues' flying and safety kit – helmet, boots, flying suits, oxygen masks. They fit all equipment expertly – remembering which pilots like their face masks tight. And they try to relax nervous visiting pilots. "We make things run smoothly. We even have a washing machine so that anyone who needs it can have a clean kit the next day," says Corporal Dave Wright. "We don't want anyone mingling with VIPs smelling of socks. It's also down to us to make certain that if anyone has to pull the 'yellow and black' – God forbid – the parachute we supply and pack will get them down safely."

THREE PHOTOGRAPHERS

The photographers double as video camera operators. They take still photographs of the team and snap them meeting VIPs and corporate groups. But their most important job is to capture every moment of every practice and every display, at home and away, on video for the Reds to analyse afterwards, looking for timing errors and aerobatic glitches.

Corporal Chris Ward joined the RAF in 1987 as an apprentice electrician, but applied to join the Red Arrows: "for the kudos. As an RAF photographer, I see the Red Arrows as the pinnacle of my trade." The most challenging part of his job is getting the right video pictures for the debriefing: "The Red Arrows demand perfection and we try to be inch-perfect in keeping the formations in frame and not letting the focus waver."

TWO FLIGHT PLANNERS

The Flight Planning officers are the team's travel organizers, providing information and back-up support whenever and wherever they travel. They make and coordinate air space reservations for transits and displays, file flight plans, book low-level routes, coordinate fly-pasts with the RAF Participation Committee, and liaise with the staff of British embassies abroad to obtain diplomatic clearance for overflying foreign territories. They plot routes and load them into the GPS navigation units used by the pilots, book facilities at landing bases and check weather data.

Corporal Alex Stockbridge was posted to the RAFAT in 2002 and has had to learn both military and civil aviation computerized route systems. Flight Planning is most pressurized during the display season. "Our office must always be staffed," she explains, "because wherever the team are, they call us to check the weather en route, that we have all the flight plans, and so on." The flight planners take their responsibilities very seriously, "When the team were on tour, they were working ten hours ahead of us and we made sure we were always here," she recalls, "Sometimes, that meant a 15-hour day."

SIX ADMINISTRATORS AND THREE GENERAL SUPPLIERS

Every organization needs administrators to make sure that routine things such as accommodation, leave and pay all run smoothly. The general supplies staff keep the squadron in the air: without them to keep the stores supplied with spare parts, the Hawks would soon be grounded.

Senior Aircraftman (SAC) Helen Ainsworth joined up in 1998 aged 17, trained as an administrator and applied to the Red Arrows because she'd heard good things about the squadron. It took a three and a half-year wait before she was posted, but she thinks it was worth the wait. "Working in a squadron is very different from working in a general office. You're there for everybody." She lives on the Scampton base in the mess which, she says, is very comfortable.

Senior Aircraftman (SAC) Claire Towns comes from an RAF family and applied to the Red Arrows because she was looking for something different. She works in supplies and her job is simply to get hold of anything that's needed – spares the aircraft need, equipment the technicians need, clothing the ground crew need, everyone's green overalls. The suppliers deal with a whole range of outside contractors and they need to know the market. "Some things are hard to get – you have to know where to go and who to speak to."

Page 190:

Top left Two Blues engineers, Senior Aircraftman Andrew Murray and Corporal Stephen Reece work on a smoke pod.

Top right The Trade Manager's office overlooks the squadron's 'Guardian' – a Folland Gnat.

Centre left A liney – a technician assigned a jet on the parking line – inspects a jet pipe for imperfections at RAF Scampton.

Centre right 'Pre-flighting' is a term used by all RAF engineers, a contraction of 'prepare an aircraft for a flight.' Here, three Blues pre-flight a jet on the line at Scampton.

Bottom left Junior Technician Brian Robb checking flaps for obstructions, RAF Scampton.

Bottom right Junior Technician Craig Allan replenishes the smoke pod. with derv and vegetable dye.

Page 191:

Top left Chief Technician Kerry Griffiths and Junior Technician Darren Budziszewski attend a Health and Safety brief.

Top right Corporal Karen McNally adjusts the flight-planning board.

Centre left Corporal David Wright, Survival Equipment Technichian, checks a life vest in the squips' room.

Centre right Suppliers, Corporal Andrew Haynes and Senior Aircraftman Michael Owen load boxes packed with the team's kit for WinterHawk.

Bottom left Corporal Mal Faulder wheels a Martin-Baker ejection seat into the 'Morgue', a blast-proof outbuilding where the explosive cylinders that fire the seat are stored in a protected environment.

Bottom right Albert, the C-130 Hercules transport, gives the Blues support team a noisy ride to winter training in Cyprus.

ROYA

XX308

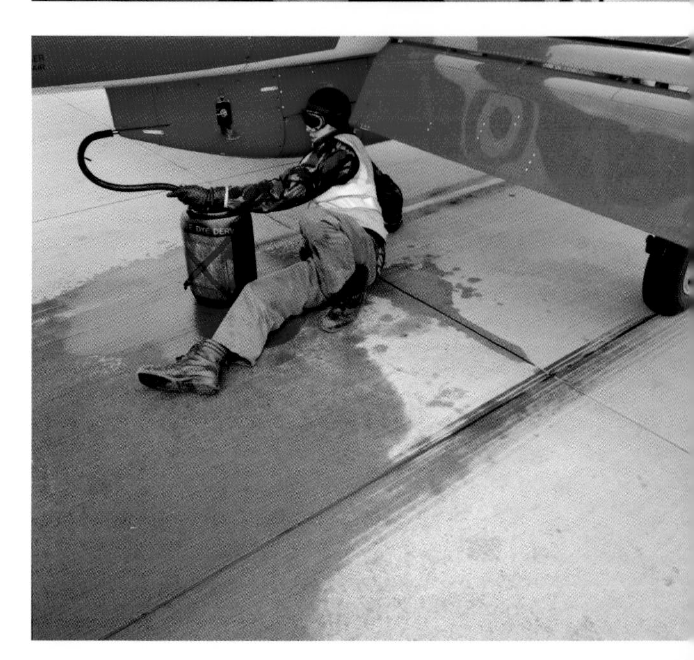

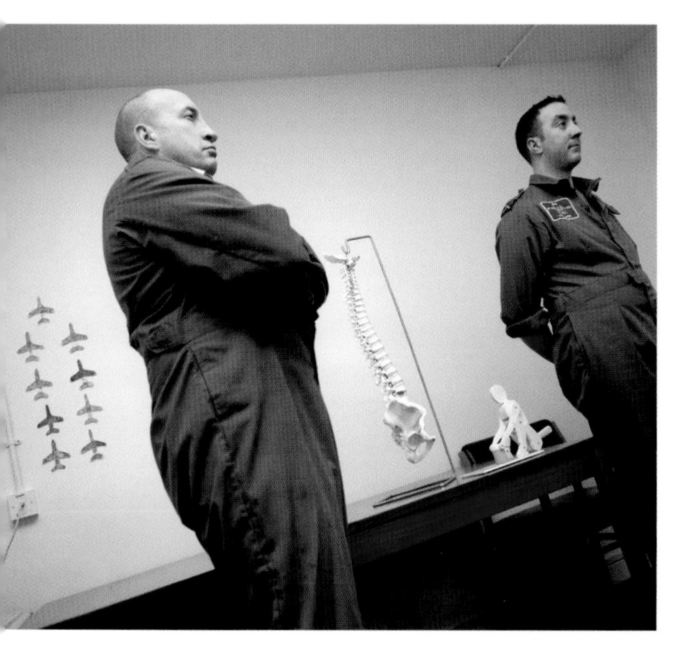

VERY HEAVY

RA-21
DANGER
FRONT SEAT
DL1217 020

NO SMOKING

AIR WEAR

In the winter, the Reds send out an order for about 40 flying suits for the Reds and 180 flame-retardant overalls for the Blues. Jays Racewear of Nelson, Lancashire, were asked to design a suit for the Red Arrows. The brief was that it must be flame-retardant, comfortable and stylish.

The Reds' suits will protect against fire for the few seconds before a pilot needs to eject. The Hawk's cockpit is air-conditioned, so the pilots' suits are not multi-layered like motorsport suits and they have an underarm panel to ventilate and prevent sweating – the Reds need to look cool at the end of every display. Jays' parent company, Dale Techniche of Barnsley, Yorkshire, manufacture the fabric – Du Pont's Nomex® 111 with 5% Kevlar, chosen because it is strong, durable and fire-retardant. They supply enough to make three suits each for the Reds dyed in Arrows Red, a non-standard colour with a heightened brightness quotient; and a batch large enough to make two suits each for the Blues dyed in standard royal blue. Staff measure each team member, and each suit is cut individually, then embroidered with names, insignia and the Red Arrows' crest. To cut, embroider, sew, inspect and pack each suit takes eight hours plus. The suits are delivered to Scampton in March or April each year and freighted to RAF Akrotiri on Albert, ready for PDA Day.

Opposite Each suit is individually cut and tailored.

Below:
Top left Bales of flame-retardant Nomex® dyed in bright Arrows Red await processing at Dale Techniche.
Top right Computer-controlled embroidery machines track some 15,000 stitches in three runs on each badge.
Bottom left Team Leader Spike Jepson checks the positioning of badges on Jez Griggs's new red flying suit.
Bottom right Blue suits drying after PDA Day in the Blues' quarters at RAF Akrotiri.

Scampton

RAF Scampton, just north of Lincoln, is the official HQ of The Royal Air Force Aerobatic Team, The Red Arrows (RAFAT). It's the physical and spiritual home of the Hawk jets, the Red Arrows brand and the 100-odd back-up staff.

Scampton is much older than RAFAT – indeed, it technically predates the RAF, having been temporarily commandeered from farmland in 1916 for use as a training station during World War I and equipped with Sopwith Camels and Dolphins. Brattleby airfield, so called because Brattleby is the nearest village, was rebuilt in 1936 and reopened as RAF Scampton. It has a distinguished war record. From March 1943, the legendary Lancaster bomber replaced Manchesters and Fairey Battles on the Scampton airstrips when 617 'Dam Busters' Squadron moved in. On 16 May 1943, 19 Lancaster bombers took off from Scampton on Operation Chastise, their raid on the Mohne, Eder and Sorpe dams using Barnes Wallis's bouncing bomb.

At Scampton, Bomber Command taught post-war pilots to fly Spitfires, Lincolns, Mosquitoes and Wellingtons. In the early 1950s the Canberra wing units were based there with their B2 jets, and the United States Air Force Bomb Group with its B29 Superfortresses. Then in 1955, the airfield was closed and a runway 2,745m or 9,000ft long was built to accommodate the new Vulcan B1 nuclear bomber; and No.617 was foremost among the squadrons that came to Scampton to fly it.

Back in 1980, the Red Arrows' home was RAF Kemble in Gloucestershire, but it was unsuitable for their new Hawk jets. In April 1984, two years after the last Vulcan squadron had withdrawn, they moved into a vacant hangar at Scampton. They were temporarily joined by their parent organization, the Central Flying School (CFS), and had to compete for flying slots with its Jet Provost trainers.

Opposite After an afternoon cloudburst, a rainbow illuminates an old Dam Busters hangar near the Red Arrows squadron building at RAF Scampton.

RAFAT HQ

RAFAT is a close-knit squadron, rather like a touring operatic company based in a provincial town. Their accommodation on the airfield is modest: just one hangar on the north side, a short walk from the main gate and the A15 into Lincoln. It looks scarcely large enough to accommodate all the jets, the offices and workshops of the 85 Blues and administration staff, all the Reds, and, of course, the hordes of visitors who report to the Guard Room at the gate every weekday.

The hangar is the atmospheric sanctuary of the jets and their support team, the Blues. Its floors are marked out with parking bays for the squadron's Hawk jets plus the occasional extra one on loan, perhaps, from the Flying Training School at RAF Valley. When RAFAT members talk about 'downstairs' they mean the Blues' offices, including the squips' room, ranged along the hangar's northwest side. There are more Blues' offices along the southeast side, along with the stores and the Line Control room, the pilots' last stop to sign for their aircraft parked out on the line, and the first stop on their way back to the briefing room after landing.

Upstairs are the Reds; their squadron building housing offices and the crew and briefing rooms was built on to the side of the hangar overlooking the runway. Lists of Red Arrows teams dating back to 1965, photographs of the current team, and awards from foreign governments decorate the walls of the visitors' reception. The offices are comfortable but solidly functional and dated. "Living in a 1930s hangar is sometimes difficult," concedes Rachel Huxford, Public Relations Officer, "we have lots of visitors and it's not built for that purpose. But we cope."

Foreign display teams may have designer HQs, but not the RAF's aerobatic team. And luxury is not one of their requirements. 'It's not part of the British character' is what they say. They have their hangar, in a good, central position, with workshops and offices, sheds and an outside stretch of concrete that leads to a wider expanse of runway, control tower and medical centre. What more do they need? "We're a team and we work as a team. And we're ingenious – if we need something, we find ways of getting it. It's not a question of throwing money at us," Rachel insists.

An atmosphere of relief and satisfaction hung over Scampton at the beginning of 2005. Since 1995 the airfield had been under threat of closure as an economy measure. In 1996, the RAFAT was moved to the Central Flying School's HQ, RAF Cranwell, also in Lincolnshire, and the base closed. But fitting the Red Arrows' flying practice and training requirements in with the CFS's flying training schedule was difficult and Scampton still had to be used, its control tower and emergency services kept manned. Sharing runways and air space and flying time was a complicated operation and the RAFAT moved back. Early in 2005, a decision came from the MoD. Scampton's future was secured and the Reds could stay. Other RAF units were to move in, but they would be ground-based.

That was a great 40th birthday present: no other jets competing for flying slots and air space. Red Arrows teams of the foreseeable future will have the skies over Scampton to themselves.

FUC
217006

The Hawks parked in the hangar at Scampton on a winter evening.

ROYAL AIR FORCE

The team's photographers film every 30-minute sortie and, during the season, every display. "It can be perishing cold in winter, but you worry more about keeping the focus sharp in strong winds," says Corporal Chris Ward.

The hangar at RAF Scampton, almost empty after the team's departure for WinterHawk training in February.

Hangar at RAF Akrotiri.

FIRE
FIRE
ACTION
RAISE THE ALARM
HOUT FOR ASSISTANCE
PERATE THE FIRE ALARM
ALL FIRE SERVICE BY:
TELEPHONE 2222
EMPT TO FIGHT THE FIRE
(IF PRACTICABLE)
LOCATION OF:
ALARMS AIR HORN ON PILLAR EITHER END OF HANGAR
HONES STORES AVIONICS
EQUIP FOAM + CO2 THROUGH OUT HANGAR
HEARING THE FIRE ALARM
ASSEMBLY POINT IS:
EASTERN SIDE OF HANGAR ON BONDU
ROYAL AIR FORCE

Aerosol markings at the Royal International Air Tattoo (RIAT),
RAF Fairford.

The Blues place a tray beneath the smoke pod of each Hawk in the hangar to collect drips of dye.

A winter sortie passes over the bright Precision Path Indicators (PAPIs) whose red lights guide landing aircraft at RAF Scampton.

Spring fog has delayed an early sortie and still blankets
RAF Scampton.

Airfield telephone, RAF Scampton.

Practising foreign object damage taxiing (FOD) to avoid dust being sucked into engine air intakes, the Reds return after a sortie at RAF Akrotiri.

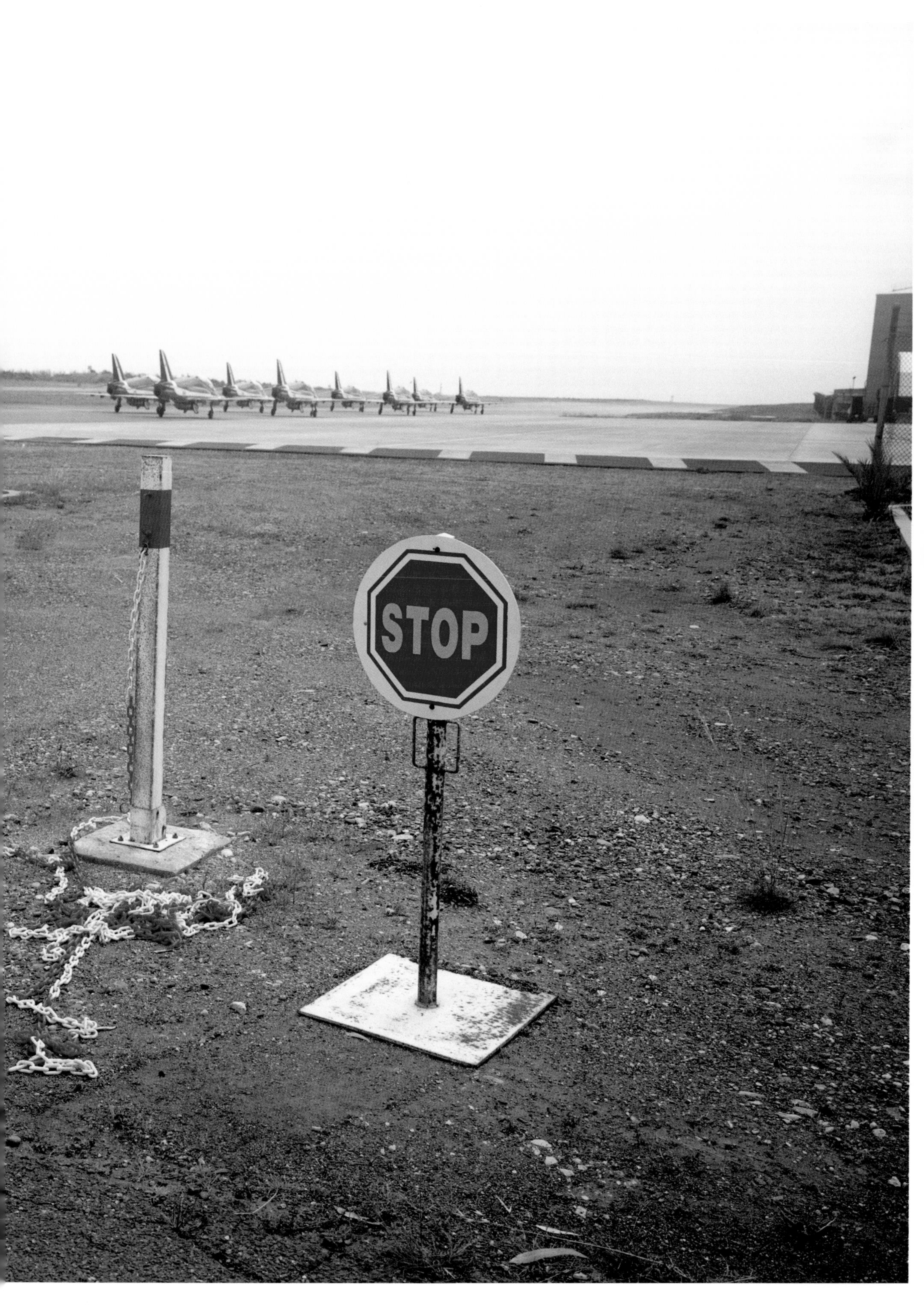
STOP

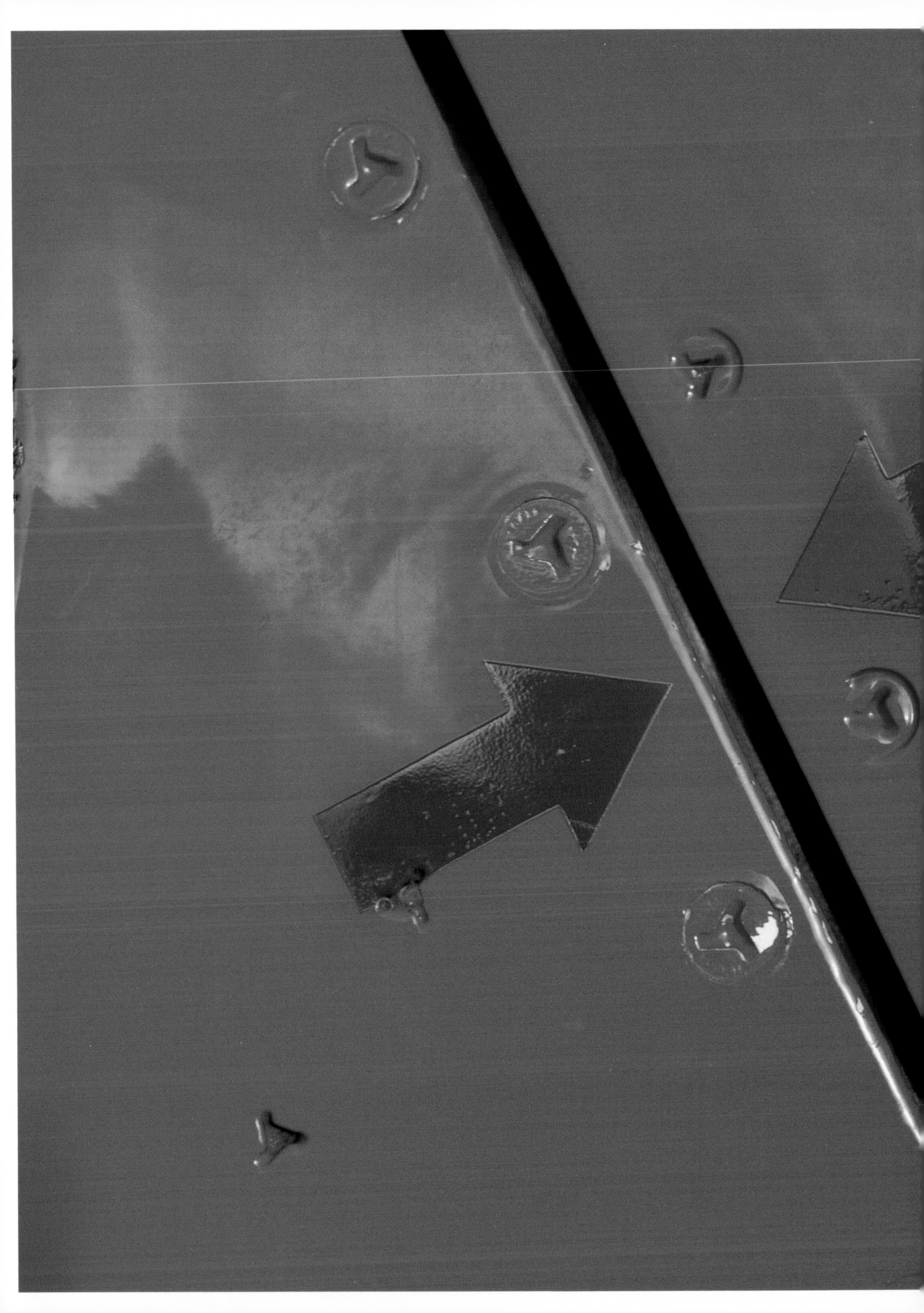

"The Hawk's side-opening canopy moves so easily," warns the T.Mk.1 Aircrew Manual, "that care must be taken not to close it accidentally and trap the fingers of the occupants or the ground crew on the cockpit rim."

SMOKE POD
013
SERVICEABLE ITEMS

Flying in a Hawk T.Mk.1 with the Red Arrows is, I suggest, one of the ten greatest kicks possible in a lifetime. The panoramas are stunning, even from the back seat. On occasions, as the Boss took off from Scampton for an afternoon sortie, with me strapped in behind him, camera in hand, I would trace across the Lincolnshire landscape below us the ruler-straight path of the A15, the former Ermine Street laid two millennia ago for Roman legions to march from Chichester to York. One afternoon, I glanced over a wing as our aircraft skimmed the clouds, its shadow chasing us before entering a spectacular rainbow of refracted sunlight. Then later, as we dipped our wing while re-entering the formation, I glimpsed a field of campers squinting up at us, waving as we flew over them.

But ask the Red Arrows pilots what it's like to fly in formation, often less than 3–4m or 12ft from their nearest neighbours, and they're likely to compare it with a spin down an expressway at 650kph or 400mph in close company with other vehicles. From the ground it looks smooth and effortless, but up there Red 1, at the head of the formation, is flying steady and true, while to me sitting behind him, our neighbours seem to bob and dip just beyond our wing tips as if jostling for position. The visor-faced pilots appear to fix us with sideways stares – just the kind of unnerving attention you don't want from a driver on the outside lane of an expressway.

The reason for the sideways stares and the bobbing and dipping is that the pilots are constantly adjusting to stay on-reference, that is, maintain their position in the formation relative to Red 1 so that the pattern the crowd sees from below doesn't blur or waver. The references change constantly as the aircraft fly through the display manoeuvres, yet to stay in their position in each formation, the pilots can allow themselves only minimal margin of error. They can deviate little more than the breadth of a helmet to the left and right of their reference points and above and below them. To achieve such accuracy during complex manoeuvres, they must know how to get the most out of the jets they fly and what degree of precision they can achieve.

The Hawk is a small jet with little by way of computers or fly-by-wire avionics, yet some of the manoeuvres the Red Arrows perform can't be achieved in larger jets fitted with state-of-the-art electronic systems. "The US Air Force display team, the Thunderbirds, demonstrate dazzling aerobatics in their fly-by-wire F-16 Fighting Falcons," says Squadron Leader John Green, "but they don't do the dynamic stuff we do. It's hard in a bigger aircraft."

Opposite A front and rear section of a smoke pod are stored in the Pod Bay while the main section is modified.

Pages 214-215, 218-219, 222-223, 230-231 Facsimiles from BAE's engineering diagrams showing the structural layout of the Hawk Mk. 51, the export version of the original Mk.1.

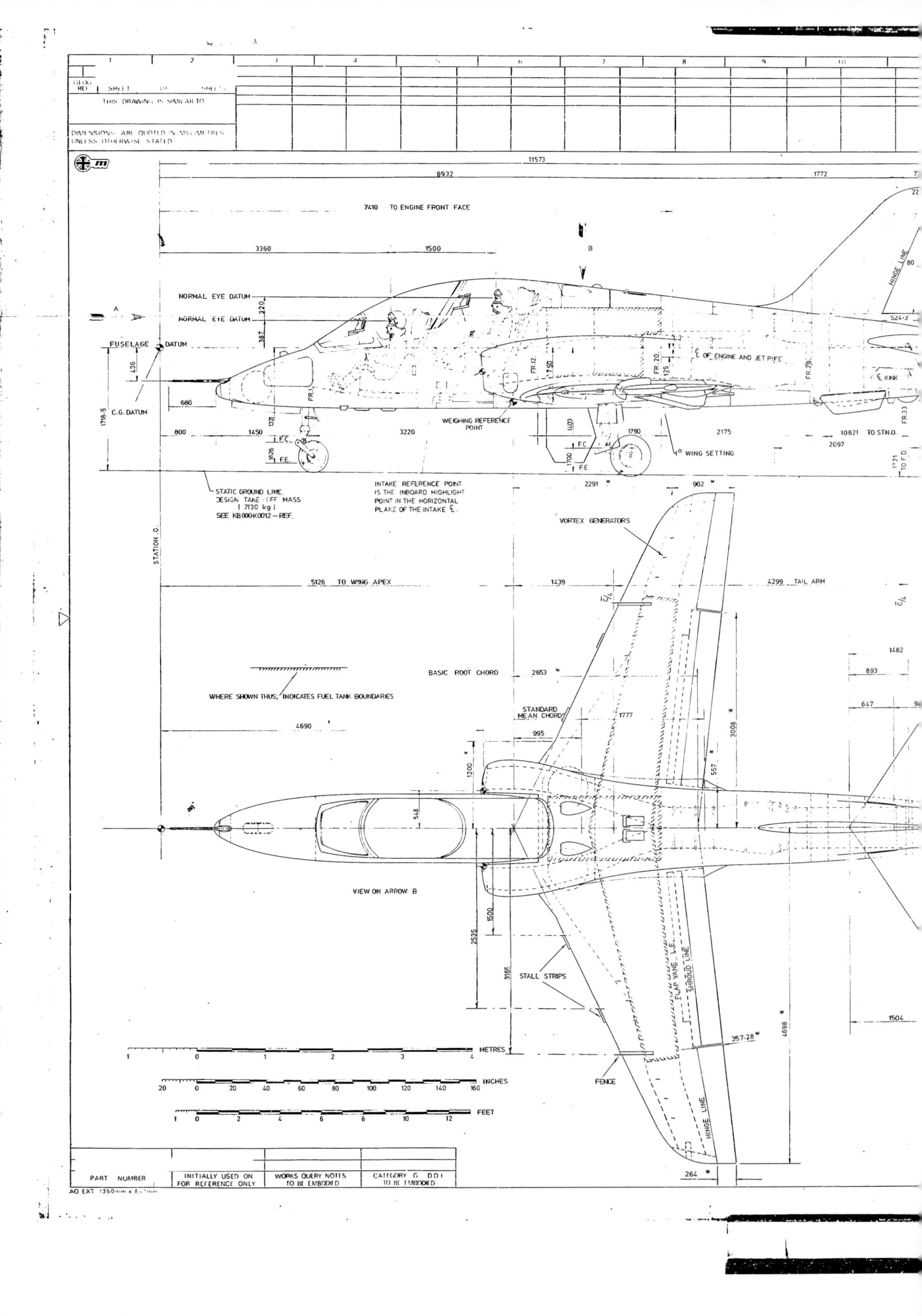
SHEET OF SHEETS
THIS DRAWING IS SIMILAR TO
DIMENSIONS ARE QUOTED IN MILLIMETRES UNLESS OTHERWISE STATED
11573
8932
1772
7410 TO ENGINE FRONT FACE
3360
1500
B
HINGE LINE
NORMAL EYE DATUM
NORMAL EYE DATUM
A
FUSELAGE DATUM
C.G. DATUM
1718·5
680
800
1450
3220
WEIGHING REFERENCE POINT
1790
2175
10821 TO STN.O.
2097
℄ OF ENGINE AND JET PIPE
℄ KINK
4° WING SETTING
STATIC GROUND LINE.
DESIGN TAKE-OFF MASS
(7130 kg)
SEE KB000-K0012—REF.
INTAKE REFERENCE POINT IS THE INBOARD HIGHLIGHT POINT IN THE HORIZONTAL PLANE OF THE INTAKE ℄.
STATION .O.
2291
902
VORTEX GENERATORS
5126 TO WING APEX
1439
4299 TAIL ARM
BASIC ROOT CHORD
2653
1482
893
647
WHERE SHOWN THUS, INDICATES FUEL TANK BOUNDARIES
STANDARD MEAN CHORD
1777
3008
4690
995
1200
548
557
VIEW ON ARROW B
1500
2535
3165
STALL STRIPS
FLAP VANE L.E.
SHROUD LINE
4698
1504
357·28
METRES
INCHES
FEET
FENCE
HINGE LINE
264
PART NUMBER
INITIALLY USED ON FOR REFERENCE ONLY
WORKS QUERY NOTES TO BE EMBODIED
CATEGORY G DDI TO BE EMBODIED

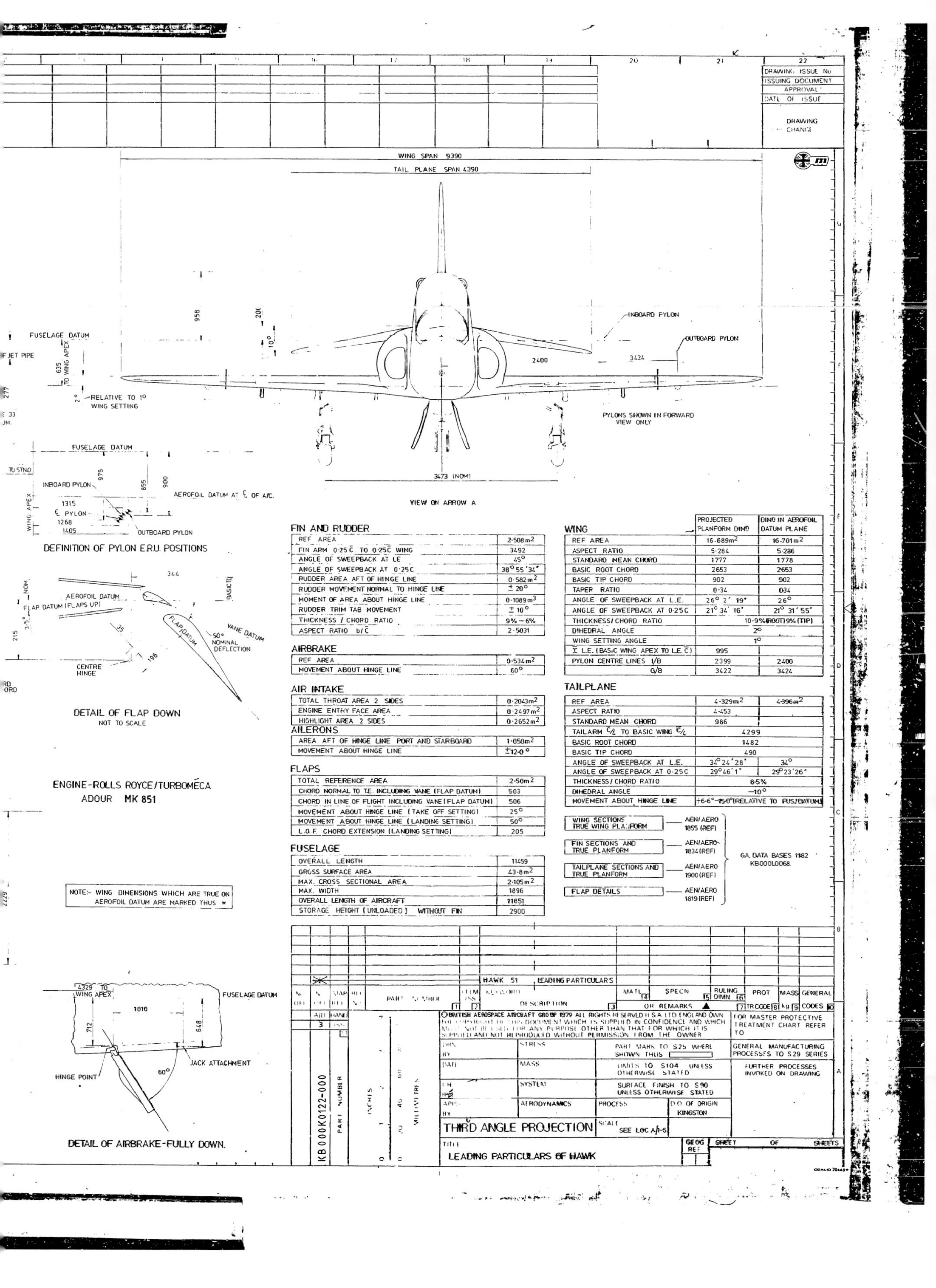

FIN AND RUDDER

REF AREA	2·508 m²
FIN ARM 0·25 C̄ TO 0·25C̄ WING	3492
ANGLE OF SWEEPBACK AT LE	45°
ANGLE OF SWEEPBACK AT 0·25C	38° 55′ 34″
RUDDER AREA AFT OF HINGE LINE	0·582 m²
RUDDER MOVEMENT NORMAL TO HINGE LINE	± 20°
MOMENT OF AREA ABOUT HINGE LINE	0·1089 m³
RUDDER TRIM TAB MOVEMENT	± 10°
THICKNESS / CHORD RATIO	9% – 6%
ASPECT RATIO b/C̄	2·5031

AIRBRAKE

REF AREA	0·534 m²
MOVEMENT ABOUT HINGE LINE	60°

AIR INTAKE

TOTAL THROAT AREA 2 SIDES	0·2043 m²
ENGINE ENTRY FACE AREA	0·2497 m²
HIGHLIGHT AREA 2 SIDES	0·2652 m²

AILERONS

AREA AFT OF HINGE LINE PORT AND STARBOARD	1·050 m²
MOVEMENT ABOUT HINGE LINE	±12·0°

FLAPS

TOTAL REFERENCE AREA	2·50 m²
CHORD NORMAL TO T.E. INCLUDING VANE (FLAP DATUM)	503
CHORD IN LINE OF FLIGHT INCLUDING VANE (FLAP DATUM)	506
MOVEMENT ABOUT HINGE LINE (TAKE OFF SETTING)	25°
MOVEMENT ABOUT HINGE LINE (LANDING SETTING)	50°
L.O.F. CHORD EXTENSION (LANDING SETTING)	205

FUSELAGE

OVERALL LENGTH	11459
GROSS SURFACE AREA	43·8 m²
MAX. CROSS SECTIONAL AREA	2·105 m²
MAX. WIDTH	1896
OVERALL LENGTH OF AIRCRAFT	11851
STORAGE HEIGHT (UNLOADED) WITHOUT FIN	2900

WING

	PROJECTED PLANFORM DIMS	DIMS IN AEROFOIL DATUM PLANE
REF AREA	16·689 m²	16·701 m²
ASPECT RATIO	5·284	5·286
STANDARD MEAN CHORD	1777	1778
BASIC ROOT CHORD	2653	2653
BASIC TIP CHORD	902	902
TAPER RATIO	0·34	0·34
ANGLE OF SWEEPBACK AT L.E.	26° 2′ 19″	26°
ANGLE OF SWEEPBACK AT 0·25C	21° 34′ 16″	21° 31′ 55″
THICKNESS/CHORD RATIO	10·9% (ROOT) 9% (TIP)	
DIHEDRAL ANGLE	2°	
WING SETTING ANGLE	1°	
X̄ L.E. (BASIC WING APEX TO L.E. C̄)	995	
PYLON CENTRE LINES I/B	2399	2400
O/B	3422	3424

TAILPLANE

REF AREA	4·329 m²	4·396 m²
ASPECT RATIO	4·453	
STANDARD MEAN CHORD	986	
TAILARM C̄/4 TO BASIC WING C̄/4	4299	
BASIC ROOT CHORD	1482	
BASIC TIP CHORD	490	
ANGLE OF SWEEPBACK AT L.E.	34° 24′ 28″	34°
ANGLE OF SWEEPBACK AT 0·25C	29° 46′ 1″	29° 23′ 26″
THICKNESS/CHORD RATIO	8·5%	
DIHEDRAL ANGLE	–10°	
MOVEMENT ABOUT HINGE LINE	+6·6° –15·0° (RELATIVE TO FUS. DATUM)	

The Hawk has been modified for air-defence roles such as close support (attacking targets that threaten friendly forces), but essentially, it's a straightforward jet trainer, lighter and more responsive than the heavy-duty, combat-orientated F-16, so more suited to certain display manoeuvres. "You can achieve greater precision in a Hawk because it's perfectly balanced," explains John Green. "You can put it where you want it. But a control-heavy fighter such as the Jaguar isn't so accurate."

The BAE Systems (formerly Hawker Siddeley Aviation) Hawk and the Red Arrows joined forces in 1979, and they developed much of their air display together. The Hawk's simplicity and its user-friendliness make it perfect for the Red Arrows. "It reacts to every input," declares Flight Lieutenant Martin Higgins, who has flown the Tucano and the Tornado F3. Without these qualities, the pace of the Red Arrows' schedule at Scampton during gruelling winter training and frantic nationwide summer display schedules would be unachievable. If the Red Arrows ever have to replace their Hawks with another aircraft, they will have to change the personality of their show.

•

The Hawk hit its 30th birthday just as the Red Arrows were coming to the end of their 40th display season. A look back through the years to 1974 shows that the Hawk has been Europe's most successful modern two-seat advanced jet trainer, the latest in a tradition of outstanding British military jet trainers such as the record-breaking de Havilland Vampire.

The light bulb moment that marks the Hawk's conception probably came about after an informal bevvy in a London pub in February 1968, following a meeting between Hawker Siddeley Aviation (HSA) executives and planners from the Ministry of Defence (MoD). What should follow the Folland Gnat T.1, which was coming to the end of its planned life as the RAF's fast-jet trainer?

In the 1950s when Folland Aircraft were developing the Gnat, its concept was so original it was startling: a lightweight fighter priced at half of anything in the air at the time. 'Teddy' Petter, Folland's Managing Director, had worked on the formidable supersonic Lightning, and wanted to buck the trend towards bigger and heavier (and more and more expensive) fighters. The idea had impact and a prototype appeared in 1955.

With a projected working life of little more than ten years, the Gnat only

Above left A Rolls-Royce/Turboméca Mk.151 engine rests on its cradle in the hangar at Scampton.

fulfilled its promise as a fighter with the Indian and Finnish air forces. In the UK it found a niche as a trainer for RAF flying students advancing from the Jet Provost to Jaguars and Lightnings. It was adaptable, super-manoeuvrable and inexpensive, had a tandem cockpit for instructor and student, and its take-off and landing distances were half those of most military jets.

Moreover, its fast climb, dive and roll rates amounted to a new design tool in the hands of first-class aerobatic pilots – such as the five Flying Training School (FTS) instructors who formed the aerobatic team, the Yellowjacks, in 1964 and impressed crowds at air shows with tight turns and nifty rolls.

Yet the Gnat was an aeroplane with foibles. Its complex fuel system was costly to maintain, its cockpit was a squeeze and, since visibility from the rear seat and its potential weapons load were both limited, it couldn't be used for tactical weapons training. For that, students transferred to the Hawker Hunter. But the Hunter was a fighter with high maintenance and fuel costs; and its two-seat version had side-by-side seating, while most of the RAF's new combat aircraft came with single or tandem seating. So dire were the options for training new pilots that the RAF was seriously considering sending its pilots abroad to hone their flying skills, or buying foreign aircraft for training.

A 'warlike trainer' was the solution put forward by HSA's team from Hawker and Folland: a fast-jet trainer capable of carrying and delivering a wide range of weapons. It could be used for weapons training and be sold as a light attack aircraft. This dual-role idea was revolutionary in 1969, when HSA submitted their proposal to the MoD, yet so unshakeable was HSA management's belief in it that the company developed the project (designated 'HS1182') privately, using company finances and relying on meticulously accurate costings, solidly based on market research.

The new advanced trainer gestated in a climate of relentless defence cuts, so the HS1182 was prudently low-priced, with low maintenance costs, low fuel consumption, and high reliability, utilisation and export potential. It was an offer the MoD couldn't refuse and about two years later, in March 1972, its Procurement Executive signed a fixed-price contract with HSA for the delivery of 176 HS1182 Mk.1s. An HSA in-house competition to find a name favoured 'Tercel' (the small male hawk used in falconry), but the RAF wanted something it thought sounded more apt for a trainer with light attack potential, and in August 1973 the HS1182 was officially named the 'Hawk'.

Only one item of Government-backed equipment was specified for the

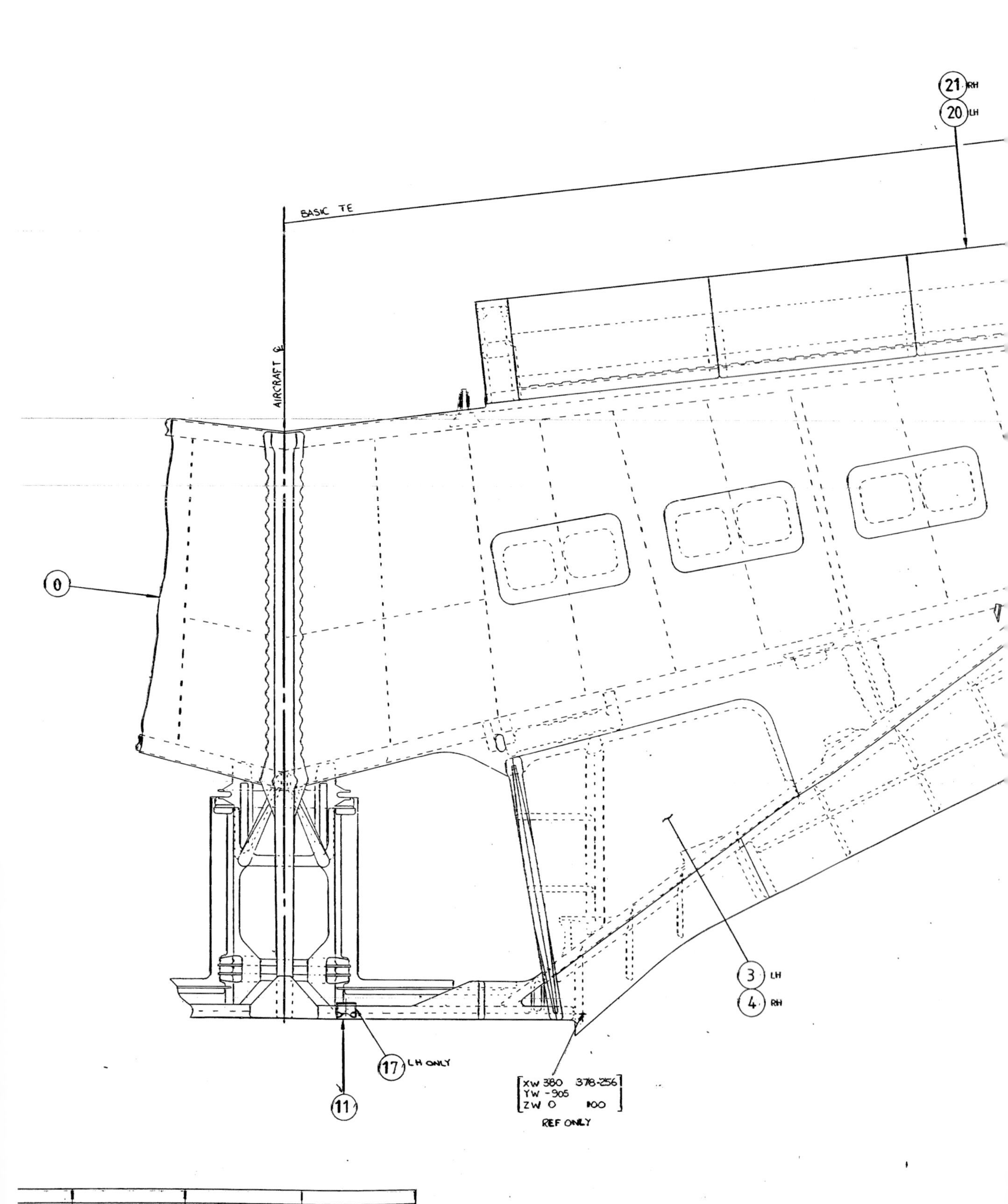
QUOTED IN MILLIMETRES
STATED
BASIC TE
AIRCRAFT ℄
21 RH
20 LH
0
3 LH
4 RH
17 LH ONLY
11
XW 380 378·256
YW -905
ZW 0 100
REF ONLY
INITIALLY USED ON
FOR REFERENCE ONLY
WORKS QUERY NOTES
TO BE EMBODIED
CATEGORY
TO BE EMBODIED

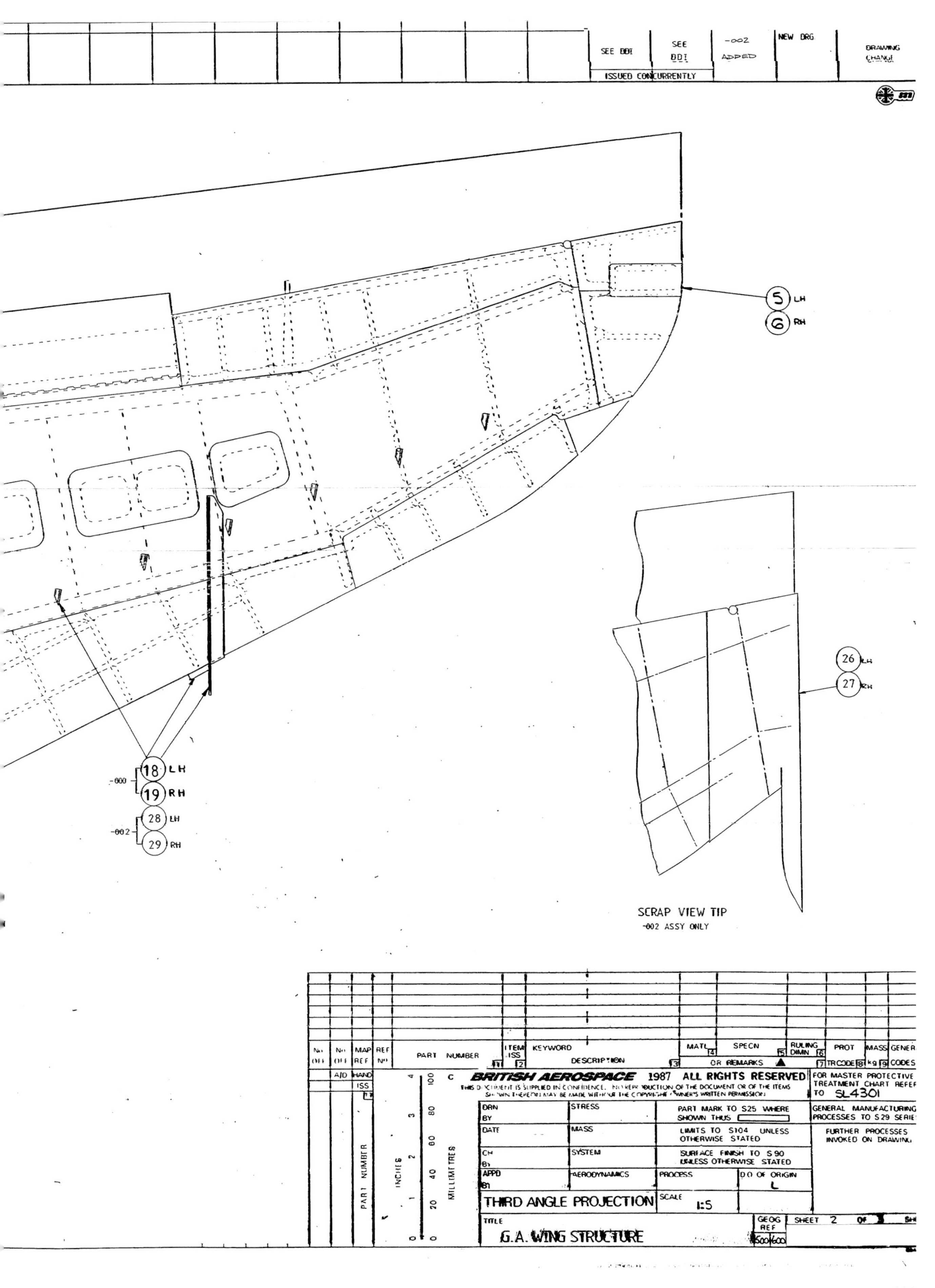
SEE DDI
SEE DDI
-002 ADDED
NEW DRG
DRAWING CHANGE
ISSUED CONCURRENTLY
5 LH
6 RH
26 LH
27 RH
18 LH
19 RH
-600
28 LH
29 RH
-002
SCRAP VIEW TIP
-002 ASSY ONLY
BRITISH AEROSPACE 1987 ALL RIGHTS RESERVED
THIRD ANGLE PROJECTION
SCALE 1:5
TITLE
G.A. WING STRUCTURE
SHEET 2
FOR MASTER PROTECTIVE TREATMENT CHART REFER TO SL4301
PART MARK TO S25 WHERE SHOWN THUS
LIMITS TO S104 UNLESS OTHERWISE STATED
SURFACE FINISH TO S90 UNLESS OTHERWISE STATED
GENERAL MANUFACTURING PROCESSES TO S29 SERIES
FURTHER PROCESSES INVOKED ON DRAWING
PART NUMBER
INCHES
MILLIMETRES
KEYWORD
DESCRIPTION
OR REMARKS
MATL
SPECN
RULING DIMN
PROT
MASS
DRN BY
DATE
CH BY
APPD BY
STRESS
MASS
SYSTEM
AERODYNAMICS
PROCESS
D.O. OF ORIGIN L
GEOG REF

Above left The Hawk's raised rear seat gives its occupant unobstructed views over the pilot's head and through the front canopy. This image was taken over Red 1's head during an In-Season Practice (ISP).

new jet trainer: the Adour engine, an Anglo-French project manufactured by Rolls-Royce of Britain and Turboméca of France. Rolls-Royce's ageing but cheap Viper turbojet had been favoured by the HSA management, while the design team wanted the Adour turbofan, already developed for the SEPECAT Jaguar in 1971. The Adour was double the price of the Viper – and in 1971 Rolls-Royce were struggling against bankruptcy. But the Viper was old technology, while the Adour was state-of-the-art and could be developed in the future for enhanced combat capability. The later-generation technology also meant that the Adour was sparing of fuel. For the RAF, fuel economy was the deciding factor, so an enhanced version of the Adour was married to the HS1182. The decision proved prophetic: two years later, in 1973, the Arab-Israeli war led to OPEC quadrupling oil prices from $3 per barrel to $12.

Outstanding among the design innovations was the cockpit layout. Seating the two crew in tandem in the Folland Gnat's cramped cockpit gave an aerodynamic advantage over side-by-seating, but the two seats were roughly on the same level. So the instructor, strapped in behind, stared at the back of the trainee's head, and had a restricted view in-flight and on landing. HSA's solution was to elevate the back seat higher than in any other aircraft. In all versions of the Hawk, the instructor has a downward view of 6°, which gives a clear sight of the touchdown point on landing and a panoramic view from the back seat that makes the Hawk ideal for weapons training.

The cockpit was designed in consultation with HSA test pilots Duncan Simpson, Andy Jones and Jim Hawkins and it has won the Hawk many friends. It's roomy enough to give the tallest pilot leg-room of extravagant dimensions (for a military aircraft), while the shortest instructor has good all-round vision from the back seat. BAE's designers worked indefatigably with their test pilots on the design of the instrument panel and equipment layout.

To reduce maintenance costs, the designers focused on ensuring that no component should need to be removed to access another. The 1970 MoD specification detailed 95 maintenance targets or 'hangar times'. HSA broke most of these and set new records. For example, pre-flight servicing was set at 15 worker minutes; HSA reached 12.8 minutes. Turnaround servicing was set at 15 minutes; HSA got it down to 8.8 minutes. The target time for changing the engine was 500 minutes; HSA reduced it to 369 minutes. The Hawk's low stance helps reduce hangar time by minimising the need to use ladders and gantries. The engine is removed through the aircraft's underside, being lowered by three winches. Furthermore, the Adour turbofan was designed in modules, each of which can be quickly removed and replaced. All this is a great advantage to the RAFAT, who service their engines every 500 hours.

By early 1974, the first Hawk T.Mk.1 (later designated XX154) was in production at HSA's factories at Kingston-upon-Thames, Brough on Humberside and Hamble in Southampton. At the outset the company went for production tooling and dispensed with prototypes. Instead, the first five aircraft, scheduled to be assembled in 1975 at HSA's test airfield at Dunsfold in Sussex, were detailed for flight development. But the catalyst that speeded up the Hawk's production was the Alpha Jet's first flight on 26 October, 1973.

The Dassault/Dornier Alpha Jet, a Franco-German advanced trainer/close support aircraft, has been the Hawk's great rival. The two jets have many similarities: both have a 9m or 30ft wingspan and are roughly the same length and height. Yet despite a thrust of 1,351kg or 2,976lb from each of its two SNECMA Turboméca Larzac 04 turbofan engines, the Alpha Jet's maximum speed is 560kt compared with the Hawk's 575kt generated by the 2,360kg or 5,200lb of thrust from its single Adour turbofan. Hawk pilots acknowledge, nevertheless, that the Alpha Jet, which is flown by the Patrouille de France aerobatic team, would be an interesting adversary in an aerial joust.

The Alpha Jet entered service as a trainer with France and Germany in 1981, and by 1991, when production ceased, 504 had been sold as military trainers and close support aircraft to 13 countries. The Hawk was the more successful of the two: it is still in production and to date more than 900 have been ordered in various versions by 18 countries.

Back in 1973, however, the situation looked dicey. Although only the first Alpha Jet prototype (of a proposed four) flew in October 1973, the jet was to make its début in September 1974 at the Farnborough Air Show. The first Hawk wasn't scheduled to be completed and flight-tested in time – but not to appear at the show would now give a commercial advantage to the Alpha Jet. The fitting of some components was put back; work was speeded up; the flight-test program was accelerated; and the first Hawk off the production line was formally rolled out for its maiden flight at Dunsfold on 21 August 1974.

Watching Hawk No.XX154 being rolled out by men in asbestos suits from a wall beside his Dutch barn were local dairy farmer Henry Bartley, on whose land the airfield's Instrument Landing System (ILS) was sited, and his brother, Peter. "We were all on first-name terms with the Hawker Siddeley pilots. We

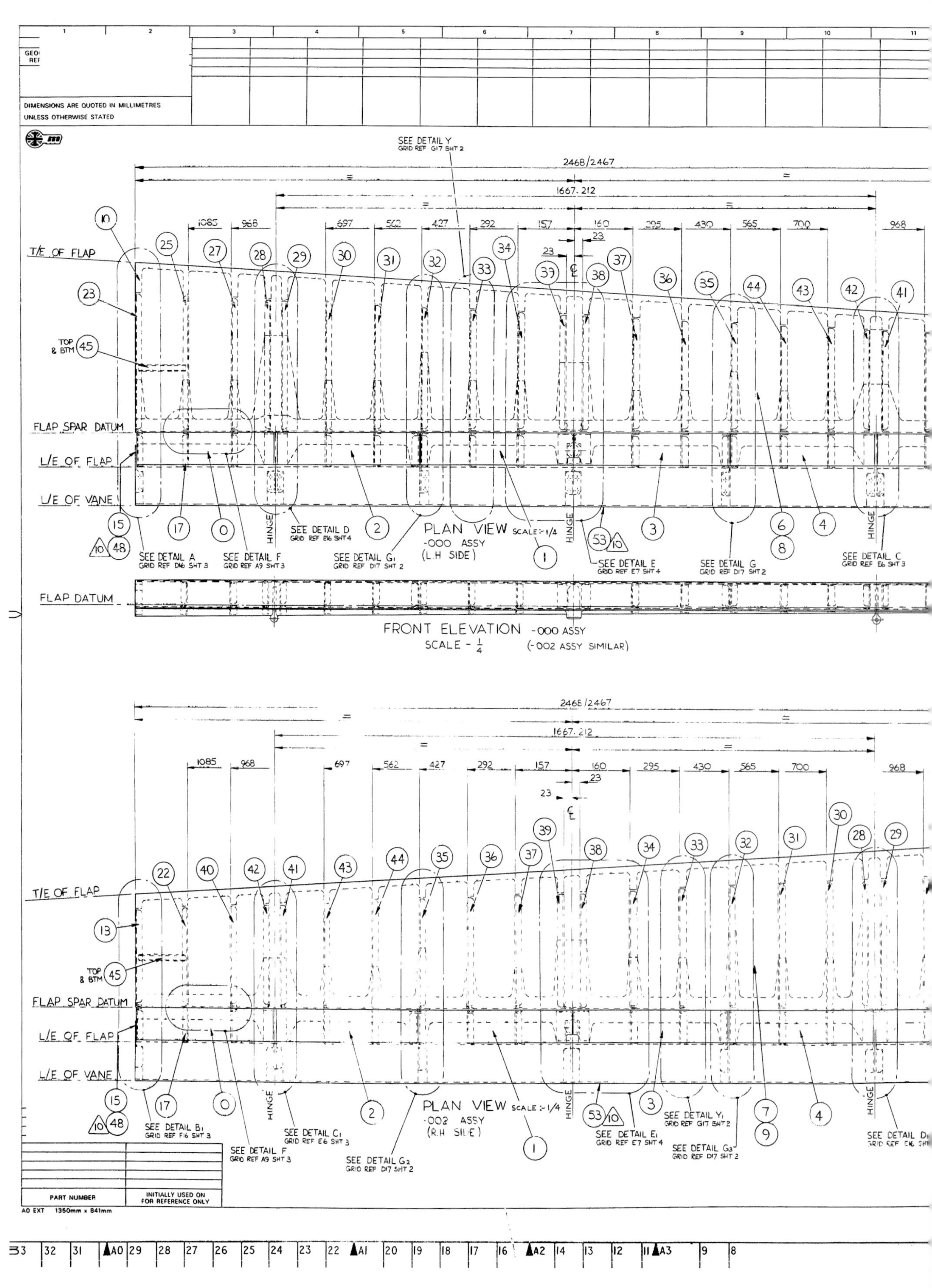

DIMENSIONS ARE QUOTED IN MILLIMETRES UNLESS OTHERWISE STATED
SEE DETAIL Y GRID REF G17 SHT 2
2468/2467
1667.212
T/E OF FLAP
FLAP SPAR DATUM
L/E OF FLAP
L/E OF VANE
TOP & BTM
HINGE
SEE DETAIL A GRID REF D16 SHT 3
SEE DETAIL F GRID REF A9 SHT 3
SEE DETAIL D GRID REF E16 SHT 4
SEE DETAIL G1 GRID REF D17 SHT 2
PLAN VIEW SCALE:-1/4
-000 ASSY
(L.H SIDE)
SEE DETAIL E GRID REF E7 SHT 4
SEE DETAIL G GRID REF D17 SHT 2
SEE DETAIL C GRID REF E6 SHT 3
FLAP DATUM
FRONT ELEVATION -000 ASSY
SCALE - 1/4
(-002 ASSY SIMILAR)
SEE DETAIL B1 GRID REF F16 SHT 3
SEE DETAIL C1 GRID REF E6 SHT 3
SEE DETAIL F GRID REF A9 SHT 3
SEE DETAIL G2 GRID REF D17 SHT 2
PLAN VIEW SCALE:-1/4
-002 ASSY
(R.H SIDE)
SEE DETAIL E1 GRID REF E7 SHT 4
SEE DETAIL Y1 GRID REF G17 SHT 2
SEE DETAIL G3 GRID REF D17 SHT 2
PART NUMBER
INITIALLY USED ON FOR REFERENCE ONLY
A0 EXT 1350mm x 841mm

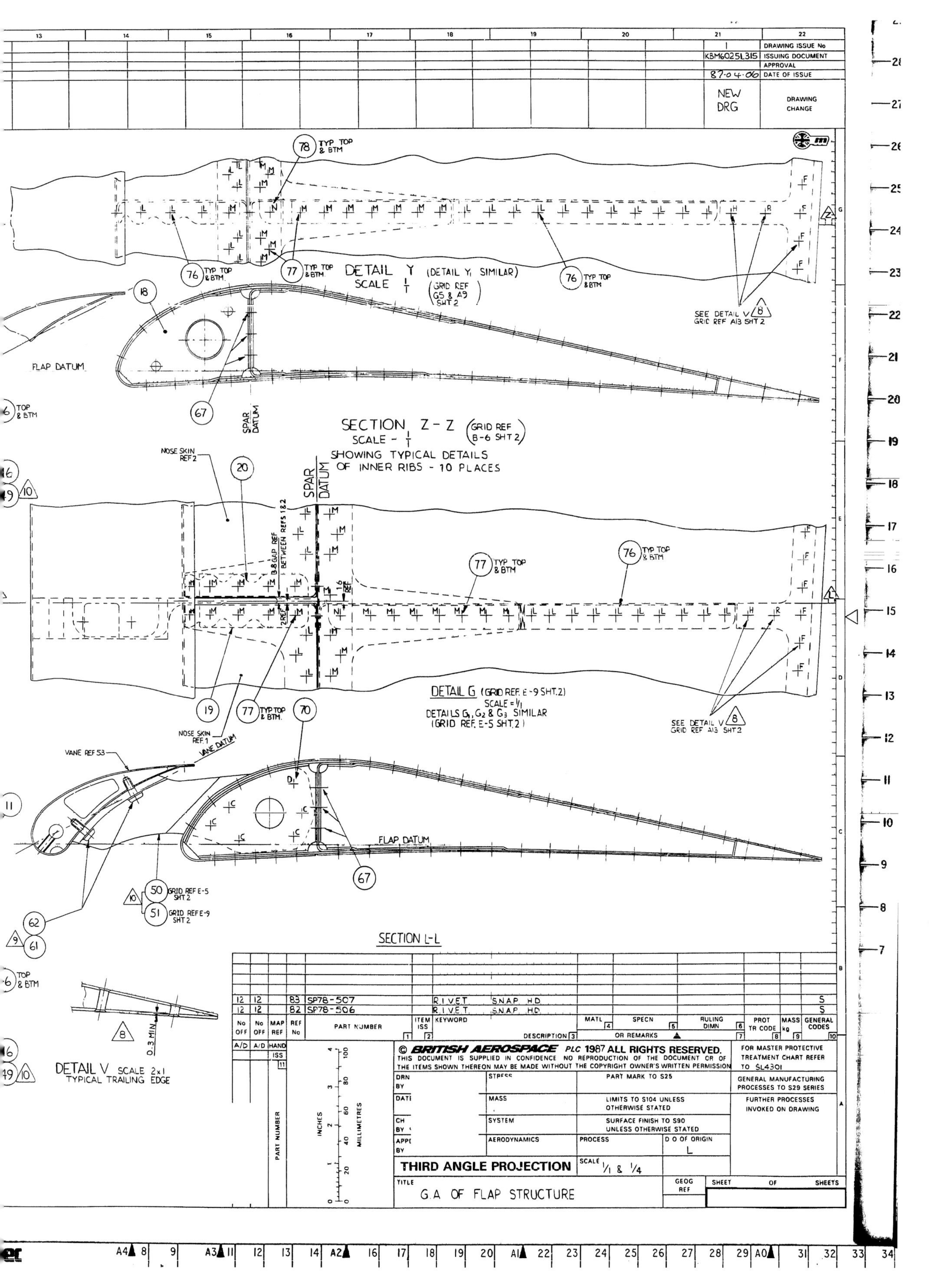

DRAWING ISSUE No
ISSUING DOCUMENT
APPROVAL
DATE OF ISSUE
DRAWING CHANGE
1
KBM6025L315
87-04-06
NEW DRG
TYP TOP & BTM
DETAIL Y SCALE 1/1
(DETAIL Y1 SIMILAR)
(GRID REF G5 & A9 SHT 2)
SEE DETAIL V
GRID REF A13 SHT 2
FLAP DATUM
SPAR DATUM
SECTION Z - Z SCALE - 1/1
(GRID REF B-6 SHT 2)
SHOWING TYPICAL DETAILS OF INNER RIBS - 10 PLACES
NOSE SKIN REF 2
3.8 GAP REF BETWEEN REFS 1 & 2
DETAIL G (GRID REF. E-9 SHT.2)
SCALE = 1/1
DETAILS G1, G2 & G3 SIMILAR
(GRID REF. E-5 SHT.2)
NOSE SKIN REF.1
VANE DATUM
VANE REF 53
GRID REF E-5 SHT 2
GRID REF E-9 SHT 2
SECTION L-L
0.3 MIN
DETAIL V SCALE 2x1
TYPICAL TRAILING EDGE
12 | 12 | 83 | SP78-507 | RIVET | SNAP HD | S
12 | 12 | 82 | SP78-506 | RIVET | SNAP HD | S
No OFF | No OFF | MAP REF | REF No | PART NUMBER | ITEM ISS | KEYWORD | DESCRIPTION | MATL | SPECN | OR REMARKS | RULING DIMN | PROT TR CODE | MASS kg | GENERAL CODES
© BRITISH AEROSPACE PLC 1987 ALL RIGHTS RESERVED.
THIS DOCUMENT IS SUPPLIED IN CONFIDENCE NO REPRODUCTION OF THE DOCUMENT OR OF THE ITEMS SHOWN THEREON MAY BE MADE WITHOUT THE COPYRIGHT OWNER'S WRITTEN PERMISSION
FOR MASTER PROTECTIVE TREATMENT CHART REFER TO SL4301
PART MARK TO S25
GENERAL MANUFACTURING PROCESSES TO S29 SERIES
LIMITS TO S104 UNLESS OTHERWISE STATED
FURTHER PROCESSES INVOKED ON DRAWING
SURFACE FINISH TO S90 UNLESS OTHERWISE STATED
STRESS
MASS
SYSTEM
AERODYNAMICS
PROCESS
D O OF ORIGIN
L
INCHES
MILLIMETRES
PART NUMBER
THIRD ANGLE PROJECTION
SCALE 1/1 & 1/4
TITLE
G.A OF FLAP STRUCTURE
GEOG REF
SHEET OF SHEETS

played cricket together, so I knew the Chief Test Pilot, Duncan Simpson, who flew that first flight," Henry Bartley recalls. "They told us in advance that the new aircraft was to fly that afternoon so we could move our cows to another field. It took off at about 6.30 and the day was still nice, light with high cloud."

Duncan Simpson's log of that day shows that the wind was less than 5kt and visibility about 15km or 10 miles, with fairly heavy cloud at 1,000–1,500m or 3–5,000ft. Filmed from an accompanying Harrier and a Hunter, XX154 rotated at 120kt, reached level flight at 600m or 2,000ft and was cleared to 1,500m or 5,000ft. The pilot then made a straight climb to 6,000m or 20,000ft at 90% rpm and at 250kt and carried out flap, undercarriage and stall tests. Firm handshakes must have been offered after Duncan Simpson landed XX154. It may have been one of those understated moments when a machine simply performs the way it's designed, unaware of its triumph.

Henry Bartley remembers the Hawk streaking across the Surrey sky on that flight. "They said it would fly from the drawing board and we were pleased to see them achieve it," he recalls. "When we saw the test pilots at the next cricket match, they asked how the cows had coped with all the noise." Watching cutting-edge test flights from the privacy of his own fields was a fairly common event in Henry's life during the 1960s and 70s, when he'd watched some of the first Harrier hover tests. Those, and the Hawk's first flights in the last week of August 1974 are indelible memories.

After a week of 24/7 working at HSA to overcome teething troubles, and with less than a day's flying hours on the clock, XX154 just made it to the Farnborough Press Preview on Sunday 1 September, 1974, with Duncan Simpson at the controls. Its appearance must have been unexpected by Dassault and Dornier representatives overseeing the Alpha Jet's display. With its flight-test program scarcely begun, the Hawk could perform only a limited range of manoeuvres, yet with this handicap and in stormy weather, Duncan Simpson demonstrated the potential of the new jet and impressed the crowds with tight turns, inverted flying and a barrel roll. On site with their Gnats for their Farnborough display, one or two of the 1974 Red Arrows team were able to inspect the jet that the team would fly at Farnborough in 1980.

The Hawk's first full display came in 1975 on the Alpha Jet's home territory. Duncan Simpson and Andy Jones demonstrated the aerobatic capabilities of the by then fully flight-tested aircraft at the Paris Air Show. The public's introduction to the RAF's new trainer was completed at Farnborough 1976,

when Duncan Simpson led nine Hawks in Arrow formation before the crowd.

Production was on target. On 4 November 1976 the RAF received the first of the 176 Hawk T.Mk.1s it had ordered; the last two were delivered in February and March 1982. As soon as each new jet arrived, its students began clocking up extra flying hours. No need to send them abroad, after all.

Above left Diesel oil or a mix of derv and coloured vegetable dye are injected through these nozzles into the efflux (exhaust) from the Hawk's jet pipe, to produce the Red Arrows' signature coloured smoke.

•

By the late 1980s, the original T.Mk.1 Hawk of XX154's day had evolved into a family of progressively more powerful and capable military variants. The 50 series, with extra fuel tanks and a weapon-control system, went to Kenya, Finland, Indonesia; the fast Mark 60 series, with carriers for Sidewinder missiles, to Abu Dhabi, Dubai, Kuwait, Saudi Arabia, South Korea, Switzerland and Zimbabwe; the 100 series with advanced avionics to Oman, Malaysia and Indonesia, and its variants to Australia, Canada and South Africa. In 2008 the RAF will take delivery of 44 Hawk 128s, the latest version, for fighter pilot training on the Eurofighter Typhoon and the Joint Strike Fighter.

So far, perhaps the biggest testament to the Hawk's success is the VTX or T-45 Goshawk, developed for the US Navy in the late 1970s. Superficially, it differs little from the Red Arrows' T.Mk.1. The contract with the US Department of Defense was worth a whopping $5,500 million for 300 aircraft, simulators, and training. The role of the T-45 is primarily to train US Navy pilots for carrier landings. It has a revised nose and main gear for catapult launches and deck landings, and an arrester hook for landings.

Ten bright red Hawk T.Mk.1s, modified for an aerobatic display role, were delivered to the Red Arrows in time for winter training 1979. The gun pod on the fuselage centreline was replaced with a smoke pod whose three compartments hold more than 300 litres – about 70gal. of derv and a derv/vegetable dye mix. During displays, these are injected into the hot efflux from the Hawk's jet pipe to generate the Red Arrows' signature white, red and blue smoke. Other modifications were made to the Adour engine to allow a quicker throttle response during aerobatic manoeuvres, and the tailplane was strengthened to take high g-forces during displays.

The Red Arrows rotate their Hawks in the formation to minimize fatigue damage. Squadron Leader Simon Davies, the team's Senior Engineering

Officer (SEngO) for the 2004 and 2005 seasons, explains: "We have to work within the fatigue limits set by BAE Systems, our Design Authority." The original Design Authority, HSA, would have set a Fatigue Index (FI) of 100 for the Hawk. By closely monitoring the aircraft, the RAFAT have been able to extend the life of their fleet, so some currently have a fuselage FI approaching a low 120. "My job," continues Simon Davies, "is to assess which airframes are taking higher g – usually those flown by Synchro – and swap them to lower g positions in between seasons to even out FI consumption across the fleet." The Hawk has a safe fatigue life of 135 FI and most of the RAF's Hawks have had replacement wings to extend their flying life, since fatigue affects mainly the wings, tailplane and rear fuselage.

Above left The Hawk's nose, with the pitot tube just above the landing light. The pitot tube measures aspects of the air speed.

The Hawk is now a classic that pilots respect when they fly and engineers love to maintain. From a training point of view, the Hawk is easy to fly. It has a natural resistance to spinning, even when mishandled, so it can be used for spin recovery training.

At high speeds the Hawk is manoeuvrable, offering exciting challenges to RAF fast-jet students. But Flight Lieutenant David Slow (Red 4) has a few criticisms. "It doesn't roll particularly cleanly," he reveals. "If you just point the nose in a straight line and do nothing but roll, the nose will dish" (be pointing down at the end of the roll); "but if you do that in the Alpha Jet the nose won't alter course." (The Alpha Jet, with twin engines and a high wing, isn't directly comparable, but it's still the closest advanced jet trainer to the Hawk).

Dave Slow also has an issue with the spool-up time of the engine (the time it takes to accelerate from idle to max. power). "That and more power!" In his view, "To make the Hawk the ideal aircraft to fly, you'd have a slightly more powerful engine, just 10–15% more. But," he admits, "all pilots say their jet hasn't enough power and that's probably because they can't get enough of it."

The Adour Mk.151 turbofan, which powers the T.Mk.1, can deliver a maximum sea-level static thrust of 2,360kg or 5,200lb at International Standard Atmosphere (ISA) conditions, using about 1,900kg or 4,200lb of fuel per hour. During display flying the Red Arrow Hawks will burn about 1,360kg or 3,000lb per hour. By comparison with, say, the Thunderbirds, who fly the Lockheed-Martin F-16 Fighting Falcon, this is low.

In fact, the wing makes a major contribution to the Hawk's fuel economy. It may not be as sleekly swept back as the Alpha Jet's, say, or the F-16's, but it's one good lifter. The Hawker-Siddeley designers considered straight, swept-back, high, mid and low configurations before settling for a low, medium-swept wing that would give good lift and induce minimal drag at low altitudes. Its wing also gives the Hawk a fast rate of climb: 12,200m or 40,000ft in 10 minutes; and good fast-jet handling characteristics.

Its cockpit views are one of the Hawk's most talked-about attractions. Such vistas are provided courtesy of the acrylic canopy that covers the tandem cockpits. But the canopy is bisected by a rib that separates the windscreen from the main shell. Pilots complain that it restricts their view. Dave Slow argues that a continuous canopy could make a big difference: "If you're sitting at a standard seat height, that canopy rib arch can fall at eye level, so you have to look over it or under it to see your references. Because of this, we have constant discussions while flying line astern: 'Do you look over or under the rib?' " Clearly, depending on their upper-body length, some pilots will look over it. That gives them a subtle change in perception from those who look under it. Moving the head has implications for accurate referencing.

BAE counter that if the seat is correctly adjusted for the pilot, the eye will be at 'design eye height' and the pilot will always look below the rib to see ahead. But the Reds follow their own requirements and the Synchro Pair, who are positioned in line astern directly behind the Boss in most formations, fly stepped down below the aircraft in front to avoid its exhaust, so they both have to look up. They have their seats permanently lowered so that they always check their references from under the rib.

The cockpit has a second rib that supports an internal windshield in front of the passenger seat. This has a safety role, as Armourer Corporal Lance Did-Dell explains: "it acts as a blast shield. If a bird penetrates the front windscreen, the internal windscreen will protect the passenger in the back from the air stream and debris. And if the pilot in the front ejects, the arch will stop all the blast from the rocket from invading the rear cockpit."

Besides the roll, the canopy rib, and a lust for enhanced engine power, the Reds have few quarrels with the Hawk. Even the rudimentary avionics – just an instrument landing system and radio navigation aids – are rarely criticized. Stick-and-rudder flying as experienced by Hawk pilots is sorely missed by most 21st-century military and airline pilots.

Flight Lieutenant Antony Parkinson has flown with the Red Arrows for four years and is about to exchange his Hawk for the Eurofighter Typhoon, one of the most sophisticated military flying machines. "It's like flying a computer.

Above left The wing profile of the Hawk's port flap with its individual serial number plate.

The Typhoon has scarcely any traditional instruments on the control panel, just a head-up display and three TV screens." The Reds respond to the challenge of flying their jets accurately through complex manoeuvres without electronic devices: "There's no Gucci kit, the Hawk talks to you. You can almost hear its speed," says Flight Lieutenant Scott Morley.

Recruits to the Red Arrows get to know their Hawks and learn how to tell by listening to the jet engine when to make manual corrections. When they approach Mach 0.9, for example, they apply rudder trim to maintain a heading in level flight. As shock waves pass over the wing, the aircraft rolls a little due to differences between their centres of pressure, and requires about half an aileron to hold and correct. All aircraft have such eccentricities.

High-level manoeuvring requires careful handling to achieve the best performance. Get it right and the Hawk has a surprising rate of turn at high levels: it needs to be turned 'just off the buffet nibble' (as it begins to shake, warning of an imminent stall) at Mach 0.75 to 0.78. Such handling techniques for entering a maximum rate of turn from low and high Mach numbers test a pilot's flying skill and good judgement. "The Hawk allows us to judge fairly accurately when we're max-performing it," explains Dave Slow.

Similar techniques enable the pilots to judge their sometimes low-level turns within the disciplines of their formation flying. For example, when flying the Carousel, Synchro fly in towards each other, then one turns clockwise and one anti-clockwise. To cross exactly at the right point, they have to fly the same 180° circle. Getting this right relies partly on reading the g-meter as they go into their tight turn and partly on careful interpretation of the amount of buffet the airframe is taking. "No matter which of the Hawks they're flying," says Dave Slow, "both pilots experience the same amount of buffet at the same point, and as long as they interpret the buffet correctly, it tells them where to turn so that both independently fly exactly the same-size circle."

Shortly after its 26th birthday, the Hawk turned steadily into the 21st century, and it may well celebrate its 40th anniversary on the wing, perhaps flying the Red Arrows' 2014 display. Air shows may be much the same then, opines Wing Commander Bill Ramsey – even in 30 years' time – as they are today, although quite how air-safety legislation changes their shape will be interesting to see. Perhaps in the aviation museums of the future, T.Mk.1 Hawks will be displayed in Arrows red.

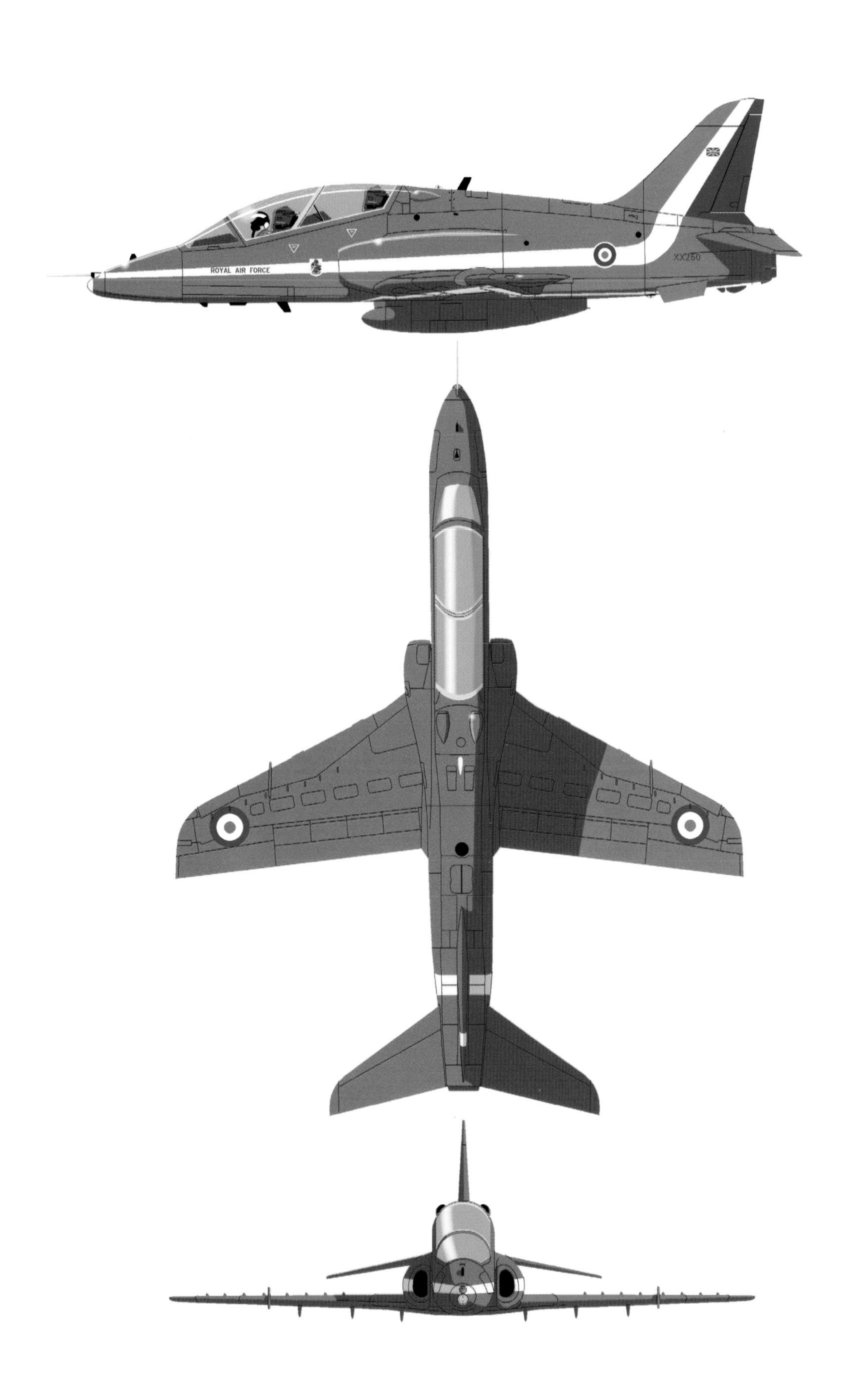
ROYAL AIR FORCE
XX260

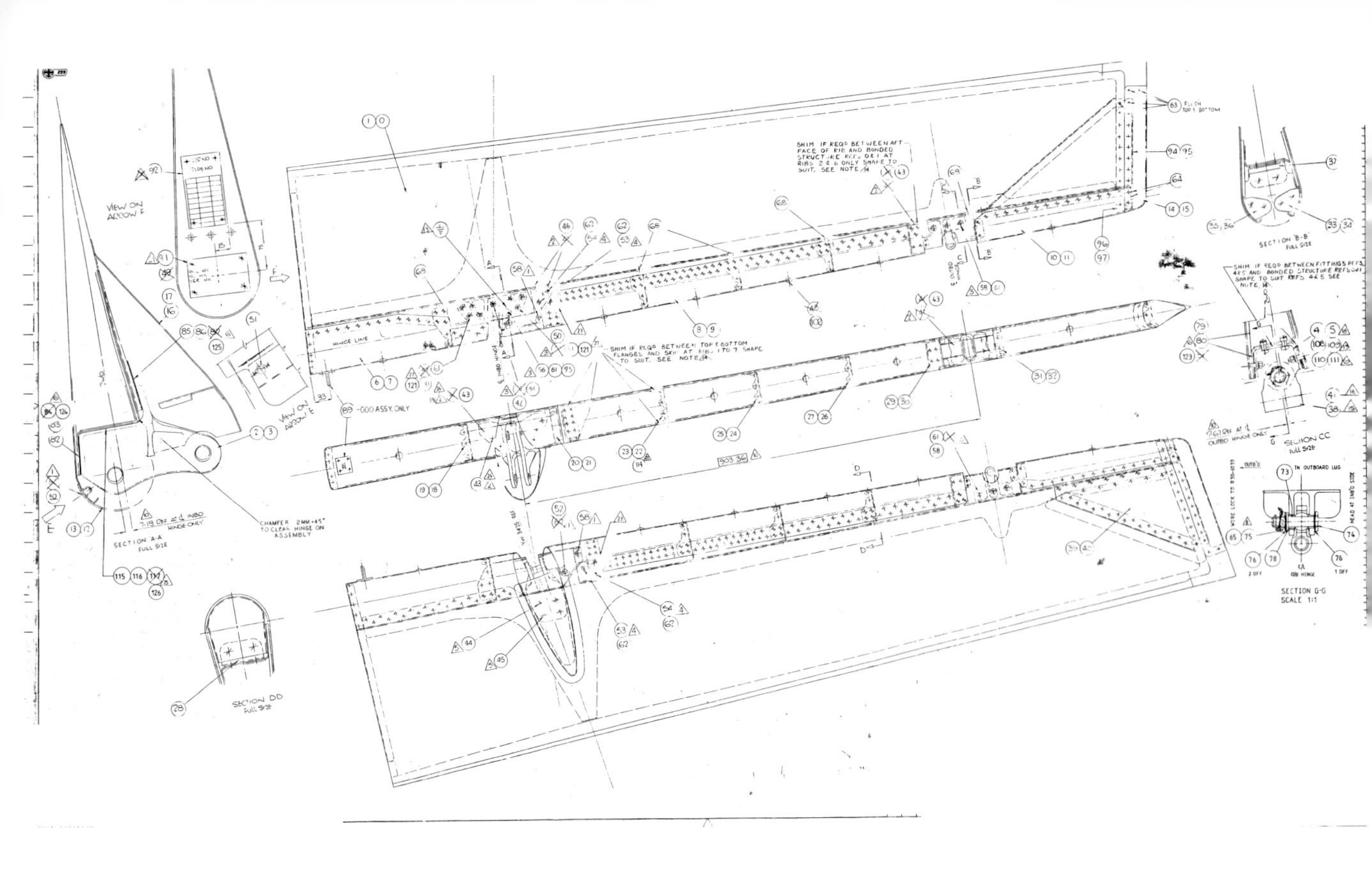
VIEW ON ARROW F
SECTION A-A FULL SIZE
CHAMFER 2MM×45° TO CLEAR HINGE ON ASSEMBLY
VIEW ON ARROW E
SECTION DD FULL SIZE
HINGE LINE
SHIM IF REQD BETWEEN TOP & BOTTOM FLANGES AND SKIN AT RIBS 1 TO 7 SHAPE TO SUIT. SEE NOTE
SECTION B-B FULL SIZE
SECTION CC FULL SIZE
SECTION G-G SCALE 1:1

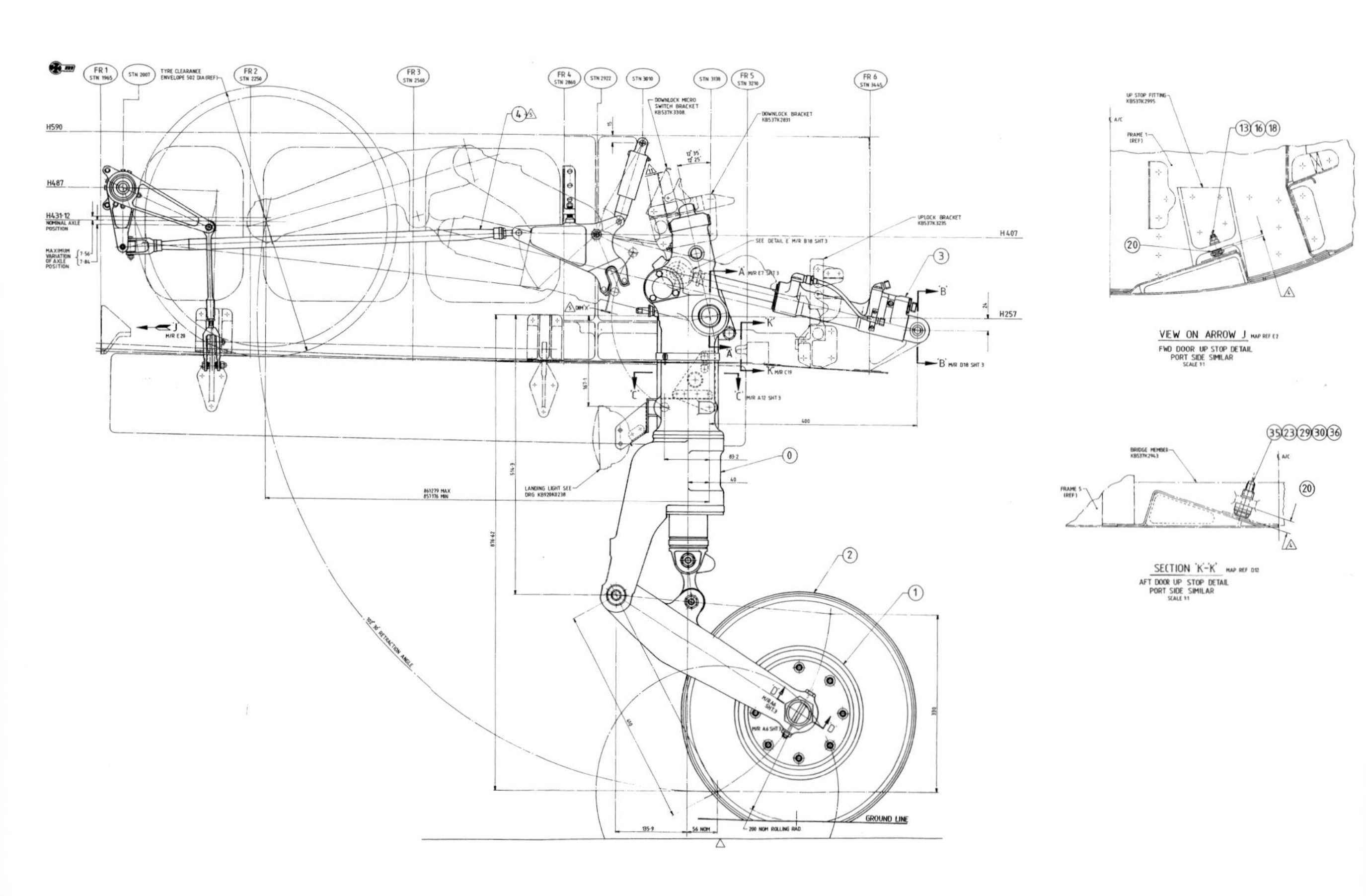
FR 1
FR 2
FR 3
FR 4
FR 5
FR 6
H590
H487
H407
H257
TYRE CLEARANCE ENVELOPE
DOWNLOCK BRACKET
UPLOCK BRACKET
GROUND LINE
VIEW ON ARROW J
FWD DOOR UP STOP DETAIL
PORT SIDE SIMILAR
SECTION 'K'-'K'
AFT DOOR UP STOP DETAIL
PORT SIDE SIMILAR

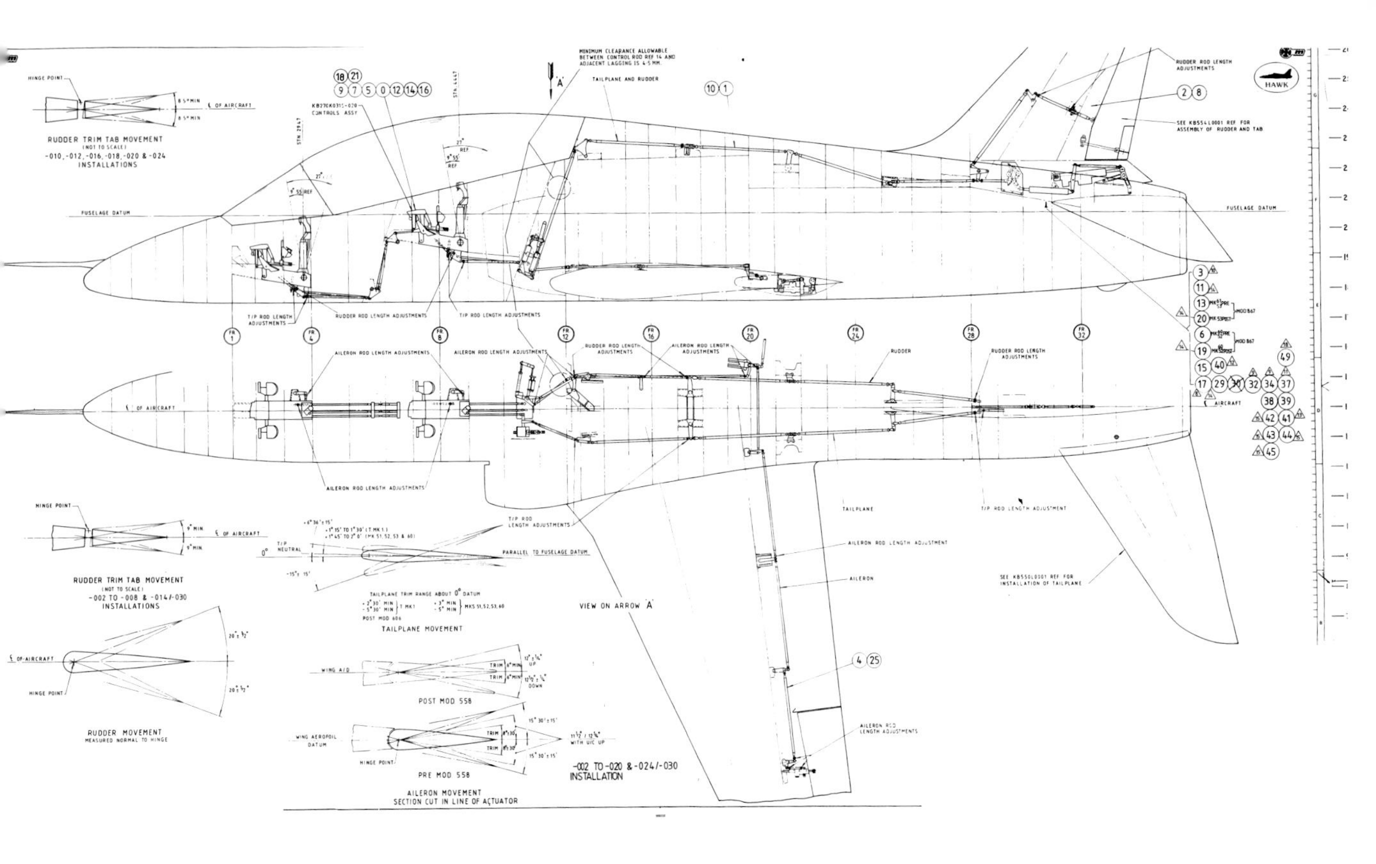
RUDDER TRIM TAB MOVEMENT
(NOT TO SCALE)
-010, -012, -016, -018, -020 & -024
INSTALLATIONS
RUDDER TRIM TAB MOVEMENT
(NOT TO SCALE)
-002 TO -008 & -014/-030
INSTALLATIONS
RUDDER MOVEMENT
MEASURED NORMAL TO HINGE
TAILPLANE MOVEMENT
POST MOD 558
PRE MOD 558
AILERON MOVEMENT
SECTION CUT IN LINE OF ACTUATOR
VIEW ON ARROW 'A'
-002 TO -020 & -024/-030
INSTALLATION
FUSELAGE DATUM
TAILPLANE AND RUDDER
RUDDER ROD LENGTH ADJUSTMENTS
AILERON ROD LENGTH ADJUSTMENTS
T/P ROD LENGTH ADJUSTMENTS
TAILPLANE
AILERON
RUDDER
HAWK

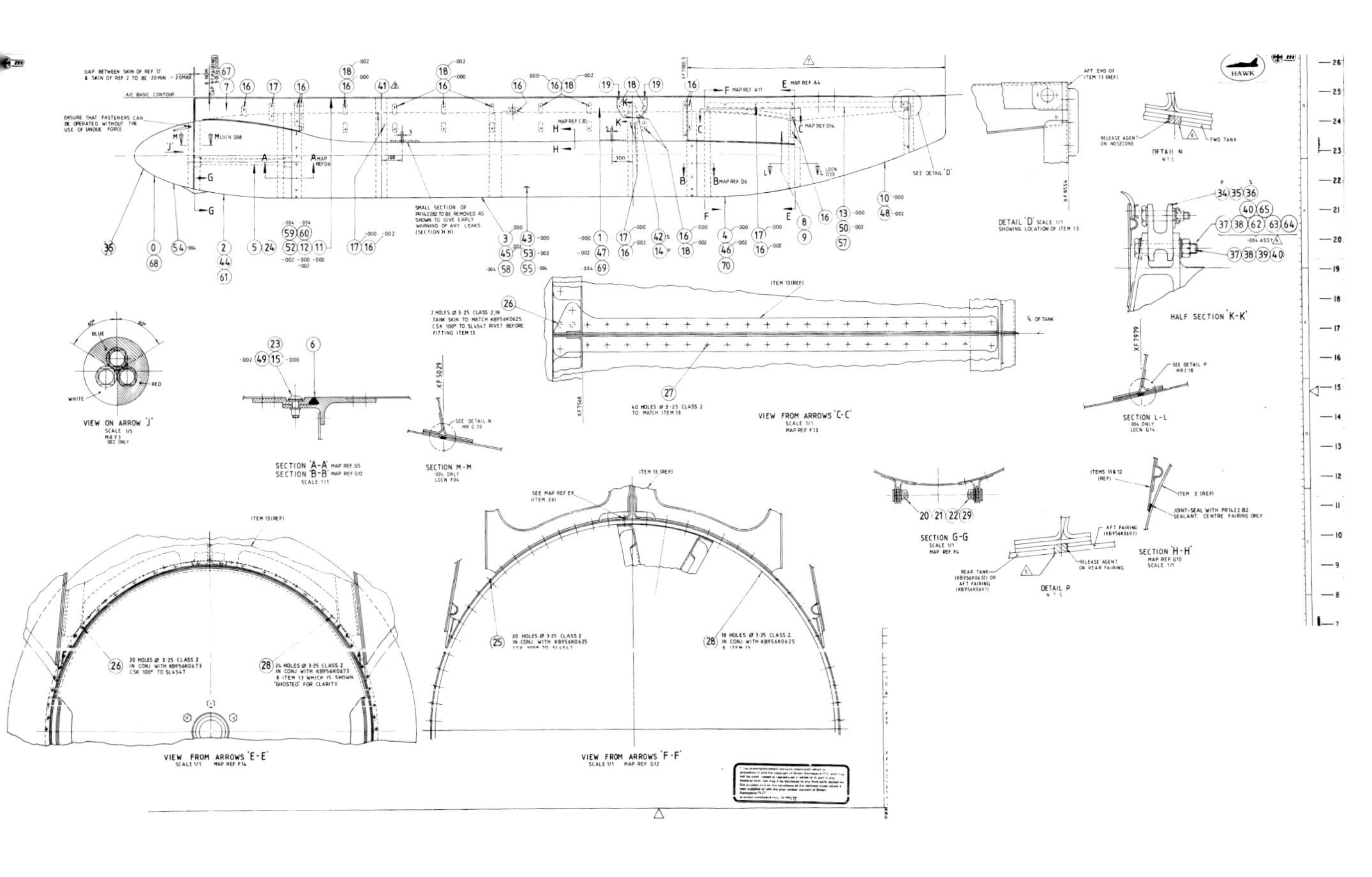
VIEW ON ARROW 'J'
SECTION 'A-A'
SECTION 'B-B'
SECTION M-M
VIEW FROM ARROWS 'C-C'
SECTION L-L
HALF SECTION 'K-K'
DETAIL 'D'
DETAIL N
SECTION G-G
SECTION 'H-H'
DETAIL P
VIEW FROM ARROWS 'E-E'
VIEW FROM ARROWS 'F-F'
HAWK

HAWK PARTICULARS

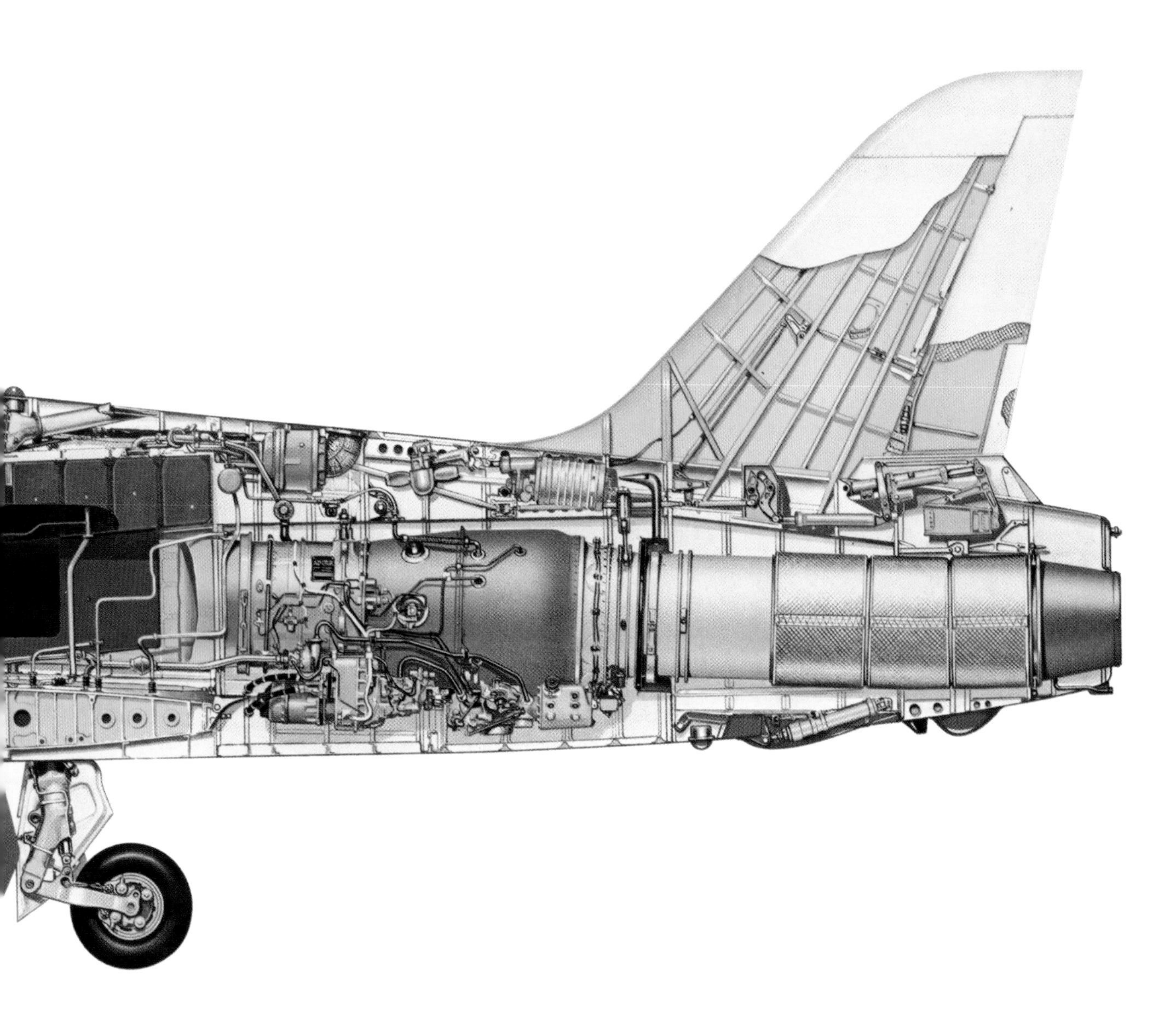

HAWK T.MK.1 SPECIFICATIONS

Wing span	9.39m (30.8ft)
Length	11.85m (38.9ft)
Height	4m (13.1ft)
Max. speed sea level	560kt (645mph/1,038kph)
Max. altitude	15,894m (48,000ft)
Empty weight	3,628kg (8,001lb)
Max. internal fuel capacity	1,272kg (2,798lb)
Max. take-off weight	5,700kg (12,566lb)
Powerplant	Single Rolls-Royce/Turboméca Adour Mk.151
Max. sea-level static thrust at ISA conditions	2,360kg (5,200lb)

MAINTENANCE AND SERVICING

The RAFAT's Hawks undergo the maintenance and servicing schedules laid down by BAE Systems. Avionics, electrical and hydraulics systems, the engine bay and the ejector seat are subject to regular maintenance patterns, shown blow. The maintenance becomes more comprehensive as the aircraft progresses from primary to major checks.

SERVICE	INTERVAL	ACTIVITIES
Primary maintenance	every 150 hours	Lubrication, fluid changes, instrument accuracy checks
Primary Star maintenance	every 300 hours	Primary maintenance plus additional lubrication and inspection tasks; and functional checks such as electrical power supplies and the Centralised Warning System
Minor maintenance	every 600 hours	All the primary checks, plus: structural checks; more detailed instrument accuracy checks; emergency undercarriage stand-by cartridges are fired and undercarriage legs are changed
Minor Star maintenance	every 1,200 hours	The minor maintenance plus additional lubrication, inspection and functional checks. The aircraft is weighed
Major maintenance	every 2,400 hours	The aircraft is taken out of service and a major servicing of airframe, systems and components is carried out

ANATOMY

While the new generation of Hawks have state-of-the-art cockpit and systems, the Red Arrows' T.Mk.1 relies on its pilots to enhance its performance. It is robust, durable, reliable, relatively low-cost to operate and technically simple to maintain.

TAILPLANE

The sweptback tailplane mirrors the wing in shape, but it takes much of the strain of the high g-forces during aerobatics. Like the wing, it is manufactured in one piece. It is all-moving and is powered by hydraulics, with an electrically powered trim system.

WINDSCREEN

The front windscreen is made from one piece of curved, stretched acrylic. A second, internal windscreen shields the passenger in the back seat in the event of bird strike or the pilot ejecting.

CANOPY

The canopy is made from a single piece of acrylic and hinges sideways for access. A Miniature Detonation Cord (MDC) zigzags around and across the top. On detonation, it fires, shattering the canopy to allow the seats to eject. For escape on the ground, the MDC can be fired from the front or the rear cockpit and from outside the aircraft by a control on either side of the front canopy frame.

COCKPIT

The cockpit is roomy, comfortable and fully pressurized and air-conditioned. The wide canopy allows sideways head movement. The back seat is positioned higher than the front seat, giving the two crew exceptional forward and sideways vision.

INSTRUMENT PANEL

Each seat has a full set of flight controls, but most non-flying controls are in the front cockpit. Controls and instruments are ergonomically laid out and easy to reach. The instruments are analogue type and the switches are lever type. Push/pull rods and mechanical links and levers transmit pilot inputs to the flying controls.

SEATS

Each crew member sits on a lightweight Martin-Baker Mark 10B zero-zero ejection seat ('zero-zero' means the seat can be operated while the aircraft is stationary on the ground). Each seat is fitted with lap, shoulder and leg restraints; an oxygen supply delivered through the Personal Equipment Connector (PEC); and emergency survival equipment such as oxygen cylinders and the Personal Survival Pack (PSP). A Personal Locating Beacon (PLB) is activated on ejection.

AVIONICS

The standard avionics equipment is housed in the forward fuselage and includes an ILS (Instrument Landing System), a VOR navigation aid, three TACAN units, two electrical inverters, a standby radio, a flight systems junction box and fatigue meters.

WING

The low, moderately swept wing is the secret of the Hawk's aerodynamic efficiency. In keeping with the minimum-maintenance and repair philosophy at Hawker Siddeley Aviation (HSA), the number of components is kept to a minimum. The major parts (skins, spars and ribs) are machined from solid billets of Duralumin. Most access panels are located on the top of the wing for ease of access. The wing is attached to the underneath of the fuselage using just 12 bolts. The two main spars and the upper and lower skins form an integral fuel tank.

ENGINE AIR INTAKES

These were originally shoulder-mounted, but were later sited lower down in the wing root. Positioning them ahead of and slightly above the wing leading edges gives extra longitudinal stability at supersonic speeds and prevents foreign objects from being sucked into the engine. In a bird strike, the main damage would be to the air intake, reducing potential damage to the engine.

FUEL TANKS

Fuel is carried in a flexible bag tank, holding 823 litres or 181gal. in the centre of the fuselage, and one integral tank, holding 837 litres or 184gal in each wing. A collector tank ensures fuel supply during negative-g conditions, and fuel can be supplied at maximum flow for up to 30 seconds in negative-g flight. The Hawk runs on AVTUR or AVTAG (a refined form of paraffin).

ENGINE

The single Rolls-Royce/Turboméca Adour Mk.151 turbofan engine is powered up by an integral gas turbine starter, which uses aviation fuel. HSA studied many single- and twin-engine configurations for the Hawk before deciding on the Adour turbofan. It is a two-spool engine with a two-stage fan driven by a single-stage turbine; and has a high bypass ratio of 0.9. The Adour has proved exceptionally reliable, economical on fuel and simple and cheap to maintain. It is designed in modules, which are easily stored and replaced.

FUSELAGE

The airframe construction is stringer and frame, with an aluminium alloy skin for simplicity and durability. For easy maintenance, 30% of the surface consists of access panels.

DYE POD

A tank beneath the fuselage contains three compartments, one filled with non-toxic derv, one with a mix of derv and red vegetable dye and the third with a derv/blue dye mix. When the pilot pushes the smoke buttons, white smoke is generated as derv is injected under pressure through a nozzle above the jet pipe to mix with the 500°C jet exhaust. Derv mixed with red dye passes through a separate nozzle to give red smoke, and a mix of derv and blue dye ejected through a third nozzle gives blue smoke. The pods hold enough for just over five minutes of white smoke, one minute of blue and one of red.

AIR BRAKE

The air brake mounted on the underneath of the rear fuselage is required to slow the aircraft down rapidly from its high cruise speed. The Red Arrows also use this feature during their aerobatic displays to accurately control the aircraft speed when in formation.

EJECT! EJECT! EJECT!

In Chapter 9 of the Aircrew Manual, the engineering bible that all Hawk pilots must plough through and memorize before they can take control, the tricky but desperately serious business of ejecting is explained in such a way that you can't fail to grasp the implications of a botched ejection sequence:

> 'When the seat starts to rise during the ejection sequence, a striker on the right side of the seat engages a lever on the MDC firing unit on the canopy frame, detonating the MDC which shatters the associated section of the canopy before contact with the seat. If the MDC fails the seat ejects through the canopy.' This has happened, with predictably tragic results.

The firing handle – the 'yellow and black' – is the coloured flexible cord handle that rests between your knees, a couple of centimetres or an inch below the Quick Release Fitting (QRF; the circular buckle securing the shoulder and lap straps) and directly behind the control column. To eject, you're instructed to jerk this handle 4cm or 1½in upwards, with a force of about 10–30kg or 20–70lb.

In the Red Arrows the armourers, who in an operational squadron deal with weaponry, look after the ejection seats, taking rigorous care over a device that may rarely be required to operate, but has to work faultlessly when a pilot pulls the 'yellow and black'. "The problem is that we can never do a functional test on it," explains Corporal Lance Did-Dell. "The only time we know whether a seat works is when it gets used." All armourers have a tacit understanding that when they work on a seat, no one takes a break until it's finished.

The Red Arrows T.Mk.1 Hawks are fitted with Martin-Baker Mk.10 ejection seats. Aircraft and seat evolved together. Martin-Baker developed their lightweight, rocket-propelled Mk.10 seat for the Hawk and the Tornado, so the company had a say in the cockpit design of these aicraft. Far from being reposing devices for half-supine passengers, like airline seats, Mk.10s maintain a state of constant readiness, perpetually less than a second away from rocket-propelled action. Like some special-effects device from a James Bond film, every seat part has a hidden function. Inside the headrest is a tightly packed parachute; the right armrest covers a personal survival pack; and a six-pack of rockets, complete with firing unit, are attached to the underside of the part you sit on. Yet by comparison with the technology packed into F-18 or Typhoon ejection seats, the Mk.10s, designed 30 years ago, are pretty basic.

The Mk.10 was developed to give pilots safe escape from a stationary aircraft to one flying at 650kt, and from ground level to 12,800m or 42,000ft. A time-release mechanism controls the parachute. When the pilot ejects at low altitudes, it opens rapidly. But at altitudes above 5,000m or 16,000ft, where high g-forces caused by deceleration might injure the pilot, and where the air pressure is too low for efficient oxygen intake through breathing, the parachute opens after a timed delay. Back-up systems are built into every phase of ejection.

The Hawk's minimal maintenance philosophy extends to its seat, which can be removed in an hour. "To take out a Tornado seat," explains Lance Did-Dell, "the riggers disarm the seat and canopy, then winch away the canopy (which is three times as thick as the Hawk's and, because the Tornado flies at higher speeds, is packed with more explosive). There are just three top explosives on the Hawk's seat, which we make safe, then we fold the canopy back on its hinge and take the seat out on a rail." Drogues and parachute are packed into a detachable container for servicing in a parachute workshop.

When the seats are due for a service, the armourers whip them out and send them back to the support unit at RAF Stafford. Mk.10s have a two-year life and spares for replacement are stored in 'the Morgue', a blast-proof outbuilding at Scampton, where the explosive devices in the seat assembly are protected. Keeping the ejection seat conveyor belt going is what takes up most of the armourers' time.

Pages 238-241 Facsimiles from the Red Arrows aircrew manual.

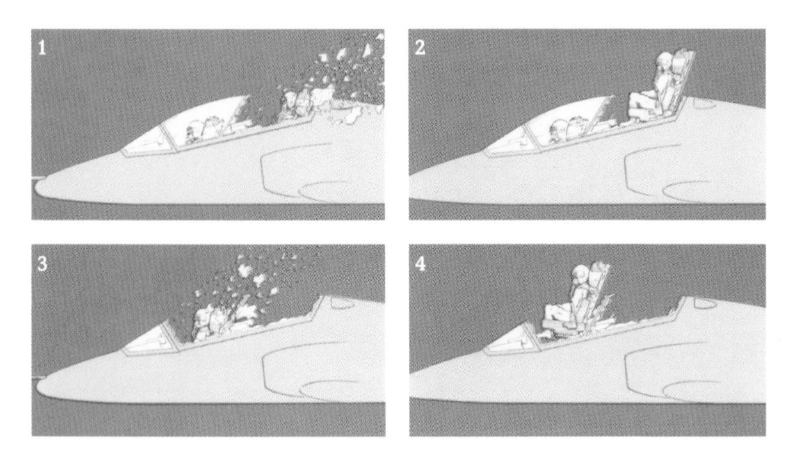

THE SEQUENCE

Each seat can be fired independently, but the rear crew can initiate the sequential firing of both seats. The rear seat fires first, diverting to the right, while the front seat goes to the left. The shape of the box that holds the parachute is rounded to make it easier for the crew to look left and right. Seat and occupant automatically separate and the seat falls to the ground without a parachute.

0 SECONDS
Pilot pulls yellow and black firing handle, initiating ejection.
1 +0.10 SECONDS
Miniature Detonation Cord (MDC) fires explosive zigzag charges in the rear canopy, which shatters.
2 +0.20 SECONDS
Three cartridges and a rocket gun propel the rear seat about 100m or 300ft above and just to the right of the aircraft.
3 +0.45 SECONDS
Forward canopy shatters.
4 +0.55 SECONDS
Front seat ejects, firing slightly to the left.

HOW IT WORKS

In an emergency, the pilot in the front seat calls 'Eject!' and pulls the yellow and black firing handle, while the passenger does the same. In less than a minute, the two crew have ejected and are free-falling, strapped to their seats. The seats separate and fall away. Pulling the firing handle initiates a complex sequence of actions:

1. A sear (catch) is pulled out from the firing unit beneath the seat, releasing a gas, which is pumped to the harness retraction unit at the top of the seat. This unit is attached to the shoulder straps of the pilot's harness, and it pulls the shoulders back into the correct upright posture for ejection – if the vertebrae (spinal bones) are not square to each other, they may be crushed by g-forces during ejection.
2. Gas from the firing unit withdraws a sear from the ejection gun, which runs down the seat back. It causes the seat to unlock from the airframe and begin to lift. Lifting of the seat:
   - disconnects the Personal Services and aircraft supplies
   - trips the emergency oxygen supply
   - trips the mechanism that causes the MDC in the canopy to fire, shattering the canopy
   - causes a rocket cartridge pack mounted beneath the seat to ignite
   - trips a drogue gun that deploys the stabilizing drogue (guide) parachutes
   - causes two nylon lines wrapped around the pilot's thighs and legs to tighten, pulling the legs back against the seat to prevent injury during ejection.
3. A rocket pack beneath the seat fires, accelerating the seat's ejection through the shattered canopy.
4. 0.30 seconds after the initial seat movement, a drogue gun at the top of the seat back fires to release two drogue (guide) parachutes, which stabilize the seat and slow its acceleration.
5. 1.5 seconds after the initial seat movement, the pilot's harness and leg restraints and the drogues are released to stream the parachute out of its pack on the upper seat back behind the pilot's head.
6. 1.5 seconds after ejecting, the parachute opens, lifting the pilot out of the seat, which falls away, and the pilot makes a normal parachute descent.

Intentionally Blank

Second Edition
July 2002

HAWK T Mk 1 & 1A

AIRCREW MANUAL

BY COMMAND OF THE DEFENCE COUNCIL

PREPARED BY HANDLING SQN

GEN0070855

Prelims Fig 1 General Layout

LEADING PARTICULARS

LEADING PARTICULARS

Name: Hawk T Mk1/1A

Type: Single engine, tandem seat trainer

Crew: One or two

Duties: Flying training. Weapons training. Air Defence/Ground Attack - T Mk1A

Main Dimensions

Wing Span: 9.4 metres (30 feet 10 inches)

Overall Length: 11.9 meters (39 feet 3 inches)

Height: 4.0 metres (13 feet 2 inches)

Wing area: 16.7 square metres (179.6 square feet)

Aircraft Mass

Maximum for Take-Off: 5700kg

Maximum (Normal) for Landing: 5000kg

Maximum (Emergency) for Landing: 5700kg

Power Plant

Engine Change Unit (ECU)

RR/Tm Adour 15101

RR/Tm Adour 15102 Red Arrows a/c

RR/Tm Adour 15103 Post Mod 630 a/c

Engine Type: Twin shaft turbofan

Thrust Rating (ISA sea level): 23.1 kN (5200 lbs)

Starting Air Supply: Aircraft mounted GTS

Engine Oil

For approved engine oil see Part 2 Chapter 2.

Oil system capacity: 11.9 litres (21 pints)

Oil tank capacity: 7.4 litres (13 pints)

Usable oil: 4.5 litres (8 pints)

Oil consumption: 1 pint/hr

Fuel

For approved fuels see Part 2 Chapter 2.

Fuel System

Table 1 - Fuel Tank Capacities - Useable Fuel

Tank	*0.79 SG Kg*	*0.77 SG Kg*	*Litres*	*Imperial Gallons*
Fuselage	645	629	818	180
Wing	627	612	795	175
Total	1272	1241	1613	355

Electrical Systems

DC generation: One engine driven 9 kW generator

Supply: 28 Volts

Batteries: 2 x 24 Volts

AC Supply: 115 Volts 400 Hz single phase.

Hydraulic Systems

Fluid: OM-15

Table 2 - Hydraulic power Sources

System	*Power Source*	*Operating Pressure*
No 1	EDP	207±10 Bars
No 2	EDP or RAT pump	207±10 Bars or 169±3.45 to 203±3.45 bars

Table 3 - Services Operated

System	*Services Operated*
No1	Aileron/Tailplane PFCUs, landing gear, wheelbrakes, flaps, airbrake.
No 2	Aileron/Tailplane PFCUs
RAT	Aileron/Tailplane PFCUs following failure of No 2 System.

Ejection Seat

Type: Martin-Baker 10B Mk 1, rocket-assisted.

Front Cockpit: 10B1 Mk 1

Rear Cockpit: 10B2 Mk 1

Oxygen Systems

Regulator: Seat-Mounted Type 517

Table 4 - Oxygen Systems

	Main System	*Emergency System*
Type	Gaseous	Gaseous
Capacity	2 x 1400 ltre cylinders	1 x 70 ltre cylinder

Air Conditioning, Pressurization and Anti-G

Air Supply: 5th stage HP compressor air.

Communications

CCS: ARI 23245/7

UHF (AN/ARC 164): ARI 23315/2

UHF (AN/ARC 164 - Havequick II): ARI 23315/10

Standby UHF (D403 MA): ARI 23159

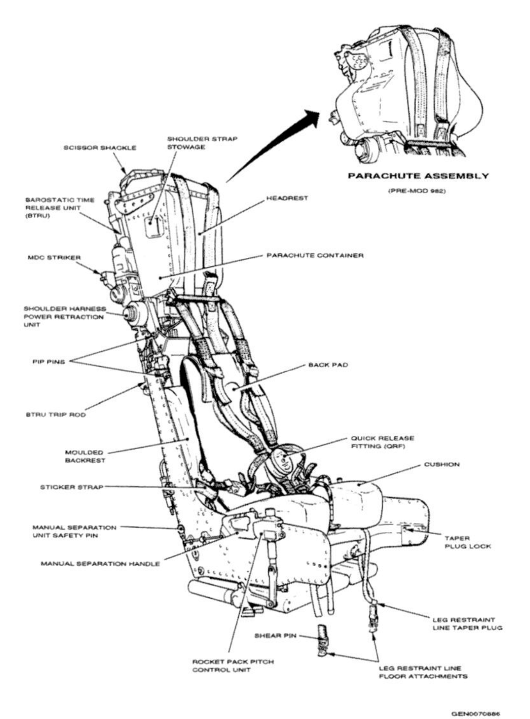

1 - 9 Fig 3 Ejection Seat - Right Side

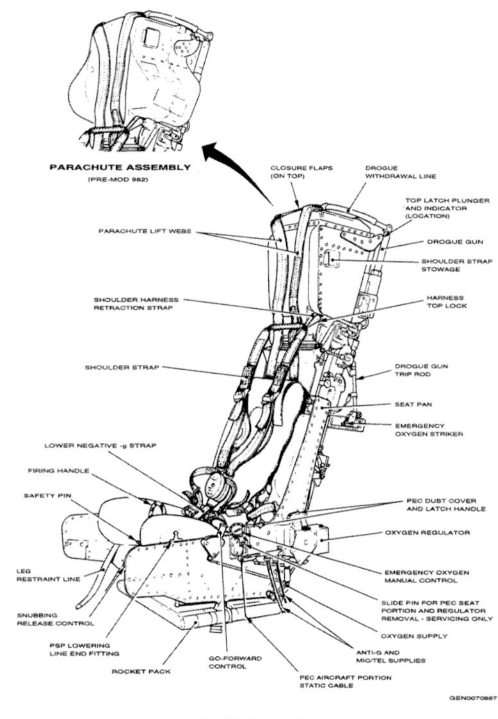

1 - 9 Fig 4 Ejection Seat - Left Side

46. The interconnection operates so long as the safety pin of the associated MDC firing unit is removed: operation is not prevented if the safety pin of the MDC firing handle on the associated canopy is still fitted.

WARNING: In each cockpit, take care to avoid inadvertent operation of the MDC firing unit, either by hand or by unauthorized stowed articles, when strapping-in or when closing the canopy.

Personal Equipment Connector

47. A PEC, on the left side of the seat pan (Fig 4), provides single action connection/disconnection of the occupant's mic/tel and personal supplies before and after flight respectively; it also provides automatic disconnection during the ejection sequence. The PEC comprises seat, aircraft and man portions:

a. *Seat Portion.* The seat portion provides for connection of the man portion on its top face and the aircraft portion on its lower face. It is locked to the seat pan and is coupled to the oxygen regulator. A catch at the front end of the seat portion enables the whole unit to be removed for maintenance. A metal dust cover, provided to protect the seat portion when the seat is not occupied, is stowed on the cockpit left wall. The dust cover is marked SELECT OXYGEN ON BEFORE CONNECTING PILOTS SERVICES. The time when the seat portion is not covered by either the dust cover or the PEC man portion (sub-para 47.c.) is to be kept to a minimum.

b. *Aircraft Portion.* The aircraft portion connects the communications system and anti-g supplies from the aircraft to the seat. It is held on the lower face of the seat portion by a lever-operated latch which is linked by static cable to the cockpit floor, so that these portions disconnect automatically during the ejection sequence.

c. *Man Portion.* The man portion is part of the flying clothing and has an oxygen tube, anti-g tube and mic/tel lead which is to be connected to the occupant's oxygen mask hose, anti-g suit and helmet mic/tel lead respectively. The man portion is connected by aligning it over the seat portion, locating its front end, and pressing down firmly on its aft end until it locks into place. It is released manually by pulling up its latch handle after pressing a thumb catch on the handle; it is released automatically after ejection by a linkage from the harness lock release mechanism. Both release methods also disconnect the leg-restraint lines.

NOTE: During the strapping-in procedure, to prevent the possibility of surplus oxygen tube and mic/tel lead fouling the pilot's elbow they should be pulled forward through the restraint flap on the life preserver to reduce to a minimum the length between the flap and the PEC.

NOTE: The man portion is not to be connected to the seat portion until after the main oxygen supply has been selected ON; it is to be disconnected and the dust cover fitted before the oxygen supply is selected OFF after flight.

Oxygen System on the Seat

48. The main oxygen system is connected to the seat at an automatic pull-off bayonet connector behind the right side of the seat pan, and thence by pipe and flexible tube to the regulator/PEC.

49. An emergency oxygen cylinder on the rear left of the seat feeds into the main supply line and has a supply release mechanism which is tripped automatically by a striker during ejection, or can be operated manually at any time by pulling sharply upwards and backwards on a control ring on the left side of the seat pan. When the control ring has been pulled a red band on its mounting is visible.

50. The oxygen systems are fully described in Part 1 Chapter 10.

Independent Ejection Sequence

51. The following sequence occurs when independent ejection is initiated, ie, the command ejection selector is at OFF or, with the selector at ON, the front seat firing handle is pulled before the rear seat handle is pulled.

52. When the seat firing handle is pulled sharply the firing unit cartridge detonates immediately and the movement of the handle releases the lock of the manual separation handle, readying that control.

53. Gases from the firing unit are distributed to:

a. The harness power retraction unit, firing its cartridge to pull the occupant's shoulders back into the seat and lock the retraction straps.

b. The ejection gun sear withdrawal unit, rotating the cross shaft to fire the primary cartridge of the ejection gun.

c. The command ejection selector valve (rear seat only), firing the command ejection cartridge. (If the command system is selected OFF, the gases are vented into the rear cockpit. If the command system is selected ON but the front seat handle is pulled first, the gases pass to the front cockpit but have no effect since the front seat has already been ejected.)

54. Gases from the ejection gun primary cartridge initiate upward movement of the seat, releasing the locking plunger from the top latch and thus unlocking the seat from the gun barrel.

55. As the seat accelerates up the guide rails, the following events occur automatically:

a. The ejection gun secondary cartridges fire in turn.

b. The MDC firing unit is engaged by the striker, detonating the MDC which shatters the associated section of the canopy.

c. The static trip rods withdraw the sears from the drogue gun and the BTRU, and static cables disconnect the command ejection system, the aircraft portion of the PEC, and the main oxygen supply.

d. The emergency oxygen supply is selected on and the regulator set to 100%.

e. The leg-restraint lines are pulled downwards through the snubbing units and restrain the occupant's legs. The units maintain the restraint after the shear pins break to free the lines from the floor.

56. As the telescopic tubes of the ejection gun separate (about 0·25 second after initiation of ejection) the rocket initiator cartridge is fired by the pull of the dispensed static cable and the gases fire the rocket pack cartridge to ignite the rocket fuel.

57. As the rocket pack completes its burn the drogue gun fires, ejecting its piston which withdraws the pin from the closure flaps on the parachute container and deploys the controller drogue. The controller drogue pulls out the main drogue which is fully developed approximately one second after initiation of ejection.

58. The remainder of the sequence is controlled by the BTRU.

a. *Above Main Barostat Altitude.* If the ejection is made above main barostat altitude, the seat descends to that altitude band and the main barostat then allows the 1·5-second time delay mechanism to operate and fire the BTRU cartridge.

b. *Below Main Barostat Altitude.* If the ejection is made below the main barostat altitude, but above the g-stop barostat altitude, the g-stop interrupts the time delay until the deceleration on the seat is below the g-stop value. The time delay is then free to operate and fire the BTRU cartridge.

c. *Below g-Stop Barostat Altitude.* If the ejection is made below the g-stop barostat altitude, the main barostat has already removed its restraint on the time delay, and the g-stop is inhibited. The 1·5-second time delay therefore operates immediately and fires the BTRU cartridge.

59. When the BTRU cartridge fires, its gases cause the drogue scissor shackle and the harness top locks to be released; the gases also release the harness bottom locks and pass to the drogue gun to fire its second cartridge (normally a redundant action).

60. The release of the harness locks frees, but does not separate, the occupant from the seat. The release of the scissor shackle transfers the drag of the main drogue to the personal parachute which is then pulled from its container.

61. The occupant is then held in the seat only by the restraint of the seat pan stickers. As the parachute develops it lifts the occupant and the PSP from the seat, pulling the seat pan stickers and PSP lowering line connector from their clips (the latter initiating PLB operation). The occupant has to release his grip on the seat firing handle at or before this stage. The seat then falls away cleanly and the leg-restraint lines run out freely through the rings on the leg garters. A normal parachute descent should then follow.

Command Ejection Sequence

WARNING: If the command ejection system is operative (ie, selected ON), removal of the rear seat firing handle safety pin renders the front seat 'live', whether or not the front seat firing handle safety pin is fitted. Therefore, the front seat occupant should always be properly strapped in whenever the rear seat firing handle safety pin is not fitted.

62. The following ejection sequence occurs when the command ejection system selector lever is at ON and the ejection of both seats is initiated by pulling the rear seat firing handle.

63. When the rear seat firing unit cartridge fires, gases are fed to the command selector valve firing its cartridge. The ejection of the rear seat continues as in the independent sequence.

64. From the selector valve cartridge gases are passed to the command breech unit in the front cockpit, and also (via a bypass) to the front harness power retraction unit which immediately pulls the occupant's shoulders back into the seat. After a 0·35-second delay the command breech cartridge fires to operate the front sear withdrawal unit which detonates the ejection gun, thus initiating seat ejection; the sequence then continues as in the independent ejection sequence.

SEAT NORMAL PROCEDURES

Checks Before Flight

65. Before dual or solo flight check that the aircraft is Safe for Parking and then carry out the Ejection Seat

air intake must not be used as a step. Vertical guide lines, from the cockpit rim to the toe-in step and the extending footstep, are provided as an alignment aid when vacating the cockpit.

3. *Extending Footstep.* The extending footstep is operated by:

a. A handhold, marked FOOTSTEP PULL-OUT, on the face of the step.

b. A lever on the front cockpit wall, forward of the LP fuel cock lever.

4. *Toe-in Step.* The toe-in step is covered by a spring-loaded flap, hinged along the upper edge.

5. *Retractable Step.* The retractable step is locked up by an integral anti-g latch. The step can be pulled down by a handhold, marked FOOTSTEP PULL DOWN, when a tongue below the handhold is raised. The anti-g latch is released when the tongue is held raised. The step is retracted under spring pressure when a plunger on the cockpit rim left side is depressed either manually, or automatically when the canopy closes. The step is to be retracted and locked up before the engine is started.

WARNING: Personnel are to be clear of the step before it is retracted.

Transparencies

6. The transparencies comprise a front windscreen and a one-piece canopy divided into front and rear sections by an integral windscreen.

7. The front one-piece, curved windscreen has good rain clearance characteristics; no rain clearance system is installed.

Canopy

WARNING: The canopy moves easily; therefore, take care to ensure that it does not close accidentally and trap the fingers of the occupants or the ground crew on the cockpit rim.

8. The sideways opening canopy rotates about four hinges on its right side. The canopy is manually operated and its weight is counterbalanced by a torque tube arrangement on its right edge.

9. A combined pneumatic damper and locking strut controls the rate at which the canopy can be opened or closed and enables the canopy to be locked in the open position. The damper/locking strut, which can secure the canopy in any desired position, is controlled by canopy operating levers via a teleflex cable. The strut is on the front cockpit right wall and is secured to the cockpit floor by a quick release pin. If a fault occurs in the strut or the controlling cable which prevents the canopy from being opened normally, remove the quick release pin to free the strut.

10. A cabin pressurizing seal strip is around the canopy base; the strip is not to be used as a handhold when entering or leaving the cockpit.

Canopy Controls

11. *Internal.* Two interconnected levers on the canopy frame, one at the left side of each cockpit, operate four interlocked canopy locking pins. The levers are spring-loaded to the forward position. The canopy is locked when the levers are fully forward and unlocked when the levers are moved aft. A thumb-operated spring-loaded safety catch in the front cockpit prevents inadvertent movement of the levers from the canopy locked position. The safety catch is linked to a thumb-operated catch in the rear cockpit and to a button integral with an external lock/unlock handle (para 12). When either the front or the rear cockpit catch is pressed outboard both levers are free to move. An UNLOCKED label in each cockpit is positioned such that when the canopy is locked each safety catch totally obscures the word UNLOCKED. If any part of the word is visible the canopy is not locked. When either safety catch is pressed the canopy seal is deflated. An arrowhead is marked on the left side of the front windscreen arch; a second arrowhead, on the canopy forward edge, is marked WITH CANOPY LOCKED ARROWS MUST BE IN LINE. When either lever is held fully aft the canopy swings partially open and the locking strut allows the canopy to be manually positioned; when the lever is released the locking strut holds the canopy in the selected position. In the front cockpit, a grab handle on the canopy frame forward of the lever may be used to position the canopy. In windspeeds in excess of 20 knots it may not be possible to open or to close the canopy without external assistance.

12. *External.* A lock/unlock handle, marked PRESS & TURN, is on the forward left side of the canopy. When a button incorporated in the handle is pressed, the safety catch in the cockpit moves outboard to free the canopy internal operating lever and to permit the handle to be turned clockwise from the horizontal to the vertical position, thus unlocking the canopy and allowing it to partially open. Using the handle, the canopy can be positioned manually and remains in the selected position when the handle is released.

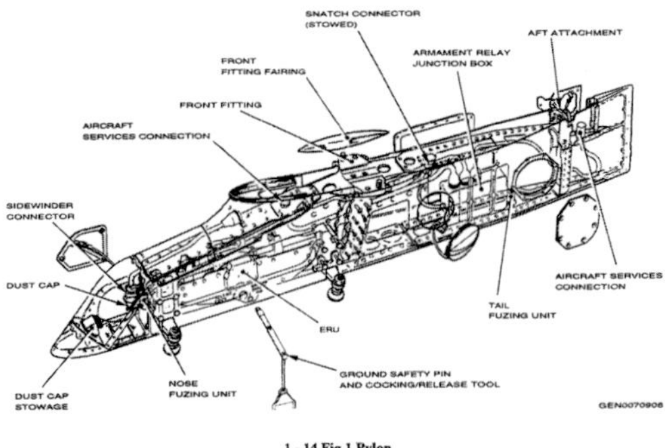

1 - 14 Fig 1 Pylon

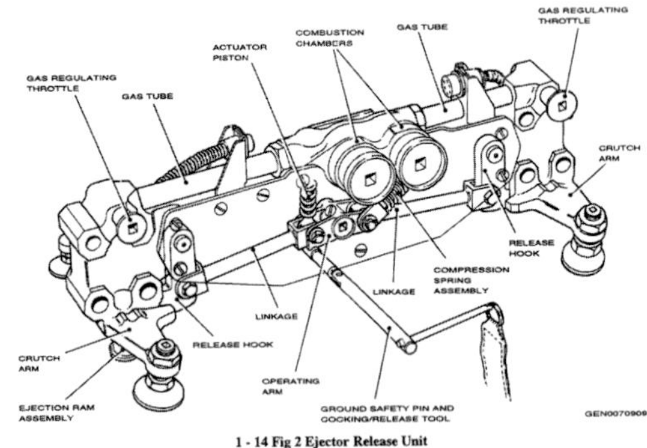

1 - 14 Fig 2 Ejector Release Unit

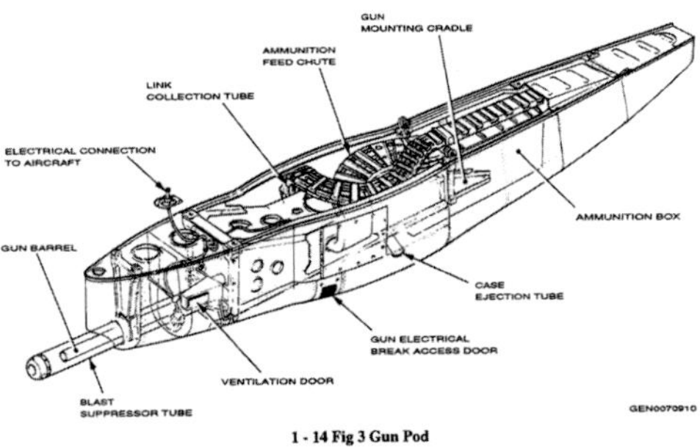

1 - 14 Fig 3 Gun Pod

7. A blast suppressor tube protrudes forward of the pod nose fairing. Expended ammunition cases are ejected downwards into the airstream through an ejection tube in the pod; empty ammunition belt links are retained in a receptacle in the pod. Whenever a gun firing safety catch, on the control column handgrip in each cockpit is raised, an electrically-operated ventilation door in the pod front fairing is opened; the door takes approximately seven seconds to open fully. If the safety catch is lowered before the seven seconds have elapsed, the door continues to the fully open position before closing.

Power Supplies

8. *T Mk 1.* On T Mk 1 aircraft two armament busbars, No 1 and No 2, are supplied from the No 1 Battery busbar and the Essential Services busbar respectively, whenever the MASS is at UNLOCK LIVE. (A simplified schematic diagram of the armament electrical system is at Fig 17) The No 1 Armament busbar provides a DC supply for store jettisoning only. The No 2 Armament busbar supplies DC for store jettisoning, weapon selection and release and for gun firing control; the supply to the gun firing circuits is broken whenever the nosewheel leg uplock microswitch is open (ie, nosewheel leg not locked up). A 2-position ground test switch in the left wheelbay allows the nosewheel leg microswitch to be bypassed and the gun firing circuits to be powered when the aircraft is on the ground with the nosewheel leg locked down. The gun installation also requires a 115 volt 400 Hz single-phase AC supply from the AC busbar; this supply is available whenever the No 2 Armament busbar is live, the gun pod ventilation door relay is energized and a gun firing trigger is pressed. The routing of the jettison supplies (ie, from both No 1 and No 2 Armament busbars) is independent of landing gear position and only requires the MASS to be set to UNLOCK LIVE.

NOTE: The two armament busbars do not physically exist in the aircraft but are so designated in this chapter to define the supplies from the No 1 Battery busbar and the Essential Services busbar after No 1 and No 2 safety relays are closed.

f. Engine instruments are to be monitored for surge throughout entry, spin and recovery. If surge is encountered, set the throttle to HP Off immediately.

g. The minimum height for initiation of spin recovery is 15,000 feet AGL.

h. Recovery action is to be taken immediately if:

(1) The IAS increases through 180 knots, or decreases through 100 knots.

(2) Transient side forces feel large to the pilot.

(3) Aerodynamic forces prevent the pilot holding the rudder at full deflection.

(4) Engine surge is encountered.

i. After recovery, the engine is to be checked for surge-free operation by noting that RPM lead TGT when the throttle is opened.

j. If recovery has not been achieved by 5000 feet AGL, the aircraft is to be abandoned.

NOTE: The probability of the conditions listed in sub-para 23.h. occurring is minimal provided that the techniques described in Part 3 Chapter 2 are used.

24. Deliberate inverted spinning is prohibited.

Aerobatics

25. The aircraft is cleared for aerobatics with flaps and landing gear retracted.

26. Flick manoeuvres and stall turns are prohibited.

27. If, during vertical manoeuvres, it becomes obvious that the manoeuvre cannot be completed without loss of control, the throttle is to be set to Idle. After recovery the engine is to be checked for surge-free operation.

Crosswind

28. The aircraft may be operated within the following crosswind component limitations:

a. Take-off and landing (dry/wet runway) - 30 knots.

b. Take-off and landing with asymmetric stores and the wind from the adverse side (loaded wing downwind):

(1) Sidewinder on one wing (launcher and adaptor on other wing) - 15 knots.

(2) BL-755 on one wing (unloaded pylon on other wing) - 8 knots.

NOTE: Landing in pairs when asymmetric stores are carried is not permitted.

29. Landing in pairs may be carried out in crosswind components up to 15 knots. Pending further tests, the result of a tyre burst on landing cannot be predicted with accuracy, and in these circumstances lateral deviations of the order of 30ft may be experienced before control can be regained.

Aircraft Approach Criteria

30. Approach criteria are as follows:

a. *Standby Pressure Instrument Allowance.* The standby pressure instrument allowance is 100 feet. This includes up to 20 feet pressure error correction.

b. *Aircraft Category.* The aircraft category for approaches is Category C.

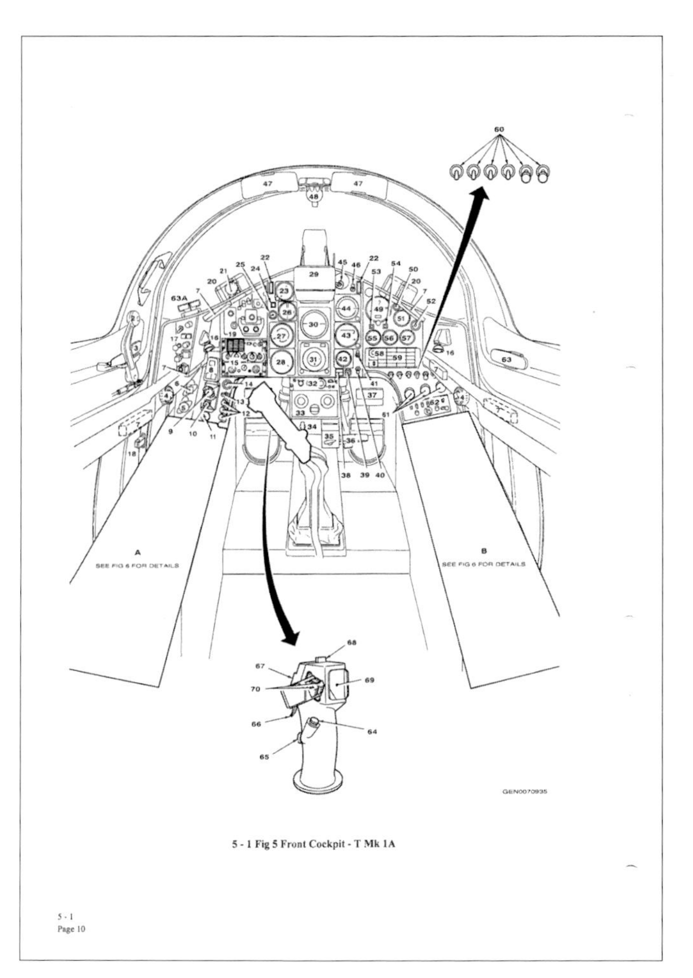

5 - 1 Fig 5 Front Cockpit - T Mk 1A

Table 5 - Key to 5 - 1 Fig 5 Front Cockpit T Mk 1A

No	*Item*	*Ref*
1	Grab handle	1 - 12
2	Canopy operating lever	1 - 12
3	Canopy operating lever safety catch	1 - 12
4	Body spray adjustable louvre (2)	1 - 8
5	Landing gear standby lowering system selector	1 - 7
6	Flap standby lowering system selector	1 - 6
7	Strip light (6)	1-12
8	Landing gear unit position indicator	1-7
9	Landing gear retraction selector button and ground emergency retraction facility	1-7
10	Landing gear lowering selector button	1-7
11	DC voltmeter	1-1
12	Reset buttons - bottom to top:	
	Generator reset	1-1
	No 2 inverter reset	1-1
	No 1 inverter reset	1-1
13	Flap position selector	1-6
14	Flap position indicator	1-6
15	UHF transceiver control panel	1-13
16	Map reading light (2)	1-12
17	Missile control panel	1-14
18	Banner target release switches	1-14
19	Weapon control panel	1-14
20	Frequency card holder (2)	1-13
21	Stopwatch holder	1-12
22	CWS attention light (2)	1-2
23	Accelerometer	1-11
24	Airbrake indicator	1-6
25	Tailplane position indicator	1-6
26	Turn and slip indicator	1-11
27	Combined speed indicator (CSI)	1-11
28	Directional gyro indicator (DGI)	1-11
29	ISIS sight head	1-14
30	Attitude indicator	1-11
31	Horizontal situation indicator (HSI)	1-11
32	AHRS control unit	1-11
33	ISIS control unit	1-14
34	Rudder pedals adjustment control	1-6
35	Bomb release intervalometer	1-14
36	Rudder bar locking handle	1-6
37	Wheelbrakes toe pad - also on left side	1-7
38	Navigation mode selector	1-13
39	ILS marker indicator light	1-13
40	Landing/taxy lamp switch	1-11
41	Communications power switch	1-13
42	Vertical speed indicator (VSI)	1-11
43	Main altimeter	1-11
44	Standby attitude indicator	1-11
45	Master armament safety switch (MASS)	1-14
46	Flight instruments power switch	1-11
47	Rear view mirror (2)	1-11
48	Standby magnetic compass	1-11
49	Standby altimeter	1-11
50	Oxygen flow indicator	1-10
51	Cabin altimeter	1-8
52	Oxygen main supply contents gauge	1-10
53	Engine LP shaft rotation indicator	1-4
54	Air producer start indicator	1-4
55	RPM indicator	1-4
56	TGT indicator	1-4
57	Fuel contents gauge	1-3
58	Fire extinguisher button	1-2
59	Central warning panel	1-2
60	Lighting switches left to right:	
	Navigation light switch	1-12
	Lower anti-collision light switch	1-12
	Upper anti-collision light switch	1-12
	Internal main lights master switch	1-12
	Internal emergency lights switch	1-12
	Standby compass light switch	1-12
61	Internal lighting rotary dimmer (3)	1-12
62	CCS station box	1-13
63	MDC firing handle	1-12
63A	Canopy/seat pin stowage	1-9
64	Camera button	1-14
65	Receiver mute button	1-13
66	Gun firing trigger	1-14
67	Gun safety catch	1-14
68	Gun safety catch indicator (Set to live)	1-14
69	Bomb/RP release button safety flap	1-14
70	Tailplane trim switches	1-6
	Detail A - See Fig 6	
	Detail B - See Fig 6	

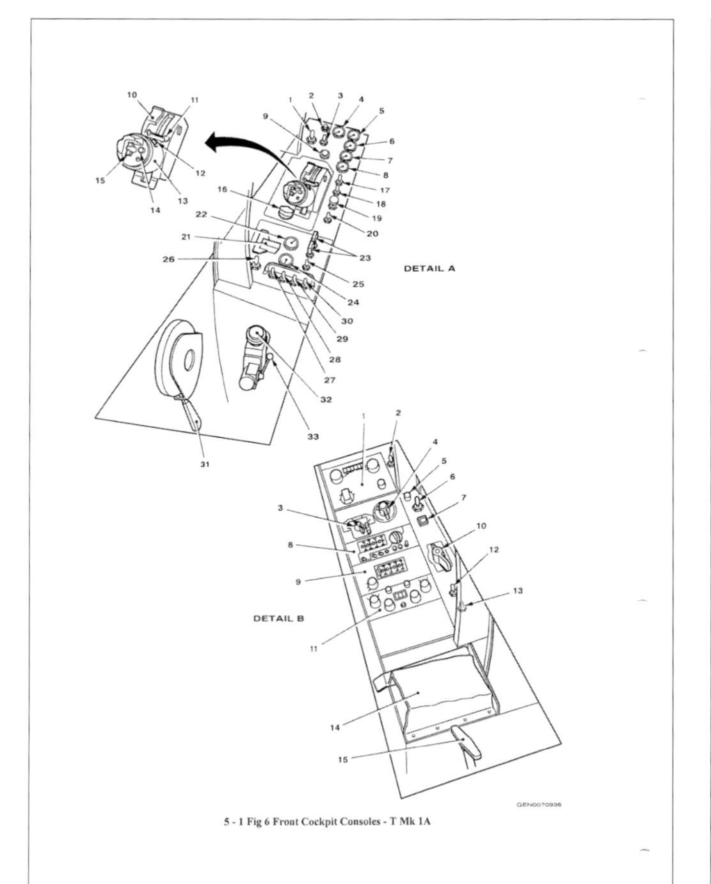

5 - 1 Fig 6 Front Cockpit Consoles - T Mk 1A

Table 6 - Key to 5 - 1 Fig 6 Front Cockpit Consoles - T Mk 1A

No	*Item*	*Ref*
	Detail A	
1	Engine ignition switch	1-4
2	No 3 inverter reset switch	1-1
3	Altimeter ground test switch	1-11
4	Left brake pressure gauge	1-7
5	Right brake pressure gauge	1-7
6	Brakes supply pressure gauge	1-7
7	No 1 hydraulic system pressure gauge	1-5
8	No 2 hydraulic system pressure gauge	1-5
9	No 2 hydraulic pump/ram air turbine (RAT) reset button	1-5
10	Full throttle stop	1-4
11	Throttle idle stop lever	1-4
12	Start/relight button	1-4
13	Throttle twist grip	1-4
14	Transmit switch	1-13
15	Airbrake switch	1-6
16	Throttle damper friction control	1-4
17	Standby UHF switch	1-13
18	Alternative receiver mute switch	1-13
19	Alternative transmit switch	1-13
20	Anti-skid switch	1-7
21	Cover for tailplane trim standby switches	1-6
22	Aileron trim indicator	1-6
23	Aileron trim switches	1-6
	Detail A	
24	Rudder trim indicator	1-6
25	Rudder trim switch	1-6
26	Engine start master switch	1-4
27	No 1 battery switch	1-1
28	No 2 battery switch	1-1
29	Fuel booster pump switch	1-3
30	Pitot static tube heater switch	1-11
31	LP fuel cock control lever	1-3
32	Anti-g system test button	1-8
33	Anti-g system control lever	1-8
	Detail B	
1	VHF transceiver control panel	1-13
2	UHF aerial selector switch	1-13
3	Cabin conditioning control switch	1-8
4	Temperature control switch	1-8
5	Telebrief light	1-13
6	External intercom switch	1-13
7	Accident data recorder (ADR) status indicator	1-12
8	IFF/SSR control unit	1-13
9	ILS control unit	1-13
10	Oxygen main supply selector	1-10
11	Tacan control unit	1-13
12	Seat pan height adjustment switch	1-9
13	Airbrake test switch	1-6
14	Map stowage	1-12
15	Parking brake T-handle	1-7

ROYAL AIR FORCE

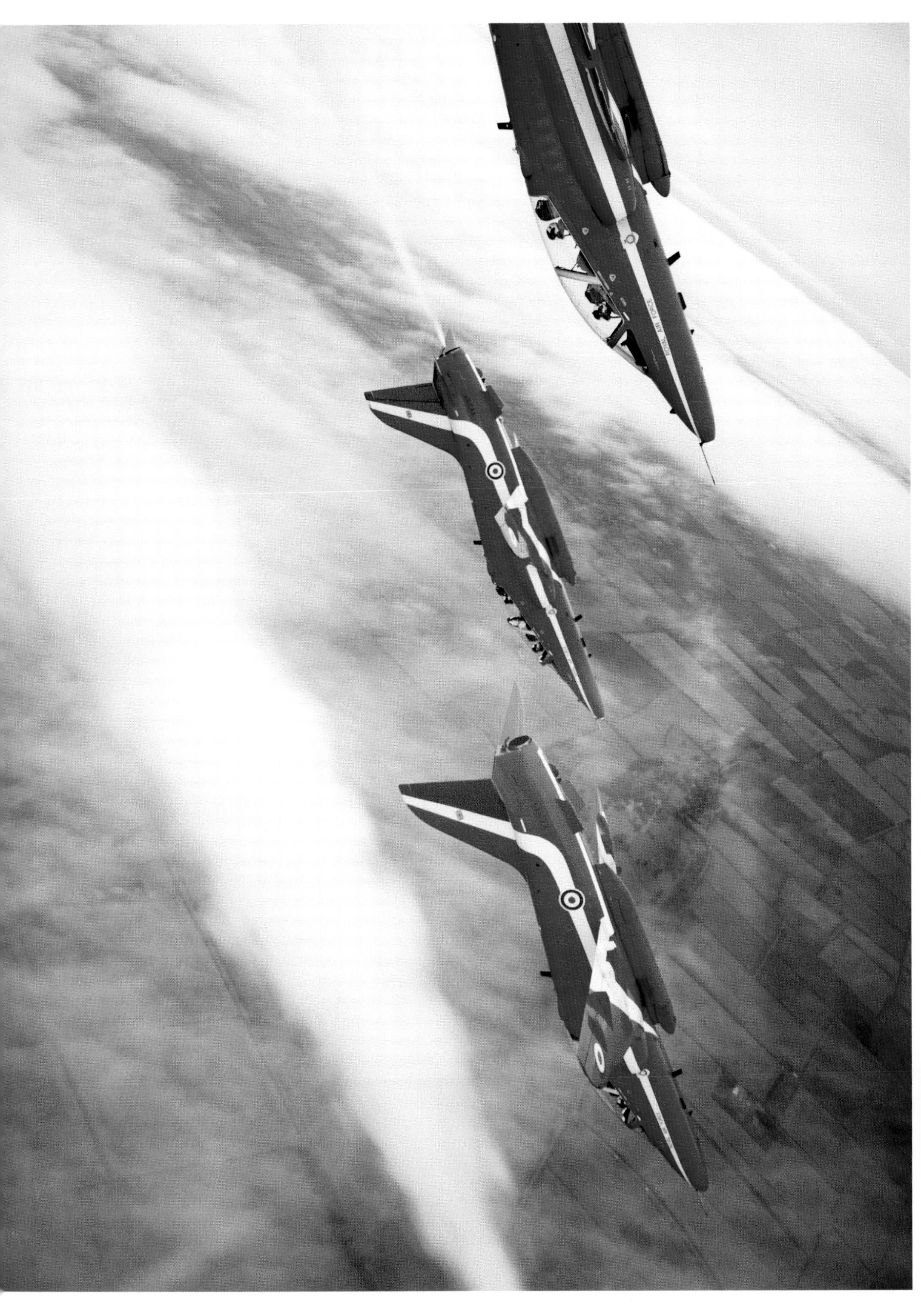
ROYAL AIR FORCE

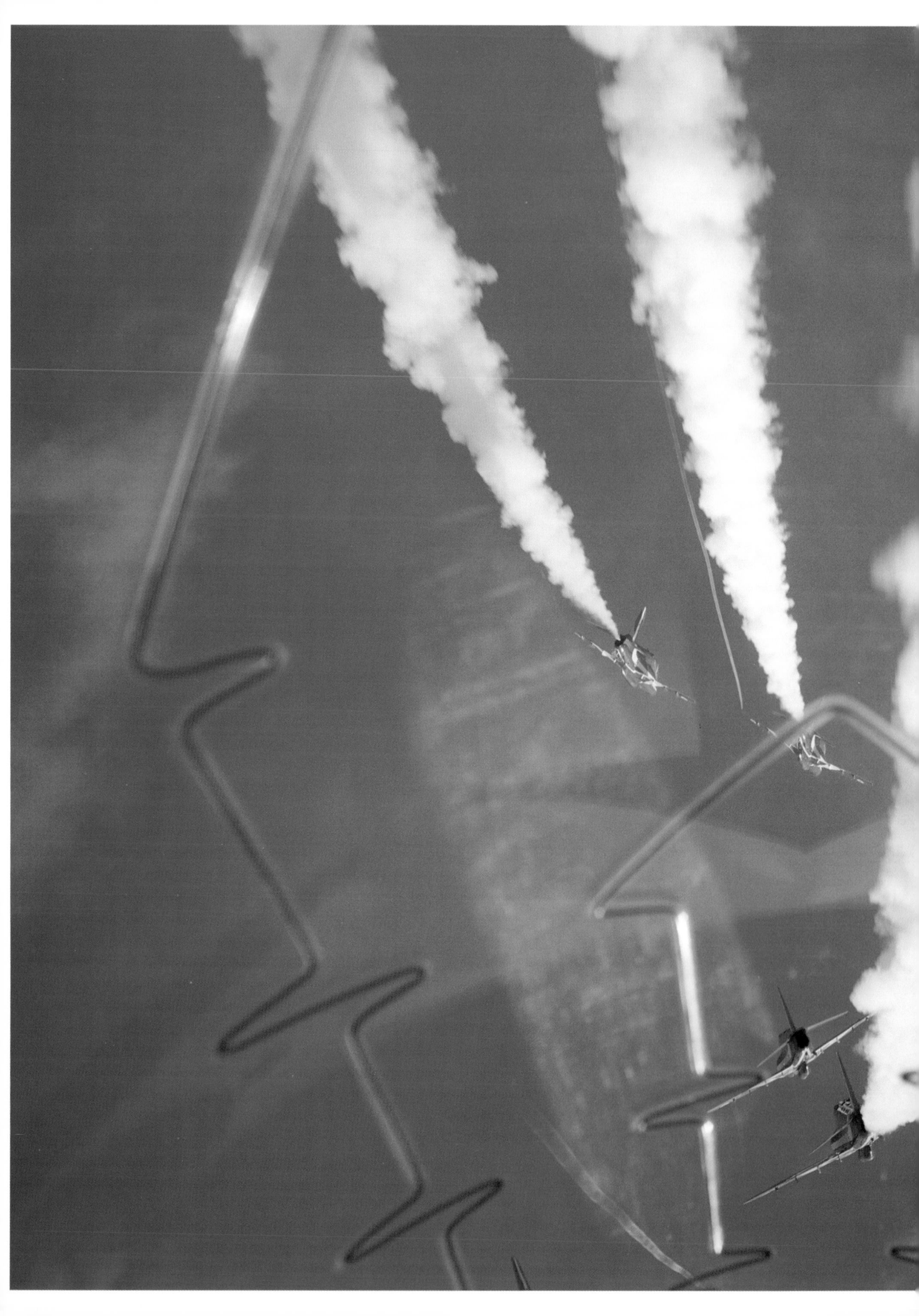

RAFSPEAK

Avionics
Aviation electronics, the radio, navigation and computer systems installed in aircraft.
Blues
The RAFAT support staff, who wear blue overalls during the display season.
Break
(v. & n.) To split off from the main formation, as in the Champagne Split.
Buffet
The shaking of an aircraft in flight, a warning of an imminent stall.
Circus
The 11 members of the Blues who are selected to accompany the Reds, often travelling in the back seats of the Hawks, during the **display season** and the back-up team who often travel to the venues in the C-130 Hercules transport.
Crisp packet
Silver dye-transfer team suit.
Crowd line
The line, usually a fence or railing, that marks the front line of the crowd at an air show. CAA regulations stipulate that the crowd line must be at least 230m or 750ft from the **display line**.
Cuckooed
Last-minute substitution of rear cockpit seat place.
Datum
The display axis, or central point on which the Red Arrows focus their air display, from where the whole display is visible to the crowd; also called the 'crowd centre'.
Derv
Diesel oil, which when mixed with vegetable dyes, creates the distinctive smoke trails.
Display line
A marked line, parallel to the forward **crowd line** and at least 230m or 750ft from the spectators at an air show, along which aircraft may fly during the display.
Display season
The time of year, usually from mid-May until late October, when the Red Arrows display to the public.
Down the hill
[To make] a steep dive: 'I'm doing 330kt down the hill' – 'I'm in a steep dive at 330kt'.
Enid
The collective name for Reds 1-5 in the Red Arrows **formation**; the name is derived from Enid Blyton's 'Famous Five' books.
Fat Albert
An RAF term for the Hercules C-130 cargo transport aircraft.
FI
Fatigue Index – the measure of the life an aircraft has experienced, similar to quoting the number of hours an aircraft has flown: 6,000 hours is roughly equivalent to 100 FI when an aircraft is flown in accordance with normal RAF usage. FI is consumed much faster if more g is experienced.
F.N.G.
An abbreviation of 'F...... new guy', RAF slang for new squadron members.
FOD
Foreign Object Damage. The smallest of debris that can be sucked into an engine intake.
FOD Plod
An inspection walk in the aircraft movement area for foreign objects.
Fairie
The RAF name for an engineer who specializes in aircraft avionics.
Figures, fuel and flies
A quick turnaround.
Flat display
A low-level display flown when the cloud base is above 300m or 1,000ft.
Forgiving (of an aircraft)
Does not overreact to sudden or clumsy use of the flight controls, as from a trainee. *See also* **Unforgiving**.
Formate
To 'hold station' off another aircraft – that is, to maintain a position relative to it; to formate on the Boss is to use Red 1 as a reference for positioning inside a formation.
Formation
A convoy of aircraft travelling in a recognisable pattern such as Arrow or Diamond Nine.
Full display
A high-level display flown when the cloud base is at least 1,400m or 4,500ft.
g, g-force
The positive or negative forces inserted on an object due to gravity.
Gate, gate safety height
The lowest altitude at which a pilot can commit to a dive; committing to a dive below this point means that the aircraft is in danger of crashing.
Greens
Standard-issue olive green RAF flying suits and overalls. The Reds and Blues wear greens during winter and spring training.
Griggo
A 3,000ft or 900m runway marker named in honour of Flt. Lt. Jez Griggs
Gucci
RAF slang for something that is desirable or good quality: 'The Hawk has no Gucci kit' – The Hawk is not fitted with state-of-the-art avionics.
Gypo
The collective name for Reds 6-9 during the flying display; the name is said to have been inspired by a member of the 1965 Red Arrows team.
Hot to trot
An aircraft that's ready to go.
ISP
In-Season Practice. The Red Arrows have a rule that if they do not fly for four or more days during the display season, they must fly a practice display or ISP before displaying in public.
kt
Knot or nautical mile, a unit of speed used by shipping and aircraft: 1kt = 1.85kph or 1.15mph.
Leckie
The RAF name for an electrician.
Line
The tarmac strip on an RAF base where the aircraft are parked; also called the **pan**.
Line abreast
A formation in which the aircraft are aligned wing tip to wing tip. **Line astern**
A formation in which the aircraft fly nose to tail in a straight line.
Liney
A technician who 'works the line', i.e. checks, cleans and refuels the aircraft parked on the line or pan.
See also **Pre-flight**.
Lineys' sunshine
Poor weather on the line.
Local
A local time zone, or as in the UK during the summer season, known as British Summer Time (BST), the Red Arrows' preferred time zone.
Loser plan
Contingency if a jet fails before a display.
Nine-ship
Nine aircraft flying in formation.
See also **Ship**.
MDC
Miniature Detonation Cord, the zigzag explosive charges that line the canopy and which shatter during the ejection sequence.

Met. brief
The morning weather reports provided by the RAF Cranwell met, or weather forecaster
Morgue
A blast-proof out-building that stores removed ejection seats and their explosive components during maintenance.
Pan
An area where aircraft are parked.
See also **Line**.
PDA
Public Display Authority – the official certification the Red Arrows need before they can display in public.
Pattern
An aerobatic formation or manoeuvre; aircraft in **formation** usually form a recognisable pattern or **shape** in the sky when seen from below.
Pick'n'mix
Sick bag.
Pre-flight
A contraction of 'to prepare an aircraft for flight'.
Pull
To pull back on the control column to bring an aircraft's nose up in a climb.
Pull up a sandbag
A frequent teller of war stories.
Push
To push forward on the control column to bring an aircraft's nose down to fly straight or dive, or to compensate for negative g-forces when climbing.
RAFAT
The Royal Air Force Aerobatic Team – the official name of the Red Arrows squadron.
Reds
The RAF name for the Red Arrows' pilots and other senior personnel who wear a red flying suit during the summer display season.
Reference
The system in aerobatic flying that uses trigonometry as the means of holding position in formation.
Rigger
The RAF name for an engineer who specializes in airframes.
Rolling display
A display flown when the cloud base is at least 750m or 2,500ft.
Round the corner
[To fly] To perform a turn in an aircraft during a display.
SAC
Senior Aircraftman (in the RAF women of this rank are called 'aircraftmen'.
Ship
RAF term meaning an aircraft. Number + 'ship': usually refers to the number of aircraft flying in a **formation**, e.g. a five-ship is five aircraft flying in formation.
Slot
An allocated time, usually for a flight or **sortie**.
Sootie
The RAF name for an engineer who specializes in aircraft engines.
Sortie
An operational flight.
SpringHawk
A period of, usually, five weeks in April and May when the Red Arrows fly to RAF Akrotiri in Cyprus for practice to put the final polish on their display.
Squip, squipper
The RAF name for a Survival Equipment Technician.
Sucker's Gap
A misjudged decision to take off in a brief respite from bad weather.
Synchro or **Synchro Pair**
Reds 6 and 7, so called because they fly synchronized manoeuvres during the second half of the display.
To flip one's kipper or Bang one up
To salute.
Transiting
Travelling to/from an airfield.
Unforgiving (of an aircraft)
Overreacts to sudden or clumsy use of the flight controls. *See also* **Forgiving**.
Up the hill
To make a steep climb during a display.
Up tits on sticks
An unserviceable aircraft on jacks.
WHAM
What's Happening Manager? A document produced by the Red Arrows' Team Manager detailing logistics information for trips away from base during the **display season**. The document was devised by a past Red Arrows' Team Manager as a written answer to the frequent question 'What's happening Manager?'
WHIPR
What's Happening in PR? A document devised by the Red Arrows' Public Relations Officer to provide a daily written calendar of public relations events to be attended during the display season.
Wave
An allocated time slot for formation practice.
Wet drill
The RAF's mandatory biannual water-rescue practice.
WinterHawk
A period of four to five weeks, usually in January to February, when the Red Arrows fly to Akrotiri RAF Base in Cyprus for a phase of their winter training.
Yellow and black
The cord handle that lies between the knees of a pilot in a fast jet and which, when pulled initiates the ejection sequence
Zulu time
The term used by the RAF and commercial aviation for Greenwich Mean Time (GMT)

JARVO

The youngest recruit in October 2003 was 29-year-old Flight Lieutenant Matt Jarvis. Having gained his Private Pilot's Licence at 17, he then won an RAF scholarship. By the time he joined the Red Arrows, he'd flown the Harrier on operational missions over the Balkans and Iraq.

His parents remember that as a child he talked aircraft all the time. Later, being a pilot became his life. He was thrilled when Squadron Leader Spike Jepson texted him to say he had made it into the Red Arrows. But he didn't realize how tough it was going to be. "It was the hardest job either of us had done," recalls Flight Lieutenant David Slow, Jarvo's best mate among the Reds. "We were dogged by self-doubt, but Jarvo was 100% suited to the job. He had wonderful traits – he was light-hearted and, best of all, he could always laugh at himself. He was a guy who always had a smile."

In April 2004, Jarvo discovered that he had a virulent cancer. Squadron Leader Spike Jepson announced it to the team at a morning brief just as they were about to depart for Cyprus. They were devastated and the news was greeted with shock and sadness when it reached the Blues.

Jarvo was grounded, his pilot's licence revoked. Yet when the team returned to Scampton after PDA, all wearing a red suit he had dreamed of putting on, Jarvo was there, waiting to congratulate them. He needed a great deal of courage but made the effort because he delighted in their achievement, his family recalls.

It seemed a natural gesture for the team to fund a flight for Jarvo in aviator Carolyn Grace's two-seater Spitfire. His family were there to see him fly and his former colleagues from No.20 Squadron appeared in their Harriers alongside the nine Hawks and the Spitfire, all wheeling over Scampton on 17 September. Below, friends and family gathered to launch a fund for Macmillan Cancer Relief, the Red Arrows' main nominated charity. He was beyond the pain threshold on that day, but he rose to the occasion, his last flight. When people read press reports of the occasion, hundreds wrote to him to express their admiration and sadness. He was astonished and humbled.

His friends meant everything to him. All through his year of illness his phone never stopped ringing and his friends and colleagues visited him all the time, say his family. Matt's last week was spent at the Sue Ryder hospice at Thorpe Hall.

He died on Sunday 20 March 2005.

ACKNOWLEDGEMENTS

Long-term photography projects such as this rely on kind-hearted people who endured my badgering and stalking. I have also been fortunate to meet countless numbers of people who shared my enthusiasm and commitment to this work, and it has been both humbling and a privilege to accept help from them as we nudged it to a conclusion.

Above all, I salute the members of the Royal Air Force Aerobatic Team, The Red Arrows. I thank them for their hospitality, camaraderie and trust, often during testing times.

In particular, I wish to thank:
Squadron Leaders Spike Jepson, Dicky Patounas, John Green and Dunc Mason; Rachel Huxford, Public Relations Officer and Squadron Leader Sally Varley, Team Manager, The Red Arrows, for their support and tireless enthusiasm; Wing Commander Bill Ramsey and Flight Lieutenant Steve Underwood (the Vintage Pair) for their bonhomie and piloting; Glyn Strong and Wing Commander Jon Taylor, External Communications RAF; Air Marshall Sir Joe French, Commander-in-Chief of RAF Personnel and Training Command; Air Commodore Glenn Edge, Flying Training; and Group Captain Jon Fynes, Commandant Central Flying School (CFS) for their official permission.

To the personnel at RAF Scampton, especially Air Traffic Controller Flight Lieutenant Barrie Robinson for general airfield advice; the various RAF and NHS medical staff for granting me clearance to fly in RAF aircraft; and met. forecaster Dave Witherden, RAF Cranwell.

Harrier and Hawk display pilots Flight Lieutenants Chris Margiotta and John Killerby for their company 'around the bazaars'. The Squirrel pilots of the Central Flying School (Helicopter) Squadron; Squadron Leader Al Dale and crew, No.28 Squadron, for the use of their splendid Merlin Helicopter at Eastbourne; and Marie Thompson and Clive Lambert-Beeson for their 'rescue' at Beachey Head; Lake Windermere Wardens, Steve Phelps and Travis Spraske for their generous assistance on the busiest of days; Shaun Gilmartin, Stacey Holland and Paul Defreitas of Carlton TV and Flight Lieutenant Kevin (Kev) Holmes for their sense of wayward fun in Cyprus; E. J. van Koningsveld and Corporal Chris Ward for air-to air modus operandi; Corporal (now Sergeant) Paul 'Fly' Taylor for showing me the ropes in my first week at Scampton; Viv and Rob Bogusz for exceptional lodgings at Robindale, Brattleby, and the Jarvis families.

Squadron Leader Chris Taylor, BAE Systems Hawk simulator, RAF Valley; Carolyn Grace, Solo Enterprises; Tony Parrini at Windermere; Glenn Moreman, Kemble Air Day; Philip Regan, North Somerset Council; Tim and Tony Feeley, Eye Show; Mike James, Caernarfon Airworld; Ray Thilthorpe, Southend Air Show; Tonia Reeve at Kielder Water; Paul Tucker, States of Jersey Government; Brian May, Hoylake Coastguard; Alan Waggett and staff, Dale Techniche Ltd; Mike Spooner, Specialised Printing Solutions Ltd; Steve Moore, RAF News; Brian Riddle, Librarian, Royal Aeronautical Society, London; Squadron Leader Dave Stewart, RAF Cranwell; Tim Lewis, MIPR RAF; Alec Ward, the Red Arrows Trust; Tim Callaway; Mike Heath; Paul Hayes-Watkins and Will Ellsworth-Jones, *SAGA Magazine*; Simon James, *British Journal of Photography*; Dagmar Seeland, *Stern*; Paul Tivnan, Process Supplies; Martin Gosling, Metro Imaging; Tony Lovatt; Elaine Sutton; Robin and Jenny Port; Paul and Pauline Jackson.

I am also indebted to Stu Smith for overall design, with assistance from Victoria Forrest and Heather McDonough.

To my friends and colleagues from IPG and Katz Pictures: Abby Johnston, Carla Rotondo, Eve Smith, James Hull, Peter Dench, Geoff Katz, Tara Bonakdar, Seamus O' Cleary, Amy Coppins, Ben Turner, Tom Stoddart, Matt Elvidge and Lina Hansson. To John Easterby, for shared passions and to Stefan Ericson who handed me this project on a silver platter.

PHOTOGRAPHY

New technical challenges presented themselves in the course of photographing the Red Arrows. From the outset, I shunned this subject's well-served association with the motor-driven 35mm zoom lens aesthetic. Instead, I chose the toolbox of quality I respect most: Fixed focal length Mamiya 6x6 and 6x7 cameras which obliges the photographer to achieve more individuality at the expense of easy handling.

Given that I have been using the same Fuji NPC 220, NPH and Superia 120 as a default film stock for many years, it was natural that I should also stay with this media.

My first surprise was that on close comparison on the ground, the jets are actually different hues of red which also change under light conditions. Some have been recently re-sprayed, others have been bleached by the sun during, perhaps, three seasons and are not so much red, as orange. Interestingly, they all look the same consistent prime colour from the air. As a complication, after PDA and during the summer, I also noticed that the pilots' red suits didn't match their aircraft either and so, during the RGB to CMYK process, I applied the colour balance that suited my preferences according to the individual image and to overall atmospheric conditions: Murky Lincolnshire winter, intensely bright Cyprus or overcast Somerset.

The fast-jet cockpit is an alien location. In all, I took six flights in various aerobatic positions within the team. Apart from my camera-less 'audition' with the Wing Commander (Red 11) and then the Boss (Red 1), I flew as Red 5 and as Red 10, the photo-chaser which can position itself in safe sky around the main display during ISPs. On all those occasions I used the 6x7 with 220 film. All straps were removed to avoid snagging any flight controls and the camera body and the pre-focussed lens was gaffer-taped. This served three purposes: to ensure nothing loosened and dropped; to reduce reflections in the canopy; to save the acrylic itself being damaged from sharp edges. The consequence of no awkward in-flight film changes was that 20 single frames had to last 24-plus minutes.

Other than digital scanning and previously-mentioned file conversions, no image manipulation has occurred.

ACCURACY

I am grateful to those members of the Red Arrows, especially Squadron Leaders John Green and Simon Davies and Public Relations Officer Rachel Huxford, who verified and corrected the factual accuracy of text and captions so exhaustively. Also to Chris Howard, BAE Systems, Brough; Robert Pogson, Jays Racewear and Del Holyland, Martin-Baker.

PICTURE CREDITS

t = top; b = bottom; c = centre; l = left; r = right:
p54 tl Flight International; pp214-215, pp218-219, pp222-223, pp230-231, pp232-233, p237, BAE Systems.

TEST ANSWERS

Spatial Reasoning, pp116-117: question 1=D, question 2=D;
Electrical Comprehension, pp118: question 1=D, question 2=C, question 3=B and question 4=C;
Mechanical Comprehension, pp119: question 1=C, question 2=A, question 3=B and question 4=E;
Memory, pp120-121: question 1=D and question 2=B.

Designed by SMITH
Printer: Star Standard Industries Pte Ltd., Singapore
Printing: Four color litho on Roland Speedmaster
Page size: 260mm x 200mm
Text paper: 170 gsm Stora Enso Matt Art
End papers: 140 gsm Woodfree
Dust jacket: 150 gsm Glossy Art